]

Studies in Contemporary Women's Writing

Series Editor

GILL RYE
Emerita Professor,
Centre for the Study of Contemporary Women's Writing,
Institute of Modern Languages Research, University of London

VOLUME 11

PETER LANG
Oxford • Bern • Berlin • Bruxelles • New York • Wien

Reimagining the Family

Lesbian Mothering in Contemporary French Literature

Robert Payne

PETER LANG

Oxford • Bern • Berlin • Bruxelles • New York • Wien

Bibliographic information published by Die Deutsche Nationalbibliothek.
Die Deutsche Nationalbibliothek lists this publication in the Deutsche Nationalbibliografie;
detailed bibliographic data is available on the Internet at http://
dnb.d-nb.de.

A catalogue record for this book is available from the British Library.

Library of Congress Cataloging-in-Publication Data

Names: Payne, Robert, 1990– author.
Title: Reimagining the family : lesbian mothering in contemporary French
    literature / Robert Payne.
Description: Oxford ; New York : Peter Lang, [2021] | Series: Studies in
    contemporary women's writing, 2235-4123 ; vol 11 | Includes
    bibliographical references and index.
Identifiers: LCCN 2021029169 (print) | LCCN 2021029170 (ebook) | ISBN
    9781788747714 (paperback) | ISBN 9781788747721 (ebook) | ISBN
    9781788747738 (epub)
Subjects: LCSH: Lesbian mothers in literature. | French literature—20th
    century—History and criticism. | French literature—21st
    century—History and criticism. | French literature—Women
    authors—History and criticism. | Families in literature. | LCGFT:
    Literary criticism.
Classification: LCC PQ307.M67 P39 2021 (print) | LCC PQ307.M67 (ebook) |
    DDC 840.9/92870904—dc23
LC record available at https://lccn.loc.gov/2021029169
LC ebook record available at https://lccn.loc.gov/2021029170

Cover picture: 'Effe' © Eddit Milkovitsch.
Cover design by Peter Lang Ltd.

ISSN 2235-4123
ISBN 978-1-78874-771-4 (print)
ISBN 978-1-78874-772-1 (ePDF)
ISBN 978-1-78874-773-8 (ePub)

© Peter Lang Group AG 2021

Published by Peter Lang Ltd, International Academic Publishers,
52 St Giles, Oxford, OX1 3LU, United Kingdom
oxford@peterlang.com, www.peterlang.com

Robert Payne has asserted his right under the Copyright, Designs and Patents Act, 1988, to be
identified as Author of this Work.

This publication has been peer reviewed.

Contents

Acknowledgements

Writing this book would not have been possible without the help of various institutions, colleagues and loved ones. I first wish to thank the School of Arts at the University of Leicester for the scholarship that enabled me to pursue the PhD research that led to the book. I would also like to thank the School of Humanities at the University of Hertfordshire for the early career fellowship that gave me the time and thinking space to complete it. Thank you also to the *Revue critique de fixxion française contemporaine* for allowing me to republish parts of the article that forms the basis of Chapter 3.

Since this volume stems from my PhD thesis, I wish to express my eternal gratitude to my supervisors, Marion Krauthaker-Coombes and Elizabeth Jones, for their advice, expertise and support, as well as for sharing and fostering my interest in my chosen subject. I would also like to thank my examiners, Claire Jenkins and Shirley Jordan, for their helpful recommendations for preparing the thesis for publication. Thank you also to Laurel Plapp at Peter Lang Oxford for her advice and guidance.

More broadly, I would like to thank colleagues and friends at the Universities of Leicester, Mulhouse and Hertfordshire for being vital sources of encouragement and laughter over the (long!) period of writing this book. The following three people deserve a special mention: Sonia Alba – for being the most amazing office buddy; Martine Fade – for her astute questioning that pushed me to refine my arguments; and Helen Monribot – for generously agreeing to cover some of my teaching duties so that I could finish this project.

Finally, I wish to acknowledge several people outside university whose constant presence and support have been, and continue to be, hugely important to me: firstly, my best friends, Rosemary Chell and Sarah Foster; and last but not least, Mum and Dad, Laura and James, Grandma Connie and Grandad Ernie.

Contextualizing Lesbian Mothering

In France, the creation of civil partnerships in 1999 and the legalization of same-sex marriage and adoption in 2013 have turned same-sex families into a subject of highly charged public debate. This has coincided with the emergence of a small but significant number of literary texts that offer privileged insights into the often marginalized but increasingly relevant experiences of same-sex parents. *Reimagining the Family: Lesbian Mothering in Contemporary French Literature* engages with this body of literature, focusing on ten texts that, taken together, illustrate the range of genres – from mass-market fiction to autobiographical writing – and narratives used by writers to talk about this phenomenon.

Published between 1970 and 2013, these texts appeared at a time when family life was changing considerably. Since the 1970s, the nuclear family has been contested by the decline of marriage and rise in divorce, the increase in alternative family groupings such as single- and step-parent families, and the widespread availability of abortion and contraception. Five of the texts studied in this volume engage with these changes by portraying lesbian mothers who have children in a heterosexual relationship that breaks down. These texts are Jocelyne François's *Les Bonheurs* [*Happinesses*] (1970); Hélène de Monferrand's *Les Amies d'Héloïse* [*Héloïse's Friends*] (1990) and *Les Enfants d'Héloïse* [*Héloïse's Children*] (1997); Axelle Mallet's *Le Choix de la reine* [*The Queen's Choice*] (2009); and Paula Dumont's *La Vie dure: Éducation sentimentale d'une lesbienne* [*The Hard Life: A Lesbian's Sentimental Education*] (2010). The other five texts revolve around the more recent emergence of planned same-sex families – that is, when a same-sex couple decide to have children together, usually by way of adoption or fertility treatment. These texts include Éliane Girard's *Mais qui va garder le chat?* [*But Who's Going to Look After the Cat?*] (2005); Laurence

Cinq-Fraix's *Family Pride* (2006); Brigitte Célier's *Maman, Mamour, ses deux mamans: Grandir dans une famille homoparentale* [*Maman, Mamour – Her Two Mums: Growing Up in a Same-Sex Family*] (2008); Myriam Blanc's *Elles eurent beaucoup d'enfants … et se marièrent: Histoire d'une famille homoparentale* [*The Women Had Lots of Children … and Got Married: The Story of a Same-Sex Family*] (2012); and Claire Bénard's *Prince Charmante: Que fait-on quand on tombe amoureuse d'une femme?* [*Princess Charming: What Do You Do When You Fall in Love with a Woman?*] (2013). The period covered by the ten texts was crucial not only for family life but also for the status of sexual minorities. The earliest texts were published at a time when LGBT+ people were beginning to fight for rights, while the later texts were published in the years between the creation of civil partnerships and legalization of same-sex marriage. This book argues that the texts not only reflect these changes but also contribute to the debates on same-sex families and to what is meant by motherhood and the family in twenty-first-century France.

Same-Sex Parenting in France

The recent emergence of same-sex parenting as a social and political issue is part of the gradual deconstruction of norms of gender, sexuality and the family that has been taking place since at least the nineteenth century. Although conservative in many respects, the nineteenth century saw the birth of feminism as an organized political movement and the beginnings of tolerance of homosexuality. The fact that aversion to homosexuality primarily concerned gay men afforded some women, especially wealthier women, licence to engage in 'romantic friendships' with other women, albeit while married to a man.[1] The nineteenth century thus laid the foundations of the sexual revolution and the women's and

1   See Judith Walkowitz, 'Sexualités dangereuses', trans. Geneviève Faure, in Geneviève Fraisse and Michelle Perrot, eds, *Histoire des femmes en Occident: le XIXe siècle* (Paris: Perrin, 2002 [1991]), 439–78 (470–8).

LGBT+ rights movements formed in the twentieth century, notably the *Mouvement de libération des femmes* [Women's Liberation Movement] (1968), the *Front Homosexuel d'Action Révolutionnaire* [Homosexual Front for Revolutionary Action] (1971) and the *Gouines Rouges* [Red Dykes] (1971). Unlike in Britain, where Margaret Thatcher's conservative administration banned the 'promotion of homosexuality', in France the socialist government under François Mitterrand passed pro-LGBT+ legislation. In 1982, it made the age of consent for homosexual acts the same as that for heterosexual acts (15 years old), thus ending an inequality (the age of consent for homosexual acts had been set at 21 by the Vichy government; it was lowered to 18 in 1974 under Valéry Giscard d'Estaing). Sexual orientation was also included in the protected characteristics of a 1985 anti-discrimination law.

While these measures helped homosexuals as individuals, the AIDS crisis of the 1980s highlighted the need to protect homosexual couples. In the twenty-first century, this need has extended to homosexual families. The creation of the *Pacte Civil de Solidarité* (PACS), or civil partnerships, in 1999 was a vital first step. Open to opposite- and same-sex couples, the PACS grants many of the rights of marriage but, crucially, not adoption or citizenship rights. In 2013, France legalized same-sex marriage and adoption, and in 2019, fertility treatment, which had been restricted to heterosexual couples since 1994, was made available to all women, irrespective of sexuality or relationship status. The legal recognition and rights of same-sex couples and families are, then, assured, yet the twenty-year gap between the PACS and *PMA pour toutes* [fertility treatment for all women] gives some indication of how contentious these issues are in France. It is in this very particular context that this volume and the texts studied in it were written.

Unlike in the US, where opposition to same-sex marriage is a defence of the institution of marriage itself, in France opposition to same-sex marriage usually stems from a reluctance to recognize same-sex families. Thus, opponents of the PACS, although the bill did not propose to allow same-sex couples to adopt, often expressed the fear that if same-sex couples were given recognition, same-sex families would be too: if same-sex couples were granted some of the rights of married, heterosexual couples, on what grounds could they continue to be refused equal access to adoption and fertility treatment?

The reason for this shift in focus lies in the somewhat peculiar types of arguments heard in the debates on same-sex marriage and families in France. Unlike in the US, where arguments against same-sex marriage are usually religious, in secular France religious arguments officially have no political weight. As Camille Robcis has shown, opponents of the PACS, even those who were catholic, therefore resorted to fields as diverse as anthropology, psychoanalysis, law and sociology, and, in particular, to the works of Claude Lévi-Strauss and Jacques Lacan.[2] They drew on some of the most complex concepts in these fields, such as the symbolic order, the Oedipus complex, the anthropological invariables of society, castration, psychosis, the Name-of-the-Father and the incest prohibition, to argue for the universality of the heterosexual family and, by extension, the indefensibility of the PACS.

The other pillar of the PACS debate was republicanism, understood as a universalist conception of citizenship and rights.[3] Positions on the PACS were not party-specific but, rather, structured around the extent to which it was compatible with republican values. Proponents claimed that the PACS epitomized universalism since, because it was open to all couples, it granted equal rights to all citizens. For opponents, the PACS 'represented another American-inspired attempt to cater to the demands of specific groups (homosexuals) and a move towards "*communitarianism*" ' – the French term for identity politics, which is strongly associated with the US.[4] Arguably, opponents of the PACS were justified in seeing it as *communautariste*; but this *communautariste* measure exists precisely because of a general unwillingness to universalize the right of marriage and treat homosexuals as ordinary citizens.

2   See Camille Robcis, 'How the Symbolic Became French: Kinship and Republicanism in the PACS Debates', *Discourse* 26/3 (2004), 110–35; see also Camille Robcis, *The Law of Kinship: Anthropology, Psychoanalysis, and the Family in France* (Ithaca, NY: Cornell University Press, 2013).

3   See Robcis, 'How the Symbolic Became French'.

4   Robcis, 'How the Symbolic Became French', 113.

Fears about same-sex families were also the basis of opposition to same-sex marriage, named 'mariage pour tous' [marriage for all] in keeping with French universalism. There were, however, some significant differences between the political landscape of the PACS and that of the same-sex marriage debate in 2012–13. Firstly, the divisions within the left- and right-wing parties over the PACS had healed; positions on same-sex marriage were broadly party-specific.[5] For the Socialists, the newly elected François Hollande had made same-sex marriage a campaign pledge. For the right, Nicolas Sarkozy's defeat to Hollande had led to a leadership crisis. Same-sex marriage was therefore an issue around which conservatives could rally.[6] Secondly, the legalization of same-sex marriage in several other countries – notably the Netherlands (2001), Belgium (2003) and Spain (2005) – invalidated the 'anthropological argument' about universal culture used to oppose the PACS.[7] As Éric Fassin demonstrates, this argument was replaced by an emphasis on the biological basis of the family.[8] The biological turn is visible in many of the slogans used by the Manif pour Tous [Demo for All], the organization formed to oppose same-sex marriage. Examples include: 'Tous nés d'un homme et d'une femme' [All are born from a man and woman]; '1 papa, 1 maman, on ne ment pas aux enfants' [One dad, one mum, we don't lie to children]; 'Non à la filiation-fiction' [No to fictional filiation]; and 'Y a pas d'ovules dans les testicules' [There are no eggs in the testicles].[9] This turn to biology served to disguise discrimination against homosexuals as a noble defence of the best interests of children.

For Robcis, the focus on reproduction in the same-sex marriage debate points to a concern over the nation: 'If homosexuals are allowed

5   Éric Fassin, 'Same-Sex Marriage, Nation, and Race: French Political Logics and Rhetorics', *Contemporary French Civilization* 39/3 (2014), 281–301 (283).
6   Michael Stambolis-Ruhstorfer and Josselin Tricou, 'Resisting "Gender Theory" in France: A Fulcrum for Religious Action in a Secular Society', in Roman Kuhar and David Paternotte, eds, *Anti-Gender Campaigns in Europe: Mobilizing against Equality* (London: Rowman and Littlefield, 2017), 79–98 (84).
7   Fassin, 'Same-Sex Marriage, Nation, and Race', 284.
8   Fassin, 'Same-Sex Marriage, Nation, and Race', 285.
9   Daniel Borrillo, 'Biologie et filiation: les habits neufs de l'ordre naturel', *Contemporary French Civilization* 39/3 (2014), 303–19 (304).

to reproduce, who will be produced through this process? What will the family look like and, more importantly, what will the future, the nation and society look like? What new norms will govern life in common?'[10] Similarly, Scott Gunther convincingly argues in an article on the Manif pour Tous that for its members 'what is at stake is not just same-sex marriage *but the definition of Frenchness*'.[11] The concern over the nation is most obviously reflected by the universalist language of the marriage law and the organization opposed to it, the Manif pour Tous. This name, chosen in response to that of the marriage law, symbolizes its claim to represent the nation, and this claim is reinforced by its campaign strategy. The first tactic used by the Manif pour Tous was its choice of iconography. Costumes worn by participants in the marches organized by the movement appropriated symbols of the republic such as Marianne. They also deployed images of the Resistance, thus associating opposition to same-sex marriage with the fight for a free France.[12]

The movement's second tactic was to portray same-sex marriage as un-French by linking it to the ongoing debate on 'gender theory', defined as queer theory and, in particular, the ideas of American philosopher Judith Butler.[13] Since 2011, several proposals have been made to include teaching on sexism and the difference between sex and gender in the school curriculum. These proposals sparked protests in the form of school boycotting, fed by disinformation about what teaching 'gender theory' involved, including a preposterous claim that children would be taught to masturbate. The frequent use of the English word 'gender', rather than the perfectly adequate

---

10   Camille Robcis, 'Liberté, Égalité, Hétérosexualité: Race and Reproduction in the French Gay Marriage Debates', *Constellations: An International Journal of Critical and Democratic Theory* 22/3 (2015), 447–61 (455).

11   Scott Gunther, 'Making Sense of the Anti-Same-Sex-Marriage Movement in France', *French Politics, Culture & Society* 37/2 (2019), 131–58 (136).

12   For more on the iconography of the Manif pour Tous, see Robcis, 'Liberté, Égalité, Hétérosexualité', 448–50.

13   For more on the French debate on 'gender theory', see Bruno Perreau, *Queer Theory: The French Response* (Stanford, CA: Stanford University Press, 2016); and Stambolis-Ruhstorfer and Tricou, 'Resisting "Gender Theory" in France'.

French equivalent 'genre', worked to portray the notion of socially constructed gender as an American import, and thus a threat to France.

The final tactic of the Manif pour Tous was to broaden the movement's appeal and, in doing so, present itself as representative of a silent French majority. Considerable effort was made to downplay the degree to which its membership was White, catholic, right wing and bourgeois. These claims were not entirely unfounded, for, as Gunther shows, some members were openly LGBT+.[14] The movement's original leaders were Frigide Barjot, a 'Roman Catholic in pop-culture drag [who] had once been the queen of gay Parisian nights'; Xavier Bongibault, a gay man; and Laurence Cheng, a supporter of the Socialist Party.[15] The movement even claimed to be areligious and accepting of homosexuality. As well as imagery associated with the republic and the Resistance, the Manif pour Tous also employed the symbols and rhetoric of the left, despite its overwhelmingly right-wing agenda and membership. Its posters recalled those of May '68; its motto – 'On ne lâche rien!' [We won't let anything get away!] – was previously used by Jean-Luc Mélenchon's left-wing party, the Front de Gauche; and another of its slogans – 'Touche pas à la filiation' [Don't touch filiation] – was inspired by the one used by the anti-racist campaign SOS Racisme, 'Touche pas à mon pote' [Don't touch my mate].[16]

The Manif pour Tous's failure to prevent the legalization of same-sex marriage hardly spelled the end of the debate. The movement has continued to campaign on a number of issues, notably filiation, fertility treatment and surrogacy, the last of which remains illegal in France. Under Hollande, the government reneged on its promise to open up fertility treatment to lesbian couples and single women. Fertility treatment has since been made available to all women, but the fact that this took six years testifies to the success of the Manif pour Tous and other opponents of same-sex parenting. The limits of the marriage law were an attempt to prop up a hierarchy of family forms based on biological filiation. Reserving fertility treatment for heterosexual couples worked to maintain the illusion that artificial

14   Gunther, 'Making Sense of the Anti-Same-Sex-Marriage Movement in France', 143.
15   Fassin, 'Same-Sex Marriage, Nation, and Race', 295.
16   See Robcis, 'Liberté, Égalité, Hétérosexualité', 448–9.

reproduction mimics biological procreation, which, as Fassin points out, was somewhat at odds with the current emphasis on being honest with children about how they are made.[17] Furthermore, considerable effort was made to prevent legislation enabling same-sex-parented children to be inserted into their non-biological parent's filiation. For instance, during the Republican primaries in the run-up to the 2017 presidential election, François Fillon pledged to revoke same-sex couples' access to *adoption plénière* [full adoption], which erases the child's filial link to its biological parents and inscribes it into the filiation of the intended parents, but to protect their access to *adoption simple* [simple adoption], which maintains the filial link to the biological parents.

Despite this turn to biology, as legal scholar Daniel Borrillo stresses filiation is a legal matter, not a biological one.[18] Its purpose is not, as opponents of same-sex parenting would have it, to instil in children a psychological identity but, rather, to provide families with legal security – for instance, in matters of inheritance. Although biology has traditionally been used as a basis of filiation, it is by no means a legal requirement. Indeed, non-biological forms of filiation have existed since a 1966 law on *adoption plénière*; it is also possible to insert a child into the filiation of a single parent. For Borrillo, the biologization of filiation has nothing to do with protecting children; it has to do with maintaining a symbolic order based on sexual difference – that is to say, the supremacy of heterosexuality.[19]

Lesbianism, Mothering and French Literary Criticism

The uniqueness of the French debates on same-sex marriage and families creates an interesting backdrop to this study of lesbian mothering

---

17 Fassin, 'Same-Sex Marriage, Nation, and Race', 290.
18 Borrillo, 'Biologie et filiation', 306; see also Daniel Borrillo, 'La vérité biologique contre l'homoparentalité: le statut du beau-parent ou le "PaCS de la filiation"', *Droit et société* 72 (2009), 361–71.
19 Borrillo, 'Biologie et filiation', 316.

in contemporary French literature. Although lesbianism and mothering have been subjects of much French literary criticism, they have almost always been treated separately. In focusing on rare but emerging texts portraying lesbian mothers, this study is the first to bring these themes together. It also brings several authors – Laurence Cinq-Fraix, Brigitte Célier, Axelle Mallet, Paula Dumont and Claire Bénard – to critical attention for the first time. While it therefore treads new ground in terms of focus and corpus, it owes much to previous studies of LGBT+ literature and women's writing.

While my primary focus is on experiences of mothering, I also examine desire, love and relationships between women, thus building on existing work on lesbian writing. Lesbian writing has traditionally received less critical attention than writing by and about gay men. In George Stambolian and Elaine Marks's *Homosexualities and French Literature* (1979), which pioneered research on homosexuality in French literature, just two chapters are exclusively dedicated to lesbian writing.[20] Efforts have since been made to redress the imbalance. A number of short, article-length analyses of lesbians in French literature focus on late nineteenth-century writers such as Rachilde and Renée Vivien.[21] These studies expose the patriarchal norms that underpinned representations of lesbians in this period: lesbianism was reduced to romantic friendships between women or, worse, associated with illness or vice.

Larger studies of lesbianism in French literature focus on the twentieth century and reveal the gradual emergence of empowered lesbian characters in this period. The most extensive of these studies are Jennifer Waelti-Walters's *Damned Women: Lesbians in French Novels, 1796–1996* (2000) and

---

20   George Stambolian and Elaine Marks, eds, *Homosexualities and French Literature: Cultural Contexts/Critical Texts* (Ithaca, NY: Cornell University Press, 1979).

21   See, for example, Tama Lea Engelking, 'Renée Vivien and The Ladies of the Lake', *Nineteenth-Century French Studies* 30/3–4 (2002), 362–79; Dominique D. Fisher, 'A propos du "Rachildisme" ou Rachilde et les lesbiennes', *Nineteenth-Century French Studies* 31/3–4 (2003), 297–310.

Lucille Cairns's *Lesbian Desire in Post-1968 French Literature* (2002).[22] Due to the lack of existing work in this area, both studies sought to make lesbian writing visible and prove that lesbians have a long-established presence in French novels. To this end, Waelti-Walters and Cairns cover impressively large corpuses of primary texts, thus providing, as Cairns puts it, 'useful, quasi-encyclopaedic reference tool[s]' for the study of lesbian writing.[23] Perhaps the most significant change to the lesbian literary landscape in the twentieth century was the shift from male- to female-authored lesbian novels.[24] With this shift came that of increasingly sympathetic portrayals of lesbians. Although still troubled, especially in early twentieth-century texts, they are no longer demonized. Lesbianism even enters the works of some of the most celebrated twentieth-century women writers such as Simone de Beauvoir, Violette Leduc and Monique Wittig. Wittig's lesbian fiction, perhaps because she was a lesbian and a hugely influential lesbian radical theorist, has attracted a wealth of criticism. Namascar Shaktini's analyses of *Le Corps lesbien* [*The Lesbian Body*] (1973) centre on its critique of phallogocentrism – that is, the structuring of language and meaning around the phallus – and attempt to reorganize language around the lesbian body, while James Davis investigates Wittig's violent reinvention of male-centred myths and language in *Les Guérillères* (1969).[25] Wittig's fiction is, then, a precursor to her theoretical works, in which language is presented as an important site of female oppression and heterosexual dominance.

This book builds on studies of lesbianism in French literature, focusing on late twentieth- and twenty-first-century texts. As well as the

22   Jennifer Waelti-Walters, *Damned Women: Lesbians in French Novels, 1796–1996* (Montreal: McGill-Queen's University Press, 2000); Lucille Cairns, *Lesbian Desire in Post-1968 French Literature* (Lewiston, NY: Edwin Mellen, 2002).

23   Cairns, *Lesbian Desire in Post-1968 French Literature*, 10.

24   Waelti-Walters, *Damned Women*, 97.

25   Namascar Shaktini, 'Displacing the Phallic Subject: Wittig's Lesbian Writing', *Signs: Journal of Women in Culture and Society* 8/1 (1982), 29–44; Namascar Shaktini, 'Monique Wittig's New Language', *Pacific Coast Philology* 24/1–2 (1989), 83–93; James D. Davis, Jr, *Beautiful War: Uncommon Violence, Praxis, and Aesthetics in the Novels of Monique Wittig* (New York: Peter Lang, 2010). See also Monique Wittig, *Le Corps lesbien* (Paris: Minuit, 1973); Monique Wittig, *Les Guérillères* (Paris: Minuit, 1969).

first study of literary representations of lesbian mothering, it offers the first sustained examination of twenty-first-century French lesbian writing, since the studies by Waelti-Walters and Cairns have cut-off points of 1996 and 1998 respectively. The texts studied here are part of the literary panorama just outlined. Indeed, the centrality of mothering in these texts may indicate an emerging trend within lesbian writing more broadly – a trend that both reflects and contributes to the dismantling of the association of lesbianism with childlessness and the opposition between homosexuality and family. Like much twentieth-century lesbian writing, the texts covered here present lesbianism as largely unproblematic. At stake in these texts is, rather, the reconcilability of lesbianism with mothering. This study thus sheds light on how lesbian writing is evolving in the twenty-first century.

Similarly, this book extends the insights of previous studies examining how women's writing exposes, questions or rebukes normative discourses of mothering. Numerous studies of mothering in French literature focus on the works of well-known twentieth-century women writers, such as Simone de Beauvoir, Marie Cardinal, Chantal Chawaf, Annie Ernaux, Jeanne Hyvrard and Violette Leduc.[26] These studies shed light on how writers challenge patriarchal discourses of maternity, particularly the prescription of mothering as women's sole or primary function. For instance, Alison Fell claims in *Liberty, Equality, Maternity in Beauvoir, Leduc and Ernaux* (2003) that the authors resist 'dominant patriarchal interpretations of motherhood as women's "natural" and patriotic duty or destiny'.[27] As Fell further argues, mothers in the works of Beauvoir, Leduc and Ernaux, and in twentieth-century women's writing in general, feature as ambiguous, ambivalent characters who subvert the patriarchal image of mothering as an idealized, selfless role.[28]

---

26   See, for example, Lucille Cairns, *Marie Cardinal: Motherhood and Creativity* (Glasgow: University of Glasgow Press, 1992); Alison S. Fell, *Liberty, Equality, Maternity in Beauvoir, Leduc and Ernaux* (Oxford: Legenda, 2003); Diana Holmes, *French Women's Writing, 1848–1994* (London: Athlone, 1996); Alex Hughes, *Violette Leduc: Mothers, Lovers, and Language* (London: W.S. Maney/ MHRA, 1994); Monique Saigal, *L'Écriture: Lien de fille à mère chez Jeanne Hyvrard, Chantal Chawaf, et Annie Ernaux* (Amsterdam: Rodopi, 2000).

27   Fell, *Liberty, Equality, Maternity in Beauvoir, Leduc and Ernaux*, 187.

28   Fell, *Liberty, Equality, Maternity in Beauvoir, Leduc and Ernaux*, 4.

The most recent studies of mothering in French literature have turned
to the works of the 'new women writers' publishing in the 1990s and early
2000s, such as Christine Angot, Paule Constant, Marie Darrieussecq,
Virginie Despentes, Véronique Olmi and Laurence Tardieu.[29] These studies
reveal how this generation of writers is, in increasingly controversial ways,
continuing to disrupt normative discourses of mothering. The most comprehensive of these studies are Gill Rye's *Narratives of Mothering* (2009)
and Natalie Edwards's *Voicing Voluntary Childlessness* (2016).[30] In response
to Marianne Hirsch's observation that mothers have traditionally been
relegated to being the objects of the narratives of others,[31] Rye posits that
mothers have begun to emerge as speaking subjects in recent women's
writing, both as authors and as narrators.[32] The texts that I have chosen
to analyse reflect this phenomenon: in most cases, the mother is the protagonist and, in some, a first-person narrator. Rye's book is also important
because, as well as returning to established authors such as Chantal Chawaf
and Marie Ndiaye, it brings to critical attention some less well-known
and previously unstudied writers such as Leïla Marouane and Geneviève
Brisac. The thematic structure, which includes chapters on ambivalence
and child death, reveals the diverse circumstances and contexts in which
mothering is being represented by contemporary women writers. Rye thus
shows how writers, contrary to dominant expectations about mothering,
present this as a potentially traumatic experience. Although narrower than
Rye's in terms of corpus size, Edwards's study considers perhaps the most
outright rejection of patriarchal images of femininity and mothering: the
decision not to be a mother. As Edwards argues, 'the authors whose work

29   The term 'new women writers' is taken from Gill Rye and Michael Worton. See
     Gill Rye and Michael Worton, eds, *Women's Writing in Contemporary France: New
     Writers, New Literatures in the 1990s* (Manchester: Manchester University
     Press, 2002).

30   Gill Rye, *Narratives of Mothering: Women's Writing in Contemporary France*
     (Newark: University of Delaware Press, 2009); Natalie Edwards, *Voicing Voluntary
     Childlessness: Narratives of Non-Mothering in French* (Oxford: Peter Lang, 2016).

31   Marianne Hirsch, *The Mother/Daughter Plot: Narrative, Psychoanalysis, Feminism*
     (Bloomington: Indiana University Press, 1989), 8.

32   Rye, *Narratives of Mothering*, 15.

forms the basis for the analyses in this book carve out new narrative forms to encapsulate new forms of female identity and, taken together, perform a radical rethinking of the connection between femininity and maternity'.[33] Edwards demonstrates how childlessness, rather than being a punishment or source of shame, is represented as a positive, thoroughly considered choice. By contrast, in the texts considered here motherhood, though not idealized, is usually presented as a desired state. My book thus deepens our understanding of the multiple ways in which non-normative modes of mothering are being represented in contemporary French literature.

In a number of smaller studies, Rye and Edwards focus on particular ways in which late twentieth- and twenty-first-century women writers rebuke received ideas about mothering. For example, in her analysis of childbirth in Christine Angot's *Interview* (1995), Virginie Despentes's short story 'A terme' [Full Term] (1995) and Camille Laurens's *Philippe* (1995), Rye argues that these texts contest the symbolic power of women's reproductive function by situating childbirth in the contexts of incest, infanticide and infant mortality, thus inscribing the birthing body as a site of trauma.[34] Furthermore, studies point out the problematization by women writers of dichotomous and subjective notions of 'good' and 'bad' mothering. For instance, in her discussion of mother–daughter relations in Paule Constant's fiction, Rye argues that the writer's portrayal of this relationship, although negative, works not to blame mothers for 'bad' mothering but to encode a process of mourning – that is, in Kleinian theory, the reworking of originary loss or separation from the mother.[35] Similarly, Edwards argues in her examination of infanticide in Olmi's *Bord de mer*

33 Edwards, *Voicing Voluntary Childlessness*, 16.
34 Gill Rye, 'Registering Trauma: The Body in Childbirth in Contemporary French Women's Writing', *Nottingham French Studies* 45/3 (2006), 92–104 (104). See also Christine Angot, *Interview* (Paris: Fayard, 1995); Virginie Despentes, 'A terme' (1995), in *Mordre au travers* (Paris: Librio, 1999), 61–3; Camille Laurens, *Philippe* (Paris: P.O.L., 1995).
35 Gill Rye, 'Lost and Found: Mother–Daughter Relations in Paule Constant's Fiction', in Gill Rye and Michael Worton, eds, *Women's Writing in Contemporary France: New Writers, New Literatures in the 1990s* (Manchester: Manchester University Press, 2002), 65–76 (71).

[*Beside the Sea*] (2001) and Tardieu's *Le Jugement de Léa* [*The Judgement of Léa*] (2004) that the authors go beyond the mad/bad framework in which infanticidal mothers are portrayed, especially in the legal system and the media, as monstrous, sadistic villains by presenting a disconcerting testimony of mental illness and maternal despair.[36] By focusing on lesbian mothers, who are stereotyped as neglectful and inappropriate role models, this book also enters the debate on subjective notions of 'good' and 'bad' mothering. Moreover, it engages with the wider deconstruction of binaries relating to mothering through a critical examination of texts foregrounding women tasked with negotiating the maternal role with a sexuality that has traditionally been regarded as preclusive to mothering. Lesbian mothers deconstruct the nexus between lesbianism and sterility and, by extension, the equation of maternity with heterosexuality. Although this study examines representations of mothering from a previously unconsidered angle, it is, then, inscribed in a critical context concerned with challenges to dominant beliefs about mothering.

At the same time as studies of the 'new women writers' emerged, another strand of criticism, pioneered by Rye, began to address mothering in non-traditional family contexts. Although short, these studies show how changing family patterns are emerging as a theme of French literary texts and, critically, how they contribute to social and political debates on the family. Rye has published two chapters on surrogate mothering – an illegal activity in France but one that is nonetheless practised informally or organized through overseas associations.[37] For Rye, the few texts depicting

---

36   Natalie Edwards, 'Babykillers: Véronique Olmi and Laurence Tardieu on Motherhood', in Amaleena Damlé and Gill Rye, eds, *Women's Writing in Twenty-First-Century France: Life as Literature* (Cardiff: University of Wales Press, 2013), 98–110 (103). See also Véronique Olmi, *Bord de mer* (Paris: Actes Sud, 2001); Laurence Tardieu, *Le Jugement de Léa* (Paris: Arléa, 2004).

37   Gill Rye, 'Marginal Identities and New Kinship Paradigms: Surrogate Motherhood in Contemporary Women's Writing in France', in Gill Rye and Amaleena Damlé, eds, *Experiment and Experience: Women's Writing in France, 2000–2010* (Oxford: Peter Lang, 2013), 109–24; Gill Rye, 'New Representations and Politics of Procreation: Surrogate Motherhood, Artificial Insemination and Human Cloning in Contemporary Women's Writing in France', in Margaret Atack, Diana Holmes,

surrogacy are suggestive of a growing trend.[38] Rye interprets these texts as interventions in the current reshuffling of family paradigms in twenty-first-century France, arguing that they 'suggest wider possibilities for the experience of parenting than the narrower understandings determined by French *filiation*'.[39]

Most significantly, as far as this book is concerned, Rye devotes a chapter of *Narratives of Mothering* to the portrayal of lesbian parenting in Éliane Girard's *Mais qui va garder le chat?* (2005) and the first edition of Myriam Blanc's *Et elles eurent beaucoup d'enfants … Histoire d'une famille homoparentale* (2005) – texts that also feature in my corpus. This chapter examines how far these texts portray lesbian families as a new family form and concludes that they regard them as both similar to and different from other family types. In a more recent chapter, Rye updates and builds on her first study, concentrating on the experience of the non-biological lesbian mother and examining how this figure in particular, as well as lesbian mothering more generally, interrogates the biologized system of filiation in France.[40] For Rye, the three autobiographical texts studied, which were published just before or just after the same-sex marriage law, offer insights into what it means to be a lesbian mother at a time when French law is beginning to recognize mothers whose mothering operates outside the limits of conventional filiation. Both of these studies of lesbian mothering focus primarily on texts treating planned lesbian families – that is to say, a family in which a lesbian couple intend to parent together from the beginning. This focus is pertinent in light of the debates on same-sex parenting in France, but it does not consider the many women who have children in a heterosexual relationship before coming out as lesbian. This volume focuses on both 'ex-heterosexual' and planned lesbian families, thus providing a

Diana Knight and Judith Still, eds, *Women, Genre and Circumstance: Essays in Memory of Elizabeth Fallaize* (Oxford: Legenda, 2012), 109–21.

38   Rye, 'Marginal Identities and New Kinship Paradigms', 113.

39   Rye, 'Marginal Identities and New Kinship Paradigms', 123.

40   Gill Rye, 'Mums or Dads? Lesbian Mothers in France', in Gill Rye, Victoria Browne, Adalgisa Giorgio, Emily Jeremiah, and Abigail Lee Six, eds, *Motherhood in Literature and Culture: Interdisciplinary Perspectives from Europe* (Abingdon: Routledge, 2017), 98–110.

more complete picture of how lesbian mothering is represented in contemporary French literature.

Although many studies of French literature address the ways in which women's writing subverts patriarchal ideals of mothering, literary representations of lesbian mothering have yet to receive in-depth critical attention. Rye's pioneering work on portrayals of mothering in non-traditional family contexts is, however, a crucial point of reference for this book. In particular, it is her claim that literature offers wider definitions of parenting than those endorsed and institutionalized by French law that is the starting point for my own analysis.

Reimagining the Family: Corpus and Structure

In his introduction to *Representation: Cultural Representations and Signifying Practices* (1997), influential cultural studies scholar Stuart Hall argues that meaning is produced by, rather than simply found in, representation.[41] Following Hall, this study postulates that literature, as a mode of representation, can foster, as well as reflect, ideological and social change. The continued popularity of reading as a leisure activity makes literature a potentially powerful force of change. A 2019 Ipsos study found that 88 per cent of French people described themselves as readers and 31 per cent had read twenty or more books in the preceding twelve months.[42] This book, then, argues that French literary portrayals of lesbian mothering not only mirror but also contribute to the debates on same-sex families and to the meaning of motherhood and the family in twenty-first-century France.

41   Stuart Hall, ed., *Representation: Cultural Representations and Signifying Practices* (London: SAGE, 1997), 5.

42   Armelle Vincent-Gérard and Julie Poncet, 'Les Français et la lecture en 2019', an Ipsos study for the Centre National du Livre (2019), <https://www.centrenationaldulivre.fr/fichier/p_ressource/17602/ressource_fichier_fr_les.frana.ais.et.la.lecture.2019.03.11.ok.pdf>, accessed 3 January 2020.

The timing and functional nature of the texts analysed here make it pertinent to read them as harbingers of change. Seven of the ten texts were published between the creation of the PACS in 1999 and the legalization of same-sex marriage in 2013. These are, then, texts that were written in a very particular context that undoubtedly influenced how they were written and guides readers' responses to them. The texts seek, sometimes explicitly, to achieve political and social aims. While they do not claim to speak for same-sex parents and their children, they inevitably give visibility and a voice to these people and offer privileged insights into their experiences. Taken together, the authors appear to be writing with several aims: to justify their own decisions to become parents; to convince readers that same-sex families are no better or worse than other families; to satirize heteronormative and homophobic discourses; or to mediate between sympathizers and opponents of same-sex families. The texts also have a clear didactic purpose, featuring interactions showing how the family might be reimagined in non-heterosexual contexts and in which the characters act as mouthpieces for the different positions in the debates on same-sex families. Subsequent chapters will further explore the functional nature of the texts in the changing political landscape in France.

Given that same-sex families have only recently become a visible social phenomenon, it is perhaps unsurprising that the number of texts portraying lesbian mothers is still quite small. The fact that most texts featuring lesbian mothers were published after 2000 may, however, indicate an emerging trend. In addition to those analysed in this volume, five other titles stand out: Claire Altman's *Deux femmes et un couffin* [*Two Women and a Crib*] (2005); Claire Breton's *J'ai 2 mamans, c'est un secret* [*I Have 2 Mums, It's a Secret*] (2005); Muriel Douru's *Deux mamans et un bébé* [*Two Mums and a Baby*] (2008); Nathalie Séguin's *Une maman, une papa: récit d'une homoparentalité* [*A Mum and a Dad in the Feminine Form: An Account of Same-Sex Parenting*] (2013); and Jennifer Schwarz's *Une histoire de famille* [*A Family Hi/Story*] (2014).[43] All five texts are autobiographical

43 Claire Altman, *Deux femmes et un couffin* (Paris: Ramsay, 2005); Claire Breton, *J'ai 2 mamans, c'est un secret* (Paris: Leduc.s, 2005); Muriel Douru, *Deux mamans et un bébé* (Paris: KTM, 2011 [2008]); Nathalie Séguin, *Une maman, une papa: récit d'une homoparentalité* (Paris: Société des Écrivains, 2013); Jennifer Schwarz, *Une*

accounts, but Breton's is unique because, as the titles implies, the text – a retrospective account of meeting other people who grew up in same-sex families – is narrated from a child's, rather than a parent's, perspective. If literary representations of lesbian mothers are, then, beginning to emerge, texts featuring gay fathers remain very rare. Currently, only three examples, all of which are autobiographical, exist in French: *Papa gay: Lettre à mon enfant interdit* [*Gay Daddy: A Letter to My Forbidden Child*] (2009) by Swiss writer Pascal Pellegrino; *Deux hommes et trois couffins: Une tranche de vie réelle* [*Two Men and Three Cribs: A Slice of Real Life*] (2013) by Jean-Yves Duthel, who was born in France but has been living in Canada for many years; and *Ton père* [*Your Father*] (2017) by French film director and young adult writer Christophe Honoré.[44] The lack of literature about gay fathering might be explained by the smaller number of gay fathers relative to lesbian mothers in the population. Although this book focuses on adult literature, it is worth mentioning that a significant proportion of literary portrayals of same-sex families are picture books aimed at young children. Notable examples include Muriel Douru's *Dis … mamanS* [*Hey … MummIES*] (2003), Ophélie Texier's *Jean a deux mamans* [*Jean Has Two Mummies*] (2004), Béatrice Boutignon's *Tango a deux papas, et pourquoi pas?* [*Tango Has Two Daddies, and Why Not?*] (2010) and Juliette Parachini-Deny and Marjorie Béal's *Mes deux papas* [*My Two Daddies*] (2013).[45] Like many of the texts for adults, these texts aim above all to raise awareness and under-standing of the diversity of family forms in contemporary France.

Although this study does not cover all representations of lesbian mothering, the corpus includes a range of genres, both autobiographical

---

histoire de famille (Paris: Robert Laffont, 2014). For a discussion of the texts by Séguin and Schwarz, see Rye, 'Mums or Dads?'.

44   Pascal Pellegrino, *Papa gay: Lettre à mon enfant interdit* (Lausanne: Favre, 2009); Jean-Yves Duthel, *Deux hommes et trois couffins: Une tranche de vie réelle* (Saint-Zénon, Québec: Louise Courteau, 2013); Christophe Honoré, *Ton père* (Paris: Mercure de France, 2017).

45   Muriel Douru, *Dis … mamanS* (Paris: Éditions Gaies et Lesbiennes, 2003); Ophélie Texier, *Jean a deux mamans* (Paris: L'École des Loisirs, 2004); Béatrice Boutignon, *Tango a deux papas, et pourquoi pas?* (Issy-les-Moulineaux: Le Baron Perché, 2010); Juliette Parachini-Deny and Marjorie Béal, *Mes deux papas* (Nice: Tom'poche, 2015 [2013]).

and fictional. Of the autobiographical texts, those by François, Dumont and Bénard are written in storytelling mode, whereas those by Blanc and Célier are non-chronological testimonies. Of the fictional texts, Monferrand's *Les Amies d'Héloïse* is notable for its use of the epistolary form, while the other texts are written in a more conventional novel format. The corpus also includes highbrow texts, such as those by François and Monferrand, and mass-market literature, such as the novels by Girard, Cinq-Fraix and Mallet, the last of which was published by a specialist lesbian publishing house, KTM Éditions. The inclusion of highbrow and mass-market texts challenges the distinction between 'high' and 'mass' culture. As Hall explains, definitions of culture tend to distinguish between 'the sum of the great ideas, as represented in the classic works of literature, painting, music and philosophy – the "high culture" of an age'; and 'the widely distributed forms of popular music, publishing, art, design and literature, or the activities of leisure-time and entertainment, which make up the everyday lives of "ordinary people" – what is called the "mass culture" or the "popular culture" of an age'.[46] This distinction carries a 'powerfully evaluative charge', whereby high is deemed to be superior and mass inferior.[47] Against this, my study values all cultural productions equally and posits that both highbrow and mass-market literature can contribute to ideological and political debate and change. It thus partially resists Roland Barthes's distinction between the *texte de plaisir* [text of pleasure] – 'the text that comes from culture and does not break with it, is linked to a *comfortable* practice of reading'; and the *texte de jouissance* [text of bliss] – 'the text that discomforts [...], unsettles the reader's historical, cultural, psychological assumptions, the consistency of his tastes, values, memories, brings to a crisis his relation with language'.[48] While it is undeniable that some texts create greater discomfort than others, and that this can be reflected or enhanced by their form, I postulate that easy-reading texts have the potential to be just as politically transgressive as ones that are linguistically challenging. Moreover, the terms employed to distinguish between high and mass culture are far

46 Hall, *Representation*, 2.
47 Hall, *Representation*, 2.
48 Roland Barthes, *The Pleasure of the Text*, trans. Richard Miller (New York: Hill and Wang, 1975 [1973]), 14.

from self-evident. To recall Hall's quotation, what are 'classic' works of art, what constitutes 'philosophy', what is 'popular' and who are 'ordinary people'? In practice, the categories 'high' and 'mass' are not dichotomous and fixed but overlapping and unstable. The same is true of autobiography and fiction. There is, of course, a widely accepted link between personal experience and literary composition. The French literary turn towards autofiction from the 1970s has further problematized the distinction between autobiography and fiction. Focusing on a range of literary genres also offers opportunities for analysing the relationship between the form of the texts and their treatment of lesbianism and lesbian mothering.

As well as a range of literary forms, the corpus comprises works by established and less well-known writers. François and Monferrand have achieved considerable success in French mainstream literary circles. François received the Prix Femina for her third autobiographical novel, *Joue-nous 'España'* [*Play Us 'España'*] (1980), and Monferrand won the Prix Goncourt for best debut novel with *Les Amies d'Héloïse*.[49] Since I am primarily concerned with the representation of lesbian mothering – that is, with what literature has to say about lesbian mothering and how it says it – texts are included for thematic reasons, rather than on account of the writers' literary reputation, gender, sexuality or parental status. It is worth noting, however, that François, Monferrand, Célier, Blanc, Dumont and Bénard are known to identify as lesbian. While an author's gender, sexuality or parental status can undoubtedly impact on her treatment of lesbianism and mothering, this book follows postmodernism's distrust of author-centred criticism.[50] In his famous essay 'La Mort de l'Auteur' [The Death of the Author] (1968), Barthes advocates the birth of the reader at the expense of the death of the Author.[51] For Barthes, reading can begin only when the author's intentions are no longer the guide to the interpretation of the text. Problematically, author-centred criticism postulates that texts have only one meaning, the author's, and overlooks the divergent meanings that

49   Jocelyne François, *Joue-nous 'España'* (Paris: Mercure de France, 1980).

50   For a discussion of the shift from author- to reader-centred criticism, see Roger Webster, *Studying Literary Theory: An Introduction* (London: Arnold, 1990), 11–27.

51   Roland Barthes, 'La Mort de l'Auteur' (1968), in Éric Marty, ed., *Œuvres complètes*, 5 vols (Paris: Seuil, 1993–2002), II (1994), 491–5.

texts have according to the conditions in which they are read. It also, as Steph Lawler notes, 'assumes that the reader could *know* what the author intends, and, indeed, it would do away with any need for analysis since the narrative would simply "speak for itself"'.[52] By decentring the author as the object of criticism, postmodern literary theory transfers the power to create meaning to the reader. This reader-centred approach to literary criticism owes much to Ferdinand de Saussure's theory of language as a system of signs consisting of a signifier, the spoken or written word, and a signified, the concept. According to Saussure, the relationship between the signifier and the signified is arbitrary.[53] Meaning, then, is not referential – that is to say, signs have no inherent quality that defines them. Rather, it is we, the speakers of a language, who construct meaning to the extent that it appears fixed and natural. By applying Saussure's theory of language to the text, Barthes concludes that texts have multiple meanings. Thus, the text is not the product of its author's meaning but of the meaning created by the reader.

As well as influencing stylistic and thematic choices, factors such as genre and an author's reputation and sexuality are likely to affect reader-ship. Lesbian readers may be more inclined to read lesbian authors and texts published by lesbian publishers out of a desire to identify with them or, on a more political level, in solidarity with them. Prestige makes an author appealing to a broader spectrum of readers who value works that are well regarded by the literary establishment; at the same time, it may put off readers who find this intimidating or who prefer easy-reading texts. The autobiographical testimonies by Célier and Blanc offer guidance to same-sex couples thinking about starting a family and heterosexual readers wishing to learn more about same-sex families. The focus on a range of authors and genres captures the diversity within the literary landscape and among readers.

---

52   Steph Lawler, 'Stories and the Social World', in Michael Pickering, ed., *Research Methods for Cultural Studies* (Edinburgh: Edinburgh University Press, 2008), 32–49 (46).

53   Ferdinand de Saussure, *Cours de linguistique générale*, 3rd edn (Paris: Payot, 1949 [1916]), 100.

This book is divided into five chapters. Chapter 1 positions the texts within the three theoretical fields most relevant to lesbian mothering – psychoanalysis, feminism and queer theory – and suggests, in broad terms, how they engage with these perspectives. I begin by discussing the limits of psychoanalysis, particularly Freudian theory, for thinking about the lesbian family. The second section takes Simone de Beauvoir's ambivalent stance on motherhood in *Le Deuxième Sexe* [*The Second Sex*] (1949) as a key starting point and goes on to trace the shift towards more positive feminist positions on mothering. I then address emerging queer perspectives on mothering that consider family forms that challenge the widely accepted view of mothering as a fundamentally heterosexual role. In keeping with my central focus on reimagining the family, I also discuss the debate on how far same-sex families significantly differ from or largely replicate heterosexual families.

Maintaining this focus, the order of Chapters 2 to 5 serves to emphasize the gradual expansion of the meaning of motherhood found in the ten texts. Chapters 2 and 3 concentrate on the five texts in which many of the traditional limits of the term 'mother' are respected: the mother is biologically related to her children; she is their only mother; and she has them with a male partner. In Chapter 2, I analyse representations of lesbian mothers who, to varying degrees, struggle to reconcile their sexuality with the maternal role, focusing on François's *Les Bonheurs*, Dumont's *La Vie dure* and Mallet's *Le Choix de la reine*. I first examine the heteronormative forces seeking to preclude lesbianism and lesbian families in the works by François and Dumont. I then consider the impact of non-traditional family forms on the mother–daughter relationship in Mallet's novel. Although the chapter is organized thematically, then, analysis of literary form and genre is interspersed throughout. Particular attention is paid to the parallel between linguistic experimentation and the subversion of sexual norms in François's *Les Bonheurs* and how this contrasts with the other texts.

Chapter 3 draws on feminist claims that maternal love is assumed to be unconditional to interpret the ambivalent relationship between the protagonist and her children in Monferrand's *Les Amies d'Héloïse* and *Les Enfants d'Héloïse*. My reading of these novels centres on the apparent tension between their traditionalist form and transgressive themes. I begin with a close analysis of the novels' form and genre, focusing on the use of the epistolary form in *Les Amies d'Héloïse* and its intertextual links to the epistolary classics of the eighteenth century. I then examine Monferrand's treatment of lesbianism and lesbian mothering.

Chapters 4 and 5 turn to the texts by Girard, Cinq-Fraix, Célier, Blanc and Bénard. Unlike those discussed in Chapters 2 and 3, these texts extend the typical definition of mothering. By depicting lesbian couples planning to parent together from the beginning, they challenge the assumption that children have only one mother and the biologistic definition of mothering. Chapter 4 examines how the texts rethink the family as a non-heterosexual, non-biological unit. I begin by examining how the texts expose and ultimately go beyond the heteronormative attitudes that preclude same-sex parenting. I then examine the reasons for which the lesbian couples opt in favour of or against incorporating a father into their families. Having examined the role of the father, I then turn to the representation of the 'other' mother – that is, the non-biological mother. This section examines the arguments and strategies used by the texts to legitimize mothering in the absence of a culturally and legally significant biological connection. As in Chapter 2, form is discussed throughout this chapter. Special attention is paid to the role of autobiography in Célier's *Maman, Mamour* and Blanc's *Elles eurent beaucoup d'enfants*.

Finally, Chapter 5 deals with issues of difference and equality. I first examine how the texts engage with the debate on how far same-sex families differ from other families. This chapter also considers the texts' engagement with the campaigns for legal equality for homosexual couples and parents, such as the same-sex marriage campaign and the debate on lesbian couples' access to fertility treatment. Finally, the chapter discusses the texts' positions on forms of identity politics, such as LGBT+ parenting associations.

The literary portrayals of lesbian mothering on which this book focuses exist alongside a wealth of feminist, psychoanalytic and queer theoretical work on gender, sexuality and the family, and it is to these fields that I now turn.

CHAPTER I

Theorizing Lesbian Mothering

Since the early twentieth century, psychoanalysis and feminism have been equally influential in shaping understandings of mothering, yet their ideas on the subject have often been at odds: in Freudian thinking, motherhood is the natural consequence of female psychological development; feminists have fought to expose this view as an instrument of patriarchy, to uncouple notions of femininity from mothering and, ultimately, to make motherhood a choice. Since the 1970s, increasing attention has been paid to lesbian mothers, initially by social scientists and with a focus on those who had children in a previous heterosexual relationship. More recently, queer theorists have started to explore how mothering might be theorized and experienced in non-heterosexual contexts.

In this chapter, I provide a critical overview of the most relevant contributions to this vast, multidisciplinary area of research, which forms the theoretical framework of this book. I begin by presenting early psychoanalytic theories of mothering. I then turn to feminist theories of mothering, including perspectives from feminist psychoanalysis. In keeping with this book's central focus on reimagining the family, I then discuss how far same-sex families are different from heterosexual families, as well as the emerging perspectives on mothering within queer theory.

Early Psychoanalysis and Mothering

In Freudian thinking, mothers and fathers have unique roles in ensuring their children's healthy psychological and social development. Freudian psychoanalysis would, then, seem to oppose same-sex parenting; Freud regarded homosexuality itself as an abnormal form of psychological development. The emphasis on the distinct roles of mothers and fathers in Freudian thinking makes it of relatively limited use when thinking about the same-sex family. Despite this, this school of thought remains politically powerful because it fuels many of the arguments used to oppose same-sex parenting in France today and is, therefore, what the literary texts studied in this book seek to challenge.

Freud's well-known theory of the Oedipus complex postulates that sexuality emerges not during puberty but in early childhood. In his 'Three Essays on the Theory of Sexuality' (1905), Freud describes infantile sexuality as 'polymorphously perverse' – that is to say, formless, multidirectional, non-procreative and uninhibited by the 'mental dams' of shame, disgust and morality that curb sexual excess.[1] Polymorphous perversity is repressed and channelled into the socialized (heterosexual and procreative) form of adult sexuality – a process that Freud calls 'infantile amnesia' – by way of the Oedipus complex.[2] During the Oedipal phase, the mother, the child's primary caregiver and love object, is rejected in favour of the father, who thus enforces the separation between mother and child and enables the child to later form its own identity. For Freud, the Oedipus complex is driven by biology: while it may be a result of socialization, fundamentally it is 'organically determined and fixed by heredity'.[3] During the Oedipal phase, the male infant desires to possess the mother and perceives the father as a rival. He then abandons his desire for the mother for fear that he will be castrated by the father, thus accepting his authority. The female infant blames the mother for her 'lack' of a penis and experiences what Freud refers to as 'penis envy' – the desire to possess a penis and the power that it would give her. The little girl therefore turns to the father, before resolving to become a mother, preferably to a son, so that she might possess a penis 'of her own'. In Freud's thinking, then, maternal desire represents the

---

1   Sigmund Freud, 'Three Essays on the Theory of Sexuality' (1905), in Elisabeth Young-Bruehl, ed., *Freud on Women: A Reader* (London: Hogarth, 1990), 89–145 (119).

2   Freud, 'Three Essays on the Theory of Sexuality', 106.

3   Freud, 'Three Essays on the Theory of Sexuality', 108.

dissolution of the girl's Oedipus complex. For Freud, the mother functions merely as an object of or obstacle to the infant's desire, while the father occupies the position of authority. As Stephen Frosh states in his introduction to Freud's work, the father acts as the 'symbol of patriarchal authority and hence of all social authority under patriarchy'; it is he who 'stands in the position of the originator of culture and of sexual difference, of what is male and female, allowable and forbidden'.[4] While the obvious male bias in this position has been thoroughly challenged, the idea that growing up with same-sex parents could prevent children from understanding sexual difference is still frequently used to oppose same-sex families.

Understandably, feminists have objected to Freud's phallocentrism and misogynistic references to penis envy. Before second-wave feminism, though, Freud's work underwent considerable extension and revision by psychoanalysts during his own lifetime. Melanie Klein, for instance, acknowledges her considerable intellectual debt to Freud, but her theory of the Oedipus complex diverges from the original in a number of ways. In her early essay 'Early Stages of the Oedipus Conflict' (1928), Klein argues that the Oedipal tendencies are triggered earlier than Freud believed, as early as the period of weaning and training in cleanliness.[5] As a result, Klein attaches considerable importance to the infant's identification and changing relationship with the mother as the Oedipal tendencies emerge. Whereas Freud considers the girl's realization of her lack of a penis to be what compels her to turn away from the mother, Klein states that this is fundamentally caused by the deprivation of the mother's breast; the lack of a penis just reinforces the rejection of the mother.[6] Klein's Oedipal model also differs from Freud's in the emphasis that she places on the violence that the infant directs towards the mother during weaning. For Klein, the infant 'desires to destroy the libidinal object by biting, devouring and cutting it, which leads to anxiety, since awakening of the Oedipus tendencies

---

4   Stephen Frosh, *The Politics of Psychoanalysis: An Introduction to Freudian and Post-Freudian Theory*, 2nd edn (Basingstoke: Macmillan, 1999 [1987]), 50.

5   Melanie Klein, 'Early Stages of the Oedipus Conflict' (1928), in *'Love, Guilt and Reparation' and Other Works, 1921–1945* (London: Vintage, 1998 [1975]), 186–98 (186).

6   Klein, 'Early Stages of the Oedipus Conflict', 193.

is followed by introjection of the object, which then becomes one from which punishment is to be expected'.[7] Klein's Oedipal model, then, reveals the considerable ambivalence in the relationship between mothers and infants and presents the mother not as a passive object or obstacle, as Freud's does, but as an active agent of child development.

The object relations school of psychoanalytic thought, with which Klein herself has sometimes been associated, further emphasizes the role of the pre-Oedipal relationship with the mother in child development.[8] Whereas Freud places instincts at the heart of mental life, object relations theory underlines the role of relationships in development. Consequently, it has, as I will discuss later with reference to the work of Nancy Chodorow, proven to be popular among feminists seeking to eschew Freudian biologistic explanations for women's mothering. Moreover, object relations theorists devote considerable attention to the role of the mother in child development. Donald Winnicott's notion of the 'good enough mother' typifies this approach. For Winnicott, a good enough mother is 'one who makes active adaptation to the infant's needs' by gradually enabling the infant to separate itself from her and to form its own identity.[9] Significantly, the emphasis placed on the role of the father by Freud is markedly absent from Winnicott's object relations theory. This, as well as his claim that a good enough mother is not necessarily the infant's biological mother, partially opens the door to a psychoanalytic model of the lesbian family.

Despite this, psychoanalysis is a relatively limited theoretical paradigm for thinking about same-sex parenting. The importance of this field should not, however, be underestimated, for it is the theories of early psychoanalysis, and the work of Freud in particular, that modern-day detractors of same-sex parenting evoke when they insist on the centrality of mixed-sex parenting to children's healthy development. Furthermore,

---

7   Klein, 'Early Stages of the Oedipus Conflict', 187.

8   For a discussion of Klein's relationship with object relations theory, see Frosh, *The Politics of Psychoanalysis*, 4–5.

9   D. W. Winnicott, 'Transitional Objects and Transitional Phenomena' (1951), in *Collected Papers: Through Paediatrics to Psycho-Analysis* (London: Tavistock, 1958), 229–42 (237).

Freud's Oedipal model is the starting point for many feminist theories of mothering, to which I now turn.

Feminism and Mothering

Feminism has an ambivalent relationship with mothering. Celebrated by some feminists as a specificity of women's identities and a metaphor for their creativity, mothering is considered by others to be instrumental in maintaining female oppression. Others still have tried to bridge the gap between these two camps by rejecting patriarchal motherhood while maintaining that maternal experience is, at least potentially, a source of female empowerment. Beginning with Simone de Beauvoir's *Le Deuxième Sexe* [*The Second Sex*] (1949), which laid the foundations of feminism's critique of mothering, this section charts the evolution of and critically reviews the most influential feminist theories of mothering.

In *The Second Sex*, Beauvoir challenges the widely held belief that womanhood is innate and intrinsically tied to mothering. Beauvoir strives to ensure that becoming a mother is a choice rather than a social obligation. To this end, her chapter on mothering in *The Second Sex* begins with a call to legalize abortion and oral contraception, and goes on to repudiate the essentialist assumption that women have a maternal instinct – that is, both a desire to have children and a natural capacity to love and nurture them.[10] In Beauvoir's view, a woman's capacity to love her children depends on the circumstances in which she becomes a mother and, most crucially, on whether motherhood is a choice. Beauvoir's ambivalence towards mothering is, in addition, a recurrent theme of her autobiographical works, in which mothers are portrayed as tender but also as manipulative, overbearing and self-effacing.[11]

10   Simone de Beauvoir, *Le Deuxième Sexe: L'Expérience vécue*, Folio Essais, 38 (Paris: Gaillmard, 1976 [1949]), 364.
11   For a comprehensive discussion of Beauvoir's treatment of mothering, see Yolanda Astarita Patterson, *Simone de Beauvoir and the Demystification of Motherhood* (Ann Arbor, MI: UMI Research, 1989).

Second-wave feminists in France and the English-speaking world reiterated Beauvoir's critique of the equation of womanhood with maternity. Betty Friedan, for instance, regards mothering as a source of female discontentment and a cornerstone of what she calls 'the feminine mystique' – that is, the image and role assigned to women by postwar American society.[12] In *The Dialectic of Sex* (1970), Shulamith Firestone advocates an overhaul of childcare and reproductive relations. For Firestone, women's responsibility for the bearing and rearing of children is the fundamental inequality between the sexes. Female emancipation therefore demands that natural procreation be replaced by artificial reproduction and that the whole of society contribute to caring for children.[13] Undeniably, these texts played a crucial role in exposing gender inequality and awakening feminist consciousness at the time of their publication, yet their negative attitudes towards motherhood are to some degree outdated. The association between women and maternity is, at least in the West, less strict than it used to be: birth rates are falling; the majority of women have access to methods of birth control; and many women today combine mothering with a career. This has, however, resulted in what is popularly dubbed the 'double burden': responsibility for paid and the majority of unpaid labour. As recently as 2015, it was found that mothers assumed an unequal proportion of childcare and household responsibilities on top of the demands of paid employment.[14] This inequality imposes a heavy mental burden recently referred to in France as 'la charge mentale' [the mental load] – that is, as one newspaper puts it, 'the syndrome of women who are exhausted with "having to think of everything"'.[15] The fact that women do more

---

12   Betty Friedan, *The Feminine Mystique* (London: Norton, 2001 [1963]), 15.

13   Shulamith Firestone, *The Dialectic of Sex* (London: Cape, 1971 [1970]), 8–12.

14   Clare Lyonette and Rosemary Crompton, 'Sharing the Load? Partners' Relative Earnings and the Division of Domestic Labour', *Work, Employment and Society* 29/1 (2015), 23–40.

15   Émilie Tôn, 'La "charge mentale", le syndrome des femmes épuisées "d'avoir à penser à tout"', *L'Express* (10 May 2017), <http://www.lexpress.fr/actualite/societe/la-charge-mentale-le-syndrome-des-femmes-epuisees-d-avoir-a-penser-a-tout_1906874.html>, accessed 20 June 2017. Unless stated otherwise, all translations are my own.

housework encourages the belief that women must also think to do it and that men, when they do help, do so only in a supporting role. In an online cartoon called 'Fallait demander' [You Should've Asked] (2017), graphic artist 'Emma' critiques the notion that women should have to ask their husbands for help.[16] Women's advancement in the paid workforce has not, then, coincided with men's increased participation in domestic work.

The publication of Adrienne Rich's *Of Woman Born* in 1976 marked an important shift in feminist thinking about motherhood. Unlike previous feminist works on mothering, Rich explicitly states that motherhood is not oppressive to women 'except as defined and restricted under patriarchy'.[17] Rich distinguishes between the experience of mothering – or the potential relationship between mothers and children and between women and maternity; and the patriarchal institution of motherhood – that is, the norms that police this experience, including the prescription of mothering as women's sole or primary function. This distinction allowed Rich both to extend feminism's critique of patriarchy and to hypothesize that mothering can, if chosen and lived freely, empower women. It thus helped to create a space within feminist theory for women who genuinely desire to have children while defending other women's wish to remain childless.

Like Rich, Nancy Chodorow suggests in *The Reproduction of Mothering* (1978) that only patriarchal motherhood is oppressive to women. Chodorow's work continues to be an important reference point for its treatment of mothering from the perspective of psychoanalysis, which, as was noted earlier, has long had an antagonistic relationship with feminism. Principally, Chodorow seeks to explain why mothering is a female rather than male role. Rejecting biological essentialist and social constructionist explanations, Chodorow argues that women's mothering is reproduced by 'social structurally induced psychological processes'.[18] In Chodorow's view, the fact that an infant's first relationship is with a woman fosters

16 'Emma', 'Fallait demander', (9 May 2017), <https://emmaclit.com/2017/05/09/repartition-des-taches-hommes-femmes/>, accessed 20 June 2017.

17 Adrienne Rich, *Of Woman Born: Motherhood as Experience and Institution*, 2nd edn (London: Norton, 1986 [1976]), 14.

18 Nancy Chodorow, *The Reproduction of Mothering: Psychoanalysis and the Sociology of Gender* (Berkeley: University of California Press, 1978), 7.

life-long expectations in children.[19] That women mother and men do not is thus internalized psychically and subsequently reproduced. Despite this, throughout *The Reproduction of Mothering* Chodorow, true to the feminist cause, remains insistent on the potential and need for change, claiming that anyone, male or female, has the relational basis for parenting and ultimately calling for men's equal participation in childcare.[20]

In Britain, one of the leading second-wave feminist theorists of mothering and women's domesticity is sociologist Ann Oakley. In *Housewife* (1974), Oakley conceives of and deconstructs a 'myth of motherhood' bearing close resemblance to Rich's more well-known theorization of motherhood as an institution. According to Oakley, the myth of motherhood consists of three common assumptions: firstly, children need mothers; secondly, mothers need their children; and thirdly, becoming a mother is a woman's greatest achievement and means of self-fulfilment.[21] For Oakley, the myth of motherhood is, as the institution of motherhood is for Rich, a principal source of women's oppression, since it confines them to the private sphere and forestalls their financial independence and access to the power of public life.[22] Yet, Oakley, like Rich, implies the potential for ideological and social change, for beyond the myth of motherhood mothering is not inherently an obstacle to women's liberation. Rather, it is the normative organization of mothering that is to women's detriment. Much of Oakley's subsequent work further unpicks discourses and norms of femininity, domesticity and mothering. In *The Sociology of Housework* (1974), Oakley investigates women's attitudes towards domestic labour and finds that social isolation and the juggling of housewifery and child-rearing lead to women's dissatisfaction with both their domestic and their maternal roles.[23] In *Becoming a Mother* (1979), Oakley draws on interviews with first-time mothers to criticize the increasing medicalization of maternity care. In Oakley's view, the medicalization of maternity care is often unnecessary,

---

19   Chodorow, *The Reproduction of Mothering*, 83.
20   Chodorow, *The Reproduction of Mothering*, 215.
21   Ann Oakley, *Housewife* (Harmondsworth: Penguin, 1976 [1974]), 186.
22   Oakley, *Housewife*, 221.
23   Ann Oakley, *The Sociology of Housework* (London: Martin Robertson, 1974).

even dangerous, and therefore demonstrates a lack of concern for mothers.[24] Like Rich and Chodorow, then, Oakley does not see mothering as de facto oppressive to women. Rather, her critique is levelled at the circumstances and discourses that impact negatively on maternal experience.

French feminists have contributed to the debate among English-speaking theorists on the reconcilability of mothering with women's emancipation. In *Parole de femme* [*Woman's Word*] (1974), Annie Leclerc celebrates mothering as a uniquely female experience.[25] Christine Delphy, on the other hand, follows in Beauvoir's footsteps by rejecting mothering. Delphy denounces Leclerc as essentialist because she posits men and women as natural entities – that is, as categories deriving from biology – and even condemns Leclerc's work as 'pseudoscientific antifeminism'.[26] As a materialist feminist, Delphy believes that female oppression is a product of ideological and social structures.

Alongside Leclerc and Delphy, a group of French feminists spearheaded by Hélène Cixous, Luce Irigaray and Julia Kristeva took up the task of rewriting Freudian and Lacanian psychoanalysis from a feminist perspective and, in doing so, extended insights into the link between mothering and female psychological development. Cixous and Irigaray aim above all to theorize feminine subjectivity outside patriarchy. In Cixous's work, references to mothering are predominantly metaphorical. In 'Le Rire de la Méduse' [The Laugh of the Medusa] (1975), in which she calls on women to inscribe feminine subjectivity in writing, Cixous states that women write in 'white ink' – a figurative reference to breast milk.[27] Furthermore, Cixous widens the conventional meaning of mothering by using the word 'mother' to refer to a woman who instils in another woman love for her own body.[28] Finally, Cixous underlines the delights of pregnancy, thus rejecting the patriarchal taboo on the gestating body, but resists prescribing

---

24 Ann Oakley, *From Here to Maternity: Becoming a Mother* (Harmondsworth: Penguin, 1986 [1979]), 15–20.
25 Annie Leclerc, *Parole de femme* (Paris: Grasset, 1974).
26 Christine Delphy, 'Proto-féminisme et anti-féminisme', *Les Temps modernes* 346 (1975), 1469–1500 (1496).
27 Hélène Cixous, 'Le Rire de la Méduse', *L'Arc* 61 (1975), 39–54 (44).
28 Cixous, 'Le Rire de la Méduse', 44.

mothering as a prerequisite of femininity.[29] Like Leclerc, then, Cixous celebrates mothering as a site of feminine subjectivity and source of women's
literary inspiration.

Irigaray's interest in mothering lies in the mother–child and, in particular, the mother–daughter relationship. Irigaray argues that under patriarchy this relationship is founded on matricide – that is, the psychological
and symbolic murder of the mother. Irigaray describes matricide as a twofold
suppression. Firstly, the infant must reject the mother as its primary love
object in favour of the father. Irigaray's lyrical mother–daughter dialogue
in *Et l'une ne bouge pas sans l'autre* [*And the One Doesn't Stir without the
Other*] (1979) presents the daughter's struggle to extricate herself from her
ties to the mother.[30] Secondly, Irigaray argues in *Le Corps-à-corps avec la
mère* [*Body against Body: In Relation to the Mother*] (1981) that Western
civilization demands that mothers be suppressed. Challenging Freud's claim
that the primitive horde was founded on the murder of the father, Irigaray
contends that this murder was in fact preceded by that of the mother.[31] It is
not obvious whom or what Irigaray blames for the mother's murder, yet her
analysis of the Greek play the *Oresteia*, in which Orestes kills his mother
Clytemnestra, implies that the son is merely an agent of a patriarchal order
that demands matricide and that pardons Orestes by curing him of the
madness that this crime entails. Since Irigaray is clear that matricide today
is more or less as it was in ancient Greece, responsibility for the mother's
murder continues to lie with Western patriarchal civilization.

Kristeva charts the rise and recent decline of the cult of the Virgin
Mary as a model of mothering in Christian societies. In 'Stabat Mater'
(1977), Kristeva shows how mothering has long been portrayed as the only
legitimate form of female subjectivity.[32] According to this cult, mothers
should, like the Virgin Mary, be asexual and devoted to their children.

In addition to the psychoanalysis-based theories of mothering offered
by Irigaray, Cixous and Kristeva, French feminist historians Élisabeth

29   Cixous, 'Le Rire de la Méduse', 52.
30   Luce Irigaray, *Et l'une ne bouge pas sans l'autre* (Paris: Minuit, 1979).
31   Luce Irigaray, *Le Corps-à-corps avec la mère* (Montreal: La Pleine Lune, 1981), 19.
32   Julia Kristeva, 'Stabat Mater' (1977), in *Histoires d'amour* (Paris: Denoël, 1983),
     225–47 (225).

Badinter, Yvonne Knibiehler and Catherine Fouquet have sought to reveal the changing nature of maternal love. Echoing Beauvoir, Badinter in *L'Amour en plus* [*The Myth of Motherhood: An Historical View of the Maternal Instinct*] (1980) rejects the existence of maternal instinct, arguing that maternal love is culturally and historically variable.[33] According to Badinter, until the end of the eighteenth century mothers felt largely indifferent towards their children due in part to the high rate of infant mortality.[34] Ann Dally makes the same argument in *Inventing Motherhood* (1982).[35] It is, Badinter and Dally claim, a natural human reaction not to become attached to what one is likely to lose. The de-Christianization of attitudes towards death and the afterlife and the difficulty in defining and quantifying love make it hard to argue that mothers today love their children more than mothers did in the past. It is more pertinent, then, to emphasize Badinter's and Dally's contention that maternal love has changed in line with patterns of childcare. As they point out, wealthier mothers, who had the opportunity to raise their children because their husbands did not require them to work, commonly handed over the task of nurturing their children to wetnurses and nannies. As Badinter shows, only after 1760 did maternal love acquire sufficient moral and social value to push aristocratic women to raise their own children.[36] This is not to say that mothers in the past loved their children less than mothers do today. Rather, it shows that modes of expression of maternal love have changed. Whereas in the past mothers were often distant figures, in the modern West mothering is often considered to be a hands-on role to the extent that distant mothers are now susceptible to criticism and scorn. This trend is described by Badinter in her more recent book *Le Conflit: La femme et la mère* [*The Conflict: Woman and Mother*] (2010) as a new threat to gender equality.[37] Badinter argues that since the 1980s there has been a resurgence

---

33 Élisabeth Badinter, *L'Amour en plus: Histoire de l'amour maternel, XVIIᵉ–XXᵉ siècle* (Paris: Flammarion, 1980), 7–11.

34 Badinter, *L'Amour en plus*, 75–83.

35 Ann Dally, *Inventing Motherhood: The Consequences of an Ideal* (London: Burnett, 1982), 44.

36 Badinter, *L'Amour en plus*, 137–9.

37 Élisabeth Badinter, *Le Conflit: La femme et la mère* (Paris: Flammarion, 2010).

of the idea that motherhood is a natural process and that this now dominant model serves to re-establish motherhood as women's primary role and put them back in the home.

Knibiehler and Fouquet's *L'Histoire des mères du Moyen Âge à nos jours* [*The History of Mothers from the Middles Ages to the Present*] (1980) is explicitly feminist in that it attempts to write the history of mothering from the perspective of mothers themselves. The authors argue that mothers have been sidelined by historians, who have tended to focus on the male-dominated spheres of politics and the state.[38] Like Kristeva, Knibiehler and Fouquet emphasize the centrality of the Virgin Mary to medieval discourses of motherhood. In the Middle Ages, womanhood was constructed in terms of two dichotomous images: the Virgin Mary, who embodied innocence, obedience and devotion to the maternal role; and Eve – the temptress, but mother to us all.[39]

Mothering has resurfaced as a subject of feminist theory in the first decades of the twenty-first century thanks in no small part to Canadian scholar Andrea O'Reilly. In 1998, O'Reilly established the Association for Research on Mothering, which became the Motherhood Initiative for Research and Community Involvement in 2010, and its associative biannual journal. In 2006, she founded Demeter Press, the first feminist publisher dedicated to research on motherhood. The very establishment of these organizations suggests the continued relevance of mothering as a focus of scholarly attention. Indeed, O'Reilly coined the term 'motherhood studies' to establish motherhood as a discrete academic discipline. O'Reilly's numerous edited collections centre on the theories and practices of empowered and/or feminist mothering and owe much to Rich's distinction between women's experience of mothering and the institution of motherhood.[40] O'Reilly posits that, despite this distinction, Rich paved the way

38   Yvonne Knibiehler and Catherine Fouquet, *L'Histoire des mères du Moyen Âge à nos jours* (Paris: Montalba, 1980), 4–6.
39   Knibiehler and Fouquet, *L'Histoire des mères du Moyen Âge à nos jours*, 11.
40   Andrea O'Reilly, ed., *Feminist Mothering* (Albany, NY: SUNY Press, 2008); Andrea O'Reilly, ed., *From Motherhood to Mothering: The Legacy of Adrienne Rich's 'Of Woman Born'* (Ithaca, NY: SUNY Press, 2004); Andrea O'Reilly, ed., *Mother Outlaws: Theories and Practices of Empowered Mothering* (Toronto: Women's

for, but did not create, a theory of feminist mothering. A feminist mother, in O'Reilly's words, 'is a woman whose mothering, in theory and practice, is shaped and influenced by feminism'.[41] While empowered mothering and feminist mothering overlap insofar as they both challenge patriarchal discourses of motherhood, the latter is explicitly informed by feminism's critique of patriarchy. Following Rich, O'Reilly argues that mothers can affect social change through anti-sexist child-rearing and can feel empowered as mothers only if the institution of motherhood is deconstructed.[42]

Since the publication of *The Second Sex*, feminist attitudes towards mothering have become increasingly favourable. Although Beauvoir, in a 1976 interview with Alice Schwarzer, still likened the decision to get married and have children to slavery, mothering has come to be regarded, particularly by O'Reilly, as not only acceptable to feminism but, potentially, as an explicitly feminist enterprise.[43] The decline of the nuclear family since the 1970s has prompted researchers to consider mothering and child development in non-traditional family groupings, including same-sex families.

Difference, Equality and Lesbian Mothering

One of the most enduring debates among feminist and queer theorists concerns the place of difference in the fight for equality. As early as the nineteenth century, feminists were divided between those who believed that women's interests would be best served by recognizing and defending

---

Press, 2004); Andrea O'Reilly, ed., *Twenty-First-Century Motherhood: Experience, Identity, Policy, Agency* (New York: Columbia University Press, 2010).

41   O'Reilly, *Feminist Mothering*, 7.

42   Andrea O'Reilly, 'Mothering against Motherhood and the Possibility of Empowered Mothering for Mothers and Their Children', in Andrea O'Reilly, ed., *From Motherhood to Mothering: The Legacy of Adrienne Rich's 'Of Woman Born'* (Ithaca, NY: SUNY Press, 2004), 159–74 (160).

43   Alice Schwarzer and Simone de Beauvoir, '*Le Deuxième Sexe*: Trente ans après' (1976), in *Simone de Beauvoir aujourd'hui: Six entretiens* (Paris: Mercure de France, 1984), 71–85 (77).

female difference and those who thought it more productive to emphasize the similarities between the sexes.[44] In the twentieth century, this
divide re-emerged in the form of a debate between essentialists, who see
men and women as naturally occurring entities determined by biological
properties, and constructionists, who view gender as a product of social
conditioning.

For Cixous and Irigaray, female emancipation lies in the social and
cultural inscription of sexual difference, rather than in its suppression.
In 'The Laugh of the Medusa', Cixous, reading Freud and Lacan, calls for
the creation and inscription in writing of an *écriture féminine* – that is,
a feminine symbolic order that celebrates the specificities of the female
body and sexuality and thus destabilizes the symbolic dominance of the
phallus.[45] Like Cixous, Irigaray seeks to theorize feminine sexuality and
subjectivity outside patriarchy. In her early work *Ce sexe qui n'en est pas un*
[*This Sex Which Is Not One*] (1977), Irigaray, referring to Freud and Lacan,
postulates that female sexuality has always been conceptualized as a lack
or inferior version of male sexuality – in other words, as 'not one' – and
endeavours to rewrite female sexuality more positively.[46] In her short but
uncharacteristically lucid essay 'Petite annonce: Égales ou différentes?'
[Women: Equal or Different?] (1990), Irigaray asks what it is that women
want to be equal to.[47] Although Irigaray supports gender equality in social
and political terms – that is, she believes unequivocally that men and women
should have equal opportunities – she opposes the suppression of sexual
difference and the assimilation of the feminine to a physical and symbolic
male norm. In Irigaray's view, feminism must embrace sexual difference and
push for the recognition of 'sexuate rights'.[48] A wholesale rejection of the

44   See Geneviève Fraisse and Michelle Perrot, eds, *Histoire des femmes en Occident: Le
     XIXᵉ siècle* (Paris: Perrin, 2002 [1991]).
45   Cixous, 'Le Rire de la Méduse', 39.
46   Luce Irigaray, *Ce sexe qui n'en est pas un* (Paris: Minuit, 1977), 28.
47   Luce Irigaray, 'Petite annonce: Égales ou différentes?' (1990), in *Je, tu, nous: Pour
     une culture de la différence* (Paris: Grasset, 1990), 9–15 (12).
48   Luce Irigaray, 'Pourquoi définir des droits sexués?' (1988), in *Je, tu, nous: Pour une
     culture de la différence* (Paris: Grasset, 1990), 101–15 (104–7).

universalist conception of equal rights, sexuate rights account for gender inequality by granting different rights to men and women.

Because they seem to posit sexual difference as a given and derived from biology, Cixous and Irigaray have frequently been accused of essentialism.[49] Irigaray seems to reduce womanhood to a physiological reality and suggests that women's empowerment can come through the body, thus overlooking the persuasive constructionist argument that culture is central to women's oppression. Beauvoir's frequently cited claim that '[o]ne is not born a woman but, rather, becomes one' is synonymous with this position.[50] For Beauvoir, gender is a learned concept; the sexed body is merely a canvas on to which social and cultural ideas about gender are inscribed. In her landmark work *Gender Trouble* (1990), Judith Butler, building on Beauvoir, challenges her predecessor's emphasis on becoming, for to 'become' a gender means to 'arrive at' a finite entity, which, for Butler, is impossible. In Butler's view, gender is constituted performatively: there is no predefined or predetermined identity 'behind' acts of gender; rather, this identity is constantly being produced by the repetitive 'doing' of gender and, as such, is always open to redefinition.[51] Furthermore, Butler challenges the neat separation within feminist theory of biological sex from culturally constituted gender. For Butler, sex does not exist prediscursively – that is to say, the body can only be understood through discourses of gender. As Butler states: 'Perhaps this construct called "sex" is as culturally constructed as gender; indeed, perhaps it was always already gender'.[52] Butler therefore defines gender as the regime that sexes human beings into the categories of male and female: 'Gender ought not to be conceived merely as the cultural

---

49 See, for example, Ann Rosalind Jones, 'Writing the Body: Toward an Understanding of "L'Ecriture Feminine"', *Feminist Studies* 7/2 (1981), 247–63 (255); Toril Moi, *Sexual/Textual Politics: Feminist Literary Theory*, 2nd edn (London: Routledge, 2002 [1985]), 142; Monique Wittig, 'The Point of View: Universal or Particular?' (1980), in *'The Straight Mind' and Other Essays* (London: Harvester Wheatsheaf, 1992), 59–67 (59).

50 Beauvoir, *Le Deuxième Sexe*, 13.

51 Judith Butler, *Gender Trouble: Feminism and the Subversion of Identity*, Routledge Classics, 2nd edn (London: Routledge, 2007 [1990]), 34.

52 Butler, *Gender Trouble*, 9.

inscription of meaning on a pre-given sex (a juridical conception); gender must also designate the very apparatus of production whereby the sexes themselves are established'.[53] Finally, Butler challenges essentialist conceptions of gender by underlining the differences between women – for example, in terms of class, race and sexuality – rather than a supposedly inherent difference between women and men. *Gender Trouble* begins by questioning the pertinence of a feminism that claims to represent women. Since, in Butler's thinking, identities are constantly unstable, the category 'woman' as a subject of political representation cannot be comprehensive and inevitably creates exclusions. In this respect, Butler echoes the criticism levelled at second-wave feminism by Black and lesbian feminists for its bias towards White, heterosexual women. For Butler, identity politics thus threatens to become an instrument of the very power relations that it seeks to dismantle.

It was while this debate between essentialists and constructionists was happening that the first studies of gay and lesbian parenting were carried out. These studies, which appeared in the late 1970s, were prompted by the growing visibility of homosexual parents and the challenge that same-sex parenting issued to traditional theories of psychosocial development, which emphasize the distinctive role of mothers and fathers in the healthy development of children. These studies were, moreover, a response to prejudice against homosexual parents in the resolution of custody disputes and creation of adoption policies. Most early studies focused on children with divorced heterosexual parents and compared the development of children with custodial lesbian mothers to that of children with custodial heterosexual mothers, since this was most relevant to the largest number of custody disputes.[54] These studies investigated three unproven fears that were frequently cited to oppose gay and lesbian parents in court: firstly, children raised by same-sex parents will display signs of abnormal sexual development – that is, they will themselves identify as homosexual in later life; secondly, same-sex-parented children are more apt to develop mental

---

53   Butler, *Gender Trouble*, 10.
54   For a comprehensive review of these studies, see Charlotte J. Patterson, 'Children of Lesbian and Gay Parents', *Child Development* 63/5 (1992), 1025–42.

health problems than those brought up in heterosexual families; finally, children of lesbians and gay men struggle to build relationships with peers. All three fears proved to be unfounded: the social, psychological and sexual development of same-sex-parented children was found to compare with that of children living in heterosexual families. These findings have since become known as the 'no differences' model – that is, a view that presents no significant developmental differences between mixed- and same-sex-parented children.

Although studies have largely questioned the assumption that gay and lesbian parents produce gay and lesbian children, Paul Cameron's findings are a notable, if controversial, exception. In Cameron's study, more than half of daughters thought that their lesbian mother wanted them to become homosexual, and Cameron argues that this pressure, coupled with same-sex-parented children's immersion in 'gay culture', could impact on children's adult sexual identity.[55] For Cameron, investigations into the relationship between parental and child sexuality are both methodologically flawed and politically biased. He argues that since studies have predominantly focused on young children, the impact of parental homosexuality on adult children, who have gone through puberty and are more likely to be sexually active, has yet to be ascertained.[56] Cameron further contends that those who deny a correlation between parental and children's sexual identity are in favour of same-sex parenting and support proposals to extend adoption rights to same-sex couples.[57] Cameron has been widely condemned for his blatantly homophobic position on same-sex parenting, evidenced by his provocative reference to contagion theory – the belief that homosexuality is a learned pathology. While Cameron's findings appear to support the hypothesis that homosexual parents produce homosexual children, Walter Schumm, in response to Cameron's work, maintains that this possibility is only problematic if one has a problem with same-sex desire and

55 Paul Cameron, 'Children of Homosexuals and Transsexuals More Apt to Be Homosexual', *Journal of Biosocial Science* 38/3 (2006), 413–18 (416).
56 Cameron, 'Children of Homosexuals and Transsexuals More Apt to Be Homosexual', 414.
57 Cameron, 'Children of Homosexuals and Transsexuals More Apt to Be Homosexual', 415–16.

affectivity in the first place.[58] Furthermore, Judith Stacey and Timothy Biblarz point out the difficulty of defining sexuality.[59] Studies investigating the impact of parental sexuality on that of their children measure sexuality as a heterosexual–homosexual dichotomy, rather than as a continuum, and fail to account for the possible mutability and indefinability of sexual orientation.

While early studies of gay and lesbian parenting played a crucial role in preventing homosexual parents from losing custody of their children and, more recently, in encouraging legislative changes that extend parenting rights to same-sex couples, recent social scientific work on gay and lesbian parenting has problematized the 'no differences' model. Stacey and Biblarz, for example, argue that by accepting heterosexual families as the standard by which gay and lesbian parents ought to be judged this model reinforces heteronormativity and assumes that differences amount to deficits.[60] The preface to Gillian Hanscombe and Jackie Forster's *Rocking the Cradle* (1981), one of the earliest books about lesbian mothers, exemplifies the defensiveness that is the object of Stacey and Biblarz's critique. The book opens with a description of the 'usual idea of a lesbian' as 'someone who isn't quite nice', who 'is possibly mad, or possibly dangerous, or possibly freakish and pitiable' and who is depicted, in books and films, as masculine-looking, flat-chested, overweight and so on.[61] Clearly, this is not the authors' position on lesbianism, yet the book's next paragraph, although not lesbophobic, seeks to assimilate lesbian mothers to a heterosexual norm: 'It will seem strange to many,' write Hanscombe and Forster, 'to hear that hundreds of lesbians are not only not half-men, but that they are perfectly normal mothers.'[62] They go on:

58 Walter R. Schumm, 'Children of Homosexuals More Apt to Be Homosexuals? A Reply to Morrison and to Cameron Based on an Examination of Multiple Sources of Data', *Journal of Biosocial Science* 42/6 (2010), 721–42 (732).
59 Judith Stacey and Timothy J. Biblarz, '(How) Does the Sexual Orientation of Parents Matter?', *American Sociological Review* 66/2 (2001), 159–83 (171).
60 Stacey and Biblarz, '(How) Does the Sexual Orientation of Parents Matter?', 162.
61 Gillian Hanscombe and Jackie Forster, *Rocking the Cradle: Lesbian Mothers: A Challenge in Family Living* (London: Owen, 1981), 9.
62 Hanscombe and Forster, *Rocking the Cradle*, 9.

> [T]here are already thousands of [lesbian mothers], all over the world, bringing up their children just like other mothers do. We want to introduce you to some of these mothers, their friends and their children, so that you can see for yourselves how normal and ordinary they are.[63]

The authors' insistence on the normality of lesbian mothers is slightly at odds with their subsequent reservations about the normative status of the nuclear family.[64] Indeed, their argument in the above passage seems to underscore lesbian mothers' conformity to the norm. One way of coming to terms with this tension is to differentiate between the structural norm, which refers to the configuration of the family in terms of the parents' gender and sexual identity, and the emotional norm – that is, the feelings that parents experience in relation to their children. While lesbian mothers clearly depart from the normative nuclear configuration, heterosexual and lesbian mothers might well share similar emotional experiences in relation to their children. It is in this sense, according to Hanscombe and Forster, that lesbian mothers are just like other mothers.

Since the 2000s, researchers have begun to embrace the possibility that same-sex families provide children with a number of advantages: firstly, same-sex-parented children display greater tolerance of diversity relative to those in heterosexual families;[65] secondly, homosexual parents, especially lesbians, are more likely than heterosexual couples to divide paid and unpaid labour equally.[66] Henny Bos's comprehensive study comparing 100 planned lesbian families with 100 heterosexual families reveals several differences

---

63 Hanscombe and Forster, *Rocking the Cradle*, 9.
64 Hanscombe and Forster, *Rocking the Cradle*, 16–17.
65 Megan Fulcher, Erin L. Sutfin, and Charlotte J. Patterson, 'Individual Differences in Gender Development: Associations with Parental Sexual Orientation, Attitudes, and Division of Labor', *Sex Roles* 58/5 (2008), 330–41; Erin L. Sutfin, Megan Fulcher, Ryan P. Bowles, and Charlotte J. Patterson, 'How Lesbian and Heterosexual Parents Convey Attitudes about Gender to Their Children: The Role of Gendered Environments', *Sex Roles* 58/7 (2008), 501–13.
66 Jordan B. Downing and Abbie E. Goldberg, 'Lesbian Mothers' Constructions of the Division of Paid and Unpaid Labor', *Feminism and Psychology* 21/1 (2011), 100–20; Lawrence A. Kurdek, 'The Allocation of Household Labor by Partners in Gay and Lesbian Couples', *Journal of Family Issues* 28/1 (2007), 132–48; Charlotte J. Patterson, Erin L. Sutfin, and Megan Fulcher, 'Division of Labor among Lesbian

between these families.[67] Compared with heterosexual parents, lesbian mothers exhibit a greater desire to have children and tend to reflect more on their motives for starting a family. Whether children conform to social norms is less important to lesbian mothers than to heterosexual parents. Relative to heterosexual fathers, non-biological lesbian mothers report greater emotional involvement with their children, display more respect for their children's autonomy and are less likely to assert their power over their children. In addition, non-biological lesbian mothers feel obliged to justify the quality of their parenting more often than heterosexual fathers. For Bos, these findings do not show either type of family to be superior in terms of child development, which was found to be similar regardless of family type, but reveal the effects of discrimination against non-traditional families.[68] Experiences of stigmatization increase levels of parental stress in lesbian families. Lesbian mothers who had experienced more discrimination also reported more behavioural problems with their children, suggesting that the threat to children's wellbeing stems not from having lesbian parents but from the very social and cultural norms of kinship that opponents of same-sex parenting defend.

Following Stacey and Biblarz, scholars have begun to assert and re-claim the specificity of same-sex families on ideological as well as empirical grounds. Sasha Lerner and Ada Sinacore, for example, contend that comparative studies of heterosexual and lesbian parenting preserve a heterosexual–homosexual dichotomy that equates homosexuality with abnormality and posits that lesbian families are tolerable only insofar as they resemble heterosexual families.[69] Shelley Park warns that the desire to legitimize non-normative modes of kinship often engenders their assimilation

---

and Heterosexual Parenting Couples: Correlates of Specialized versus Shared Patterns', *Journal of Adult Development* 11/3 (2004), 179–89.

67   Henny M. W. Bos, *Parenting in Planned Lesbian Families* (Amsterdam: Amsterdam University Press, 2004).

68   Bos, *Parenting in Planned Lesbian Families*, 108.

69   Sasha Lerner and Ada L. Sinacore, 'Lesbian Mother–Heterosexual Daughter Relationships: Toward a Postmodern Feminist Analysis', *Journal of GLBT Family Studies* 8/5 (2012), 446–64 (457).

to the norm, thus nullifying their subversive potential.[70] Maureen Sullivan argues that, although same-sex families are but one example of the changes to sexuality and family life dating from at least the second half of the twentieth century, the results of these changes should ultimately be understood as novel configurations of kinship that depart radically from the traditional model.[71] For Sullivan, the effects of same-sex families on gender relations are potentially ground-breaking. If, as many feminists have argued, the heterosexual family is the site for the reproduction of patriarchy, this cycle might be broken by same-sex family formations.[72] Although Sullivan's argument is persuasive, it is important not to overstate or idealize the subversive potential of same-sex families. Same-sex parents do not automatically have non-normative attitudes towards gender, just as mixed-sex parents do not necessarily hold gender-conservative views. The transgressive potential of parenting lies in how children are raised rather than in the gender of the parents.

French social scientists share their North American colleagues' reservations about the 'no differences' model. Martine Gross, perhaps the most prolific researcher on same-sex parenting in France, maintains that acknowledging difference is necessary. For Gross, although the term 'homoparentalité' (a neologism coined by the *Association des Parents et Futurs Parents Gays et Lesbiens* [Association of Gay and Lesbian Parents and Future Parents] to refer to any family in which at least one adult who identifies as homosexual is the parent of at least one child) marks the same-sex parent context as divergent from the 'ordinary', heterosexual norm by underlining the homosexuality of parents, the denomination ultimately ensures the visibility of same-sex parenting.[73] In *La Famille en désordre* [*The Family in Disarray*] (2002), Élisabeth Roudinesco makes a similar argument:

---

70 Shelley M. Park, *Mothering Queerly, Queering Motherhood: Resisting Monomaternalism in Adoptive, Lesbian, Blended, and Polygamous Families* (Albany, NY: SUNY Press, 2013), 8.

71 Maureen Sullivan, *The Family of Woman: Lesbian Mothers, Their Children, and the Undoing of Gender* (Berkeley: University of California Press, 2004), 17.

72 Sullivan, *The Family of Woman*, 11–12.

73 Martine Gross, *Qu'est-ce que l'homoparentalité?* (Paris: Payot & Rivages, 2012), 7–8.

> It is also necessary to acknowledge that homosexual parents are different from other parents. That is why our society must accept that they exist as they are [...]. And it is not by forcing themselves to be 'normal' that homosexuals will be able to prove that they are fit to raise their children.[74]

Roudinesco's stance on same-sex parenting views aspirations to 'normality' as futile and difference as a means of achieving equality between mixed- and same-sex families. In *Les Mères lesbiennes* [*Lesbian Mothers*] (2010), the first French-language book devoted entirely to lesbian mothering, Virginie Descoutures argues that the aim should not necessarily be to normalize the lesbian family but to decentre the heterosexual family as the norm.[75] Instead of asking how far same-sex families resemble those headed by a heterosexual couple, Descoutures inverts the terms of the sameness–difference debate by uncoupling the nexus between normality and heterosexual parenting. Descoutures further argues that 'it is when the "universal" model is redefined as a social construction resulting from already existing power relations that the question of equal rights and treatment can be examined'.[76] For Descoutures, then, equality for lesbian mothers will only be achieved when the authority of the ideologically dominant, heterosexual family is questioned. Despite her own position, Descoutures's interviews with lesbian families show that mothers tend to assert their similarity to heterosexual mothers.

French scholars could be said to display a greater concern than those in the US with documenting the many structures of same-sex families and with theorizing the extent to which they depart from the normative nuclear triangulation. In *Qu'est-ce que l'homoparentalité?* [*What Is Same-Sex Parenting?*] (2012), Gross distinguishes principally between two-parent same-sex families and same-sex families with multiple parents, which are usually created when two same-sex couples decide to conceive a child together.[77] In *Des parents comme les autres* [*Parents Who Are Just Like Other Parents*] (2002), anthropologist Anne Cadoret identifies four types

---

74   Élisabeth Roudinesco, *La Famille en désordre* (Paris: Fayard, 2002), 238.
75   Virginie Descoutures, *Les Mères lesbiennes* (Paris: PUF, 2010), 122–3.
76   Descoutures, *Les Mères lesbiennes*, 134.
77   Gross, *Qu'est-ce que l'homoparentalité?*, 91–2.

of same-sex family: those created when one parent enters a homosexual relationship following the breakdown of a heterosexual partnership; co-parenting arrangements – that is, when a same-sex couple seek the help of an opposite-sex person or couple to conceive and raise a child together; those created via adoption; and those created through fertility treatment.[78] Éric Garnier's *L'Homoparentalité en France [Same-Sex Parenting in France]* (2012) follows Cadoret's model but differentiates between families created via surrogacy and those created via artificial insemination, as well as between co-parenting arrangements and step-parent families, thus distinguishing between six forms of same-sex family and, in this way, eschewing essentialism.[79] Whereas Gross therefore classifies same-sex families in numerical terms, Cadoret and Garnier group them according to the circumstances of their formation, and this in itself testifies to the different ways of thinking about the family in twenty-first-century France.

Some studies of same-sex families have endeavoured to go beyond a view of homosexual parents as either similar or different. In her comparative study of Irish and Swedish lesbian mothers, for instance, Róisín Ryan-Flood suggests that it might be more productive to see them as 'inhabiting norms differently'.[80] Stephen Hicks rejects the assimilation–transgression dilemma, arguing that it reiterates either/or-type arguments, reinforces the normative status of heterosexuality and confines same-sex families to essentialist positions.[81] Instead, Hicks advocates an approach that investigates how and why same-sex parents utilize claims to both conformity and difference in their everyday lives.[82] This is not to reject outright the ways in which these families reimagine the family, parenting and sexuality, but Hicks maintains that experiences of difference are only ever the result

---

78 Anne Cadoret, *Des parents comme les autres: Homosexualité et parenté* (Paris: Odile Jacob, 2002), 14–15.

79 Éric Garnier, *L'Homoparentalité en France: La Bataille des nouvelles familles* (Vincennes: Thierry Marchaisse, 2012), 16–22.

80 Róisín Ryan-Flood, *Lesbian Motherhood: Gender, Families and Sexual Citizenship* (Basingstoke: Palgrave Macmillan, 2009), 3.

81 Stephen Hicks, *Lesbian, Gay, and Queer Parenting: Families, Intimacies, Genealogies* (Basingstoke: Palgrave Macmillan, 2011), 8.

82 Hicks, *Lesbian, Gay, and Queer Parenting*, 4.

of dominant discourses and never a product of essential characteristics.[83] The arguments of Ryan-Flood and Hicks constitute the beginnings of a theoretical shift from sameness or difference to sameness and difference.

As well as social scientific studies of same-sex families, a handful of scholars have begun trying to 'queer' mothering. In this category, two titles in particular stand out: Shelley Park's monograph *Mothering Queerly, Queering Motherhood* (2013) and Margaret Gibson's edited collection entitled *Queering Motherhood* (2014). Park's study brings together adoptive, blended, lesbian and polygamous families on the grounds that, despite the specificities of each family type, they have something in common: the presence of two or more mothers. To queer motherhood, according to Park, is to legitimize and make visible the polymaternal family – that is to say, a family that comprises two or more women who both identify as mothers.[84] This demands that mothering be thought of in social as well as biological terms, just as queer theorists regard gender and sexuality as social constructs. Park further argues that, to some degree, to queer motherhood is to understand lesbian mothering as a prototype for other configurations of mothering.[85] It is, moreover, essential to look beyond the mother–child relationship and focus equally on the relationship between mothers. Drawing on Eve Sedgewick's point that bonding between men is traditionally posited as rivalry over a woman, thus reconfiguring queer desire as heterosexual desire, Park argues that interfemale bonding is frequently made intelligible by structuring it around a child, thus reframing it as reproductive desire.[86] In polymaternal families, Park writes, female bonding over children is thought of as rivalry. For instance, it is not inconceivable, given the cultural and legal importance of the biological in matters of parenting, that non-biological lesbian mothers should exhibit some anxiety or jealousy vis-à-vis their partner's relationship with their child.

Gibson, whose introduction begins with the caveat that queer eschews definition, suggests that to queer motherhood is, broadly speaking, to pull it outside the expectations of reproduction, sexuality, culture, kinship, race

83   Hicks, *Lesbian, Gay, and Queer Parenting*, 9.
84   Park, *Mothering Queerly, Queering Motherhood*, 3.
85   Park, *Mothering Queerly, Queering Motherhood*, 12.
86   Park, *Mothering Queerly, Queering Motherhood*, 11.

and embodiment.[87] Queer motherhood can therefore begin where any of these expectations are challenged. As Park's focus on a multitude of family types also implies, Gibson thus contends that, while much can be gleaned from hearing about the experiences of queer parents, the project of queering motherhood is not limited to studying mothers who identify as queer and especially not within existing heteronormative frameworks.[88] Moreover, Gibson asks if it is possible to queer motherhood by questioning methodological and theoretical norms of academic writing on motherhood.[89] This book does not seek to offer an answer to this question or to challenge 'scholarly norms' but, rather, to examine how French literary representations of lesbian mothering contribute to political and theoretical debates on gay and lesbian parenting. That said, Gibson's question is one about the pertinence of the binarized distinction between narrative and theory.

Many French-authored studies of same-sex families are also concerned with unpicking the negative discourses associated with them, perhaps due to the ongoing debates on gay and lesbian parenting in France. Gross's *Parent ou homo, faut-il choisir?* [*Parent or Homosexual: Does One Have to Choose?*] (2013), for instance, identifies the most prevalent arguments and stereotypes voiced to oppose gay and lesbian parenting.[90] Descoutures conducts interviews with twenty-four biological and twenty-four non-biological lesbian mothers to construct a picture of the experience of forming and belonging to a lesbian family. In addition, Descoutures employs the interviews to interrogate the heteronormative framework in which her interviewees' experiences take place and the discourses that inform this experience.

The question of how to deal with difference is the most enduring, and perhaps the most important, debate among scholars of same-sex parenting. Early social scientific research concluded that the sexuality of parents had little impact on the social, psychological and sexual development of children, leading to the 'no differences' model. This conclusion has since been

87   Margaret F. Gibson, ed., *Queering Motherhood: Narrative and Theoretical Perspectives* (Bradford, ON: Demeter, 2014), 1.
88   Gibson, *Queering Motherhood*, 5–6.
89   Gibson, *Queering Motherhood*, 10.
90   Martine Gross, *Parent ou homo, faut-il choisir? Idées reçues sur l'homoparentalité* (Paris: Le Cavalier Bleu, 2013).

challenged on ideological and empirical grounds. Scholars began to question the heteronormative assumption that it was only by resembling heterosexual families that same-sex families could be acceptable. Later studies also concluded that same-sex families differ from heterosexual families in several positive ways, notably children's attitudes towards gender roles. Most recently, scholars have suggested that, rather than trying to determine whether the same-sex family is largely the same as or broadly different from the heterosexual family, it may be more productive to look at how same-sex families utilize claims to both similarity and difference in their daily lives. As will be shown in Chapter 5, the sameness–difference debate is a dominant theme in literary works about lesbian mothering, as well as a longstanding issue for theory. The theories presented in this chapter will, then, be central to the theoretical framework of Chapter 5, and attempts will be made to position the literary corpus within this theoretical context.

Concluding Thoughts

As this chapter has revealed, the family is constantly being reimagined over time and in different theoretical paradigms. In early psychoanalytic thinking, the heterosexual family in which the father represents authority is essential to social and psychological development. Feminists have endeavoured to challenge this patriarchal model of the family and, in some cases, even theorize the family as a potential source of female empowerment. More recently, social scientists and queer theorists have problematized the view of the family as an inherently heterosexual unit. Although these insights might, then, be the most valuable for thinking about the same-sex family, the literary texts analysed in subsequent chapters also engage with feminist and psychoanalytic notions of the family, particularly, in the case of psychoanalysis, in order to contest them.

While same-sex families are an established research field in the social sciences, cultural studies scholars have yet to really examine how same-sex families are being presented in artefacts of cultural production. This book, which begins to fill this gap, is premised on the idea that such artefacts, of which literature is an example, have the power not only to passively reflect social phenomena but to actively contribute to debates on them. As Shirley-Ann Jordan aptly puts it in a chapter on the family in contemporary women's writing:

> [F]iction is a primary site for 'figuring out' the family: for interrogating its structures and ideologies at given historical junctures; for exploring family relationships and the place of the individual within them; and for developing productive figures or tropes which re-imagine family in distinctive ways.[91]

How, then, do the literary texts analysed in this book reimagine the family? How do they not only reflect but also contribute to political and theoretical debates on same-sex families in contemporary France? It is to these questions that the following chapters hope to offer answers.

---

91 Shirley-Ann Jordan, 'Figuring Out the Family: Family as Everyday Practice in Contemporary French Women's Writing', in Marie-Claire Barnet and Edward Welch, eds, *Affaires de familles: The Family in Contemporary French Culture and Theory* (Amsterdam: Rodopi, 2007), 39–58 (39).

CHAPTER 2

From Lesbianism or Mothering to Lesbian Mothering

As the title of Martine Gross's *Parent ou homo, faut-il choisir?* [*Parent or Homosexual: Does One Have to Choose?*] (2013) implies, homosexuality is not typically associated with parenthood. Indeed, a study by Maxime Cervulle of over 450 articles published at the time of the same-sex marriage debate shows that in the national press it became common to link heterosexuality to fertility and homosexuality to sterility.[1] Although patently untrue, the equation of homosexuality with infertility serves to cast doubt on homosexuals' capacity to raise children and reinforce the supremacy of the heterosexual family.

In this chapter, I examine three texts – Jocelyne François's *Les Bonheurs* [*Happinesses*] (1970), Axelle Mallet's *Le Choix de la reine* [*The Queen's Choice*] (2009) and Paula Dumont's *La Vie dure: Éducation sentimentale d'une lesbienne* [*The Hard Life: A Lesbian's Sentimental Education*] (2010) – that engage with the heteronormative claim that a woman cannot be a lesbian and a mother and the patriarchal belief that her sole or primary concern is her children's welfare.[2] In these texts, the mothers end their lesbian relationships in order to have or prioritize their children. In *Les Bonheurs*, a devastated Anne breaks up with an equally distraught Sarah and agrees

1   Maxime Cervulle, 'Les Controverses autour du "mariage pour tous" dans la presse nationale quotidienne: du différentialisme ethno-sexuel comme registre d'opposition', *L'Homme & la Société* 189–90 (2013), 207–22 (213).
2   Jocelyne François, *Les Bonheurs* ([n.p.]: Lacombe, 1982 [1970]); Axelle Mallet, *Le Choix de la reine* (Paris: KTM, 2009); Paula Dumont, *La Vie dure: Éducation sentimentale d'une lesbienne* (Paris: L'Harmattan, 2010); subsequent references to these works are provided as in-text citations in the following forms: (B p.), (CDLR p.), (VD p.).

to marry Michel, with whom she has two children. Meanwhile, Sarah begins a long-term affair with a married man, Jean, before she and Anne are eventually reunited. *Le Choix de la reine* begins when 15-year-old Marion, unaware that her mother, Elena, is a lesbian, walks in on her in bed with Louise, who is Marion's teacher. Angry and shocked, Marion schemes to end the affair by contacting her mother's lost lesbian lover, Raphaëlle, whom Elena left when her ex-husband, Marion's father, threatened to abandon Marion if the relationship continued. Mother and daughter ultimately reconcile, and Elena chooses to be with Raphaëlle. In *La Vie dure*, Pascale is abandoned by her lover, Catherine, who decides to marry a man and start a family. Twenty years later, Catherine, now a mother of two, contacts Pascale, and they enjoy an intermittent reunion before Catherine leaves Pascale for another woman.

Although attitudes towards homosexuality changed considerably during the period that the texts cover – *Les Bonheurs* is set in the 1950s, *La Vie dure* in the 1980s and *Le Choix de la reine* in the 2000s – the fact that the characters end their lesbian relationships points to the difficulty of being an openly lesbian mother throughout this period. Indeed, it is significant that *Les Bonheurs* and *La Vie dure* are set before same-sex couples were given the right to become civil partners in 1999 (it is worth noting too that although *Le Choix de la reine* begins in 2006, Elena breaks up with Raphaëlle in the early 1990s). In this period, there was no legal provision for and little public awareness of gay and lesbian parents, who, as late as the 1970s, could lose custody battles on the grounds of their sexuality. The difficult circumstances in which the lesbian mothers in the texts are positioned are therefore hardly surprising.

The texts are, then, similar in terms of plot and setting, but they differ greatly in form and genre. Based on the taxonomy of literary genres developed by Philippe Lejeune in *Le Pacte autobiographique* [*The Autobiographical Pact*] (1975), *Les Bonheurs* and *La Vie dure* can be classified as autobiographical novels. Lejeune describes autobiography as a 'pact', a sort of contract, between author and reader, the implication of which is that the author pledges to write as truthfully as possible about his or her life.[3] For Lejeune, this pact can only be established if the text's author, narrator

---

3   Philippe Lejeune, *Le Pacte autobiographique*, new edn (Paris: Seuil, 1995 [1975]), 44–6.

and protagonist bear the same name, and if this is indicated in the text.[4]
If the author's name differs from that of the narrator or protagonist, as is
the case in *Les Bonheurs* and *La Vie dure*, the text is an autobiographical
novel. François and Dumont have confirmed the overtly autobiographical
nature of their works. Moreover, in *La Vie dure* the connection between
author and protagonist is strongly implied by their similar names – Paula
Dumont and Pascale Delmont. As the author's brief biographical statement
makes clear, they also share numerous biographical characteristics: Dumont
and Pascale are similar in age; they both live in Montpellier; they are both
teachers; they both identify as lesbians; and they are both members of gay
and lesbian rights groups. Although these texts belong to the same genre,
they are, as I will discuss below, stylistically different. Their titles attest to
this: if Dumont's title, *La Vie dure*, clearly expresses the difficulty of assuming a lesbian relationship in a homophobic and patriarchal context,
François's title, because its optimism is out of keeping with the mostly
sad story, encourages the reader to reflect on language as well as plot. The
striking use of the plural form of 'bonheur' [happiness] particularizes the
notion of happiness, implying that it exists at specific moments rather than
as a general state, and suggests that François plays with language to a greater
extent than Dumont. Moreover, the presence of the word 'roman' [novel]
on the front cover of *Les Bonheurs* indicates that the text blurs categories
of genre in a way that *La Vie dure* does not.

Le Choix de la reine is a romance novel of the popular fiction variety.
Popular fiction, as Suzanne Juhasz notes, typically relies on plot rather than
form to serve as the 'primary agent for the representation of meaning'.[5]
Diana Holmes seconds this point and, in addition, observes that popular
fiction is also characterized by the presence of an omniscient narrator and
'real'-seeming characters.[6] Mallet's novel exhibits these conventions. It is
plot-centred: it has a clear beginning, middle and end; and the ending

4   Lejeune, *Le Pacte autobiographique*, 15.
5   Suzanne Juhasz, 'Lesbian Romance Fiction and the Plotting of Desire: Narrative
     Theory, Lesbian Identity, and Reading Practice', *Tulsa Studies in Women's Literature*
     17/1 (1998), 65–82 (67).
6   Diana Holmes, 'The Comfortable Reader: Romantic Bestsellers and Critical
     Disdain', *French Cultural Studies* 21/4 (2010), 287–96 (288–9).

provides the reader with a strong degree of closure. It is also stylistically transparent: the narrative is divided into dated, chronologically ordered sections; the language is clear; and there is a lot of dialogue, which enables the plot to unfold quickly.

I begin my discussion of the struggle to be an openly lesbian mother by focusing on the autobiographical novels, François's *Les Bonheurs* and Dumont's *La Vie dure*, before turning to Mallet's romance novel, *Le Choix de la reine*.

Lesbian Mothering in a Homophobic Milieu

In *French Autobiography: Devices and Desires* (1993), Michael Sheringham writes that '[a]utobiography is a self-centred business'.[7] Yet, in line with the theoretical shift towards postmodernism, autobiography now frequently problematizes the notion of selfhood as a finite, stable and unified entity.[8] In particular, women's autobiography, as Natalie Edwards shows, often 'resists the traditional notion of an individual, unitary self at the heart of autobiography and instead inscribes subjectivity as in some measure non-unitary'.[9] One way in which this is expressed is by the unconventional use of the first person. Although the connection between author and protagonist that is fundamental to autobiography is most often marked by the first person,[10] writing 'I', as Edwards points out, 'has traditionally been problematic for any individual outside the dominant group'.[11]

---

7   Michael Sheringham, *French Autobiography: Devices and Desires: Rousseau to Perec* (Oxford: Oxford University Press, 1993), vii.

8   See Philippe Gasparini, *Est-il je? Roman autobiographique et autofiction* (Paris: Seuil, 2004); Elizabeth H. Jones, *Spaces of Belonging: Home, Culture and Identity in 20th-Century French Autobiography* (Amsterdam: Rodopi, 2007); Jeanette M. L. den Toonder, *'Qui est-je?' L'écriture autobiographique des nouveaux romanciers* (Bern: Peter Lang, 1999).

9   Natalie Edwards, *Shifting Subjects: Plural Subjectivity in Contemporary Francophone Women's Autobiography* (Newark: University of Delaware Press, 2011), 13.

10 Lejeune, *Le Pacte autobiographique*, 15–17.

11 Edwards, *Shifting Subjects*, 12.

Broadly, François's *Les Bonheurs* problematizes the traditional notion of selfhood to a greater extent than Dumont's *La Vie dure*, and this is evident in the authors' different uses of the first person. Whereas Dumont uses 'I' for one person only, the author-protagonist, in François's work the first person is used to refer to the author-protagonist, Anne, and her lesbian lover, Sarah. Part 1 of the text is recounted entirely in the first person, initially from Sarah's point of view but then, in the form of a diary, from Anne's perspective. Following this italicized extract, 'I' again refers to Sarah. In Part 2, which is told from Anne's point of view, the first person is abruptly replaced by the third person. Part 3 then switches back to the first person and to Sarah's point of view. The switching between different points of view communicates the difficulty of inscribing a lesbian self that exists in the margins of heteronormative society. Strikingly, François's answer to this seems to be to construct her textual self by writing about her relationship with, and from the point of view of, her lover. The subject is thus rendered a highly unstable entity in François's autobiographical novel. It expresses this instability most explicitly when Sarah reflects: 'Nous sommes deux, nous sommes nous, nous sommes Anne et Sarah, mais c'est un spectacle auquel nous n'assistons pas. Nous sommes Je' [We are two, we are we, we are Anne and Sarah, but it is a performance that we are not attending. We are I] (B 206). François's experimentation with the first person invites the reader to reflect on a question posed by Philippe Gasparini: 'Is it the author who is recounting his life or a fictional character?'.[12] Indeed, it is not always immediately apparent in *Les Bonheurs* whose perspective François is writing from. A striking example that illustrates Gasparini's reference to the sometimes unclear distinction between author and protagonist occurs at the beginning of the extract from Anne's diary: ' "J'ai appelé les mots comme le berger rassemble son troupeau. Comme le berger, j'ai usé de sons bizarres, d'onomatopées sans signification immédiate mais pour moi d'une infaillible efficacité. Les mots sont venus" ' ['I called out the words like a shepherd herding his flock. Like the shepherd, I used odd sounds, onomatopoeias that had no obvious meaning but that I found incredibly effective. Words came'] (B 46). Although these are supposedly

12   Gasparini, *Est-il je?*, 9.

the character's words, they could in fact be said to summarize the author's written style, for François's text is ambiguous, dense and marked by a taste for linguistic experimentation and metaphor. Whereas Dumont portrays lesbianism in a largely transparent style, in François's text there is a strong parallel between the experimental form and subversive themes.

Although the texts ultimately reconcile lesbianism with mothering, they primarily focus on the challenges facing lesbian mothers in the mid-to-late twentieth century. In this sense, they are not transgressive texts but, importantly, ones that explore the norms of the family and offer insights into the often difficult experiences of lesbian mothers in this period. Forming a lesbian family is portrayed as a desired but unrealistic possibility until the end of both texts. In *Les Bonheurs*, Anne fears that she will lose custody of her children if she leaves her husband for Sarah, which foregrounds the discrimination against lesbian mothers in the legal system at the time. In *La Vie dure*, Catherine does not respond to Pascale's proposal that they have children together, and Pascale herself later recalls: 'Catherine m'avait demandé un jour si j'aurais aimé avoir un enfant avec elle et je n'avais pu m'empêcher d'ouvrir de grands yeux devant une idée aussi extravagante' [Catherine had once asked me if I would have liked to have a child with her, and I had not been able to prevent my eyes from widening at such an extravagant idea] (VD 174–5). The characters' reservations about lesbian families testify to their invisibility and unworkability in the social and cultural context of the plot. Indeed, Pascale accepts that the family life for which she hopes would be impossible while Catherine's homosexuality remains a secret, and she fears that, even if Catherine came out, the children would only ever regard her as a rival for their mother's affection. Pascale thus acts as a mouthpiece for the normative assumption that children have one and only one mother, the woman from whom they are born. Again, this view represents that held by society in the 1980s, when planned same-sex parenting – that is, when a homosexual couple decide to become parents together – was a largely unacknowledged possibility. Indeed, the limited options available to lesbians wanting to mother prior to the availability of reproductive technologies in the 1970s, which only became available to lesbian couples in France in 2019, mean that Catherine's decision to have children with a man is arguably made in the absence of alternatives.

Catherine further reifies the supposed irreconcilability of lesbianism with mothering by enforcing a strict division between her lesbian affair and her life as a mother. Significantly, her children feature only as subjects of conversation, and Pascale, to her frustration, never meets them: ' "Je ne connais pas ses gamins, je ne connais rien de sa vie, seulement ce qu'elle m'en a dit, ou écrit!" ' ['I don't know her kids, I don't know anything about her life, only what she has told me or written to me about'] (VD 134). Catherine, Pascale believes, 'était persuadée qu'il fallait qu'elle élève ses enfants dans la stabilité et elle n'envisageait pas un seul instant de leur révéler, en pleine adolescence, son homosexualité' [was convinced that her children needed a stable upbringing and could not for one second imagine revealing to them, mid-adolescence, her homosexuality] (VD 28). As well as the difficulties of mothering a child through adolescence, which I will discuss later with reference to *Le Choix de la reine*, this underscores Catherine's association of a stable childhood with heterosexuality. Catherine's virtual disappearance from the plot once she and Pascale separate might be interpreted as symbolic of the silencing of lesbian mothers. This is in tune with the social and cultural context of the plot, when the very existence of lesbian mothers was overlooked or suppressed, even in feminist and queer circles. Indeed, as recently as 2013 Shelley Park pointed out that '[i]nsofar as mothers are "breeders" and breeders are the presumed antithesis of queer, the notion of queer mothering is rendered oxymoronic'.[13] Catherine's disappearance might, then, be interpreted as a reflection of lesbian mothers' invisibility within these movements. *La Vie dure* also demonstrates an acute awareness of the norms of femininity and heterosexuality that compel Catherine to sacrifice her lesbian relationship. Pascale believes that Catherine 'était tellement marquée par le grand schéma dominant de la jeune femme qui doit à toute force se marier et avoir des enfants' [was so marked by dominant ideas about young women who must at all costs get married and have children] (VD 9), and that 'sans doute son désir de maternité était-il lié étroitement au besoin de respectabilité' [her desire to become a mother was probably closely linked to the need for respectability] (VD 16). As such, she endorses the normative equation of womanhood with mothering

13   Park, *Mothering Queerly, Queering Motherhood*, 1.

and, moreover, the assumption that this is viable only when women are in a heterosexual relationship.

These texts should not, however, be read as ideological condemnations of same-sex parenting but as pragmatic descriptions of a heteronormative reality. Although the texts emphasize the challenges facing lesbian mothers, they nonetheless envisage the possibility of non-heterosexual family forms. *Les Bonheurs* takes a progressivist view of the family when Anne asks Sarah: ' "Aimerais-tu mes enfants si tu vivais avec eux tous les jours?" ' ['Would you love my children if you lived with them every day?'] (B 122). Similarly, *La Vie dure* portrays characters that anticipate the emergence of the same-sex family as a social and cultural phenomenon when Pascale suggests to Catherine that they raise a family together with help from a gay male friend: ' "Tu pourrais avoir des enfants, avec un ami homosexuel par exemple, et nous les élèverions ensemble" ' ['You could have children, with a gay friend for example, and we would raise them together'] (VD 16). It is significant too that at the end of *La Vie dure* the reader learns that Catherine's children discovered her sexuality and affair with Pascale at the beginning and, importantly, that they were untroubled by the news. This suggests that being raised by a lesbian mother has no adverse effects on children's development – an important point, given the claims about the unsuitability of gay and lesbian parents. Echoing much feminist and queer theory, *La Vie dure* also goes some way towards redefining mothering as a care-giving function rather than a purely biological process and, in this sense, looks ahead to the argument that I will make about the texts studied in Chapters 4 and 5, which are premised on this view. Adrienne Rich, for example, notes that '[m]ost women have been mothers in the sense of tenders and carers for the young, whether as sisters, aunts, nurses, teachers, foster-mothers, stepmothers'.[14] While Pascale states plainly that she has never been emotionally able to have children 'of her own' – ' "Ça ne m'est pas possible" ' ['It's not possible for me'] (VD 219) – she remains open to performing a care-giving role. As a teacher, for instance, Pascale believes that the student–teacher relationship bears resemblance to that between

---

14   Rich, *Of Woman Born*, 12.

a mother and child. Moreover, Pascale is willing to become a step-mother to Catherine's children on the basis that 'les enfants de la femme qu'on aime sont un peu les vôtres' [the children of the woman you love are kind of your own] and, as we noted earlier, is frustrated by her exclusion from this part of Catherine's life (VD 94).

Although the texts portray these family forms as largely unfeasible in the context of the plot, they do not endorse the stereotype that lesbians make 'bad' or inappropriate mothers. *Les Bonheurs* suggests that lesbians do not necessarily lack the desire to mother that is normatively associated with heterosexual women:

> [D]ès l'instant où j'ai vécu avec Michel, j'ai désiré des enfants, un enfant. Je n'avais rien d'autre à attendre que des enfants. Eux seulement pouvaient donner un sens à cette coexistence. Je ne me le suis jamais caché. Maintenant, ils sont merveilleusement là. Le travail, la fatigue, tout cela est secondaire quand je les regarde. Mais évidemment, cela ne change rien, ne modifie pas la relation que j'ai avec Michel même si tout est plus tendre, plus facile, contenu dans une espèce de joie. (B 34–5)

> [From the moment I lived with Michel, I wanted children, a child. Children were all I could expect. They alone could give meaning to this coexistence. I've never hidden this from myself. Now, they're here, and it's wonderful. The work, the tiredness, all of that is secondary when I look at them. But obviously, this changes nothing, doesn't alter the relationship I have with Michel, even if everything is tenderer, easier, enclosed within a sort of joy.]

Here, motherhood is portrayed as a means for the protagonist to make sense of her unwanted marriage. It might even be said that the text undermines the stereotypical equation of lesbianism with neglectful mothering by strategically portraying a positive mother–child relationship. Indeed, François seems to try to dissociate the protagonist's feelings about mothering from the complications of her marriage and, by extension, from her sexuality: 'Eux n'étaient pas en cause, jamais elle ne regretterait leur présence. Qu'ils soient nés de son désordre et de son errance, peu importait: ils étaient là, ils dépassaient totalement ses propres dimensions, elle les aimait' [They were not the issue. She would never regret their presence. It didn't matter that they had been born of her mess and waywardness; they were here, they were larger than she was, she loved them] (B 166).

It is significant that the text encourages a reading of the mother–child relationship from the perspective of psychoanalysis. In one scene, Anne states: '[L]a femme cherche une compensation affective dans des soins exagérés' [Women look for affective compensation through excessive care-giving] (B 35). In context, we understand that this statement is a reference to the protagonist's dissatisfaction with her husband, but the vocabulary would seem to have distinctly Freudian undertones. The phrase 'compensation affective' [affective compensation] resonates strongly with Freud's notion of penis envy. This might be interpreted as ironic, were it not for the fact that Anne later describes the mother–child relationship as 'une possession dépossédée' [a possession of which one is robbed] and feels that the children 'allaient vers leur amour et non vers moi' [were heading towards a love of their own and not towards me] (B 90) – quotations that echo the infant's rejection of the mother and subsequent love for the father that are the result of the Oedipus complex. Unlike Freud, who emphasizes the role of biological drives in the psychic development of infants, object relations theory holds that the formation of the self occurs through social relations. In Nancy Chodorow's account, infants develop chiefly in relation to the mother since it is she who is the primary carer.[15] They therefore experience themselves as one with her and acquire a sense of self only when, during the Oedipal phase, they learn that they are separate from the mother. Anne's description of her relationship with her children as a reciprocated possession thus evokes Chodorow's model of the early mother–child relationship. While this recourse to psychoanalysis is perhaps surprising, given the field's traditional heterosexism and role in opposing same-sex parenting in France, it has the effect of portraying lesbian mothers and the relationships that they have with their children as no different from those in traditional families. This was invaluable at the time of the text's publication, when lesbian mothers were regarded as inappropriate role models for children, and remains pertinent today in view of the continued prejudice against same-sex parents.

Although *Les Bonheurs* represents a distinctly unproblematic mother–child relationship, it does not idealize maternal experience and challenges

---

15   Chodorow, *The Reproduction of Mothering*, 77–8.

the obligation to mother in a patriarchal framework. For example, Anne fosters some resentment towards the gendered division of paid and unpaid labour. Whereas Michel resumes working and pursuing leisure activities after becoming a father, Anne's time is taken up by childcare. Furthermore, Michel does not attend his children's births or accompany Anne on her visit to the hospital:

> Dans la salle d'attente, des jeunes femmes accompagnées de leur mari ou de leur mère feuilletaient des albums de 'Prénatal' ou ces revues qui encourageaient la maternité heureuse et l'allaitement naturel. J'étais seule et fortement émue en contemplant comme une chose neuve ces visages inconnus, légèrement marqués de brun clair par endroits, aux yeux agrandis et brillants. (B 52–3)

> [In the waiting room, young women accompanied by their husbands or mothers were flicking through copies of 'Prénatal' or magazines encouraging happy motherhood and natural breastfeeding. I was alone and deeply moved as I contemplated like a new thing the faces of these strangers, which bore light brown spots in places and had widened and shining eyes.]

The contrast between the solitary Anne and the women accompanied by their husbands or mothers underlines the protagonist's sense of isolation and suggests the problems in her marriage. Furthermore, the text voices the reservations about the medicalization of antenatal care and child-rearing that appear in feminist tracts of the same period. Ann Oakley, for instance, qualifies the role of medicine in reducing infant mortality rates, claiming that medical practices that aid a minority of mothers are applied needlessly to the majority.[16] *Les Bonheurs* seems to sympathize with Oakley's critique of excessively medicalized maternity care when Anne, while in labour with her first child, only reluctantly accepts medical intervention: ' "Je peux supporter. Je dois vraiment prendre ce remède?" ' ['I can bear it. Do I really have to take this medicine?'] (B 64). For Anne, the pain of childbirth is almost a rite of passage to mothering: 'La douleur me tenait et moi, je me tenais dans la douleur et mon cœur était empli d'une joie hauturière. Pour rien au monde je n'aurais échangé cette nuit contre une autre' [Pain clung to me, I clung to myself through the pain and my

16   Oakley, *From Here to Maternity*, 15–18.

heart was filled with a pelagic joy. I would not have swapped this night for another for anything in the world] (B 63). François thus offers an account of the often taboo experience of childbirth and would seem to position herself within ongoing debates on the relationship between medicine and motherhood.

As well as the norms that prevent lesbian families and impinge on the experiences of lesbian mothers, both texts also engage with contemporary attitudes towards lesbianism more broadly. As Lucille Cairns demonstrates, in *Les Bonheurs* two discourses seek to prohibit lesbian love and preserve men's control of the female body and sexuality: religion, embodied in Anne's priest, who first convinces her to abandon Sarah; and phallocentrism, represented by her husband, Michel.[17] As such, *Les Bonheurs* nods towards lesbian feminism's conception of heterosexuality as a political regime that seeks to regulate women.[18] It is Anne's priest who compels her to conform to heterosexuality through the threat of damnation and the demonization and pathologization of same-sex desire: ' "Ne m'obligez pas à vous dire: de l'enfer parce que je n'aime pas brandir ce mot et nul ne sait ce qu'il recouvre mais je pense que vous la sauverez de la perte de Dieu" ' ['Don't make me talk to you of Hell because I don't like throwing this word around and no one knows what it really means, but I think you will save her from the loss of God'] (B 86–7). The priest's role foreshadows that played by the Church in opposing same-sex marriage, both in France and across the Western world. Like the priest, Michel reinforces the normative status of heterosexuality by naturalizing institutional relationships, such as heterosexual marriage, over non-contractual love: ' "Ce n'était pas une parole entre vous. C'était un vice, une passion mauvaise, une horreur. Un mariage est une parole donnée selon la loi et selon la nature" ' ['There was no vow between you. It was a vice, an evil passion, an abomination. Marriage is a given vow according to the law and according to nature'] (B 137). Michel's reference to vice recalls the pre-nineteenth-century view of homosexuality

17   Cairns, *Lesbian Desire in Post-1968 French Literature*, 212.
18   See, for example, Adrienne Rich, 'Compulsory Heterosexuality and Lesbian Existence', *Signs: Journal of Women in Culture and Society* 5/4 (1980), 631–60; Monique Wittig, 'The Straight Mind' (1980), in *'The Straight Mind' and Other Essays* (London: Harvester Wheatsheaf, 1992), 21–32.

as something not just unnatural but also immoral and criminal. Moreover, he accepts the phallocentric assumptions that female desire is necessarily heterosexual and that sexual pleasure is exclusively male, as evidenced by his assertion that ' "[L]e clitoris, ça n'existe pas" ' ['The clitoris doesn't exist'] (B 152). For Michel, then, lesbian relationships are de facto platonic, as evidenced by his understanding of Anne and Sarah's relationship as an 'amitié' [friendship], rather than love (B 147).

In *La Vie dure*, Catherine's husband's reaction to her coming out bears comparison with Michel's; he too expresses the homophobic discourse of illness and inversion. Like Michel, he allows Catherine to continue to live with him so that she can raise the children, thus reifying the nexus between women and mothering. Pascale's pragmatic, 'it-could-be-worse' attitude towards Catherine's situation says little for the way in which lesbian mothers were treated in the social and cultural context of the plot. More generally, however, *La Vie dure* critiques the invisibility and marginalization of lesbianism in the late twentieth century. Pascale recalls the fear of and stigma attached to being a lesbian, or an 'homme manqué' [failed man] (VD 13), and the challenge of coming to terms with her homosexuality in a social and cultural context in which lesbianism went unnoticed: '[D]irais-je jamais [à Catherine] combien j'avais pu, adolescente, me sentir infirme, monstrueuse, vouée à jamais à la solitude quand je m'éprenais d'une fille de mon âge?' [Would I ever tell Catherine how much I, as a teenager, had felt crippled, monstrous, forever doomed to loneliness, whenever I fell for a girl my age?] (VD 42). In particular, the image of the monster emphasizes Pascale's sense of abnormality and exclusion, and recalls the many male-authored novels of the nineteenth century that portray lesbians as monsters.[19]

The authors engage with or, in François's case, anticipate the argument put forward by feminist and queer thinkers in the 1990s that human desire and sexuality are constructed in the interests of reproduction – that is, according to the sex to which we are attracted.[20] As such, *Les Bonheurs* and *La Vie dure* go beyond a simple description of the heteronormativity and

19   See Waelti-Walters, *Damned Women*.
20   See, for example, Judith Butler, 'Is Kinship Always Already Heterosexual?', *differences: A Journal of Feminist Cultural Studies* 13/1 (2002), 14–44 (14).

homophobia that obstruct lesbian desire and love to a thorough deconstruction of the norms of gender and sexuality. Most radically, the texts reframe desire and sexuality in terms of affectivity rather than gender. As Anne tells Michel in *Les Bonheurs*: ' "Ce n'est pas la femme que j'aime en Sarah, c'est Sarah et c'est moi Anne qui suis aimée" ' ['It's not the woman that I love about Sarah, it's Sarah, and it's me, Anne, who is loved'] (B 191). It is also likely that Sarah is bisexual, as several scenes make it abundantly clear that, despite her love for Anne, she enjoys sex with her male lover, Jean. The sexual ambiguity of the characters is deepened by François's use of *tu* [you] to refer to Anne, Sarah, Michel and Jean at various points in the text. For example, towards the end of a particularly explicit sex scene between Sarah and Jean, here referred to as *tu*, the second person abruptly begins to refer to Anne:

> Tu étais à nouveau en moi, je te contenais, je bougeais autour de tes mouvements, tu gémissais et j'aimais ton désir de moi, ce désir que tu pouvais contenter à mesure car tu me savais maintenant à portée de toi. Tu m'avais à peine parlé d'Anne en me revoyant ce soir, mais aurais-je voulu parler ? Sans doute l'avais-tu senti. Non, il valait mieux nous aimer, être ensemble dans cette chambre que nous étions seuls à connaître. J'étais au plus profond du plaisir quand je t'ai sentie m'embrasser partout, me tenir, me toucher. Oui, un jour nous serions heureuses ensemble, nous nous donnerions ce que Jean me donnait mais augmenté de nous. (B 44)

> [You were inside me again, I contained you, I moved according to your movements, you were moaning, and I liked your desire for me, that desire that you could satisfy gradually because you knew I was within reach. You had barely talked to me about Anne when you saw me again tonight, but would I have wanted to talk? You had probably felt it. No, it was better to love each other, to be together in this room that only we knew. At the height of pleasure, I felt you kissing me everywhere, holding me, touching me. Yes, we would one day be happy together, we would give each other what Jean was giving me but enhanced by us.]

The abrupt transition from *tu*-Jean to *tu*-Anne is marked by the feminine inflections on the verb 'sentie' [felt] and the adjective 'heureuses' [happy]. In *Les Bonheurs*, then, sexuality is both reflected by and inscribed in linguistic play, suggesting a parallel between form and theme. The switching between *tu*-masculine and *tu*-feminine strongly connotes bisexuality and thus portrays the heterosexual–homosexual binary as less stable than it is conventionally perceived.

The linguistic experimentation in François's text recalls feminist theoretical developments that emerged in France around the time of its publication – namely, Hélène Cixous's theory of *écriture féminine*. Because of
its overt concern with language and female sexuality and subjectivity, *Les
Bonheurs* could, in many ways, be said to be an example of *écriture féminine*.
In common with Cixous's theory, *Les Bonheurs* experiments with imagery
and language to the extent that, at times, the meaning is opaque, as in the
following passage in which Sarah, in a flashback, describes her and Anne's
burgeoning relationship:

> La nuit et les étoiles, je les ai sues par toi. Ce n'est pas original, tous les amants se
> donnent le monde. Mais notre amour non nommé était une giroflée sauvage accrochée
> entre deux pierres anonymes. Il ne savait que l'espace étroit de ses racines, mais à lui
> seul il était plus important que l'édifice en son entier. (B 20)

> [The night and the stars, I knew them through you. This is not original, all lovers
> give the world to each other. But our unnamed love was a wild gillyflower hung be-
> tween two anonymous stones. It only knew the tight space of its roots, but it was
> more important than the structure in its entirety.]

Here, the text alludes to the taboo on lesbianism within the social and
cultural context of the text – that is, in this extract, the late 1940s or early
1950s, when the age of consent in France was 21 years for homosexual
relations compared with 15 for heterosexual relations. The phrase 'amour
non nommé' [unnamed love] clearly refers to the silence on lesbianism,
and the 'espace étroit de ses racines' [tight space of its roots] evokes its
lack of a place in a heterosexist and homophobic world. This is, however,
described as less important than the love itself. Indeed, François valorizes
lesbianism through clever imagery and metaphor: Anne and Sarah's love
is described as a wild flower – that is, as something beautiful and natural – yet positioned between two hard and imposing stones, which sym-
bolize the obstacles to lesbian love presented in the text – religion and
phallocentrism – or, alternatively, Michel and Jean. François thus deploys
the normative alignment of women with nature and men with strength
only to inscribe anti-patriarchal lesbian love. The linguistic experimentation contained in the passage quoted above is equally evident in the
sex scene mentioned earlier: 'J'aimais ton sexe glissant de ma faim, tu te
caressais en moi, tu caressais de ta main mon clitoris et ensemble nous

étions heureux et dès notre souffle redevenu égal nous repartions, nous étions déjà repartis vers un autre plaisir' (B 43) [I liked your penis slipping from my hunger, you were stroking yourself inside me, you were caressing my clitoris with your hand and together we were happy and as soon as we had our breath back we went again, we had already gone to another pleasure]. Although patently a description of penetration, the first clause of this quotation further exemplifies the text's linguistic experimentalism. This allusion to penetration suggests that *Les Bonheurs* is an exploration of not only lesbian sexuality but also female eroticism more broadly. The ambiguity in *Les Bonheurs*, as in Cixous's 'Le Rire de la Méduse' [The Laugh of the Medusa] (1975), engenders an open-ended mode of representation that fosters multiple interpretations. For Cixous, this functions to resist patriarchal codes of femininity and circumvent the recodification of female norms. Indeed, Cixous refuses to define *écriture féminine*: 'It is impossible to *define* a feminine practice of writing, and this is an impossibility that will remain, for this practice can never be theorized, enclosed, coded – which doesn't mean that it doesn't exist'.[21] Comparably, the ambiguity of *Les Bonheurs* works to open up lesbian desire and love and to resist its recodification in what, in Cixous's terms, would be the language of phallocentrism. Indeed, Cixous claims that female sexuality cannot be represented in such a language. *Écriture féminine*, she argues, 'will always surpass the discourse that regulates the phallocentric system; it does and will take place in areas other than those subordinated to philosophico-theoretical domination'.[22] Taking the connection between François's and Cixous's texts further, then, it might be argued that François suggests that lesbianism, as a female-centred sexuality, cannot be represented in normative, phallocentric language.

Although not characterized by the same linguistic experimentalism as François's text, Dumont also challenges the conventional notion of lesbianism. Pascale wonders while contemplating her relationship with Catherine:

---

21   Hélène Cixous, 'The Laugh of the Medusa', trans. Keith Cohen and Paula Cohen, *Signs: Journal of Women in Culture and Society* 1/4 (1976 [1975]), 875–93 (883).

22   Cixous, 'The Laugh of the Medusa', 883.

Quand comprendrait-elle que le mot 'homosexuelle' que je revendique pourtant par ailleurs [...] s'appliquait mal à mon cas personnel puisque j'étais cent fois plus affamée d'amour que de caresses, les secondes me bouleversant seulement si je les sentais émaner du premier? (VD 139)

[When would she understand that the word 'homosexual', to which I actually lay claim, [...] did not really work for me, as I was a hundred times more desirous of love than physical contact, the latter moving me only when I could feel them coming from the former?]

As this discussion suggests, the texts share or, in the case of *Les Bonheurs*, foreshadow queer theorists' distrust of sexual identity categories. In her landmark work *Gender Trouble*, Judith Butler argues that sexual identity categories – heterosexual, lesbian and so on – fail to adequately account for the nuances of human sexuality since they structure desire first and foremost around a binary conception of gender. Although Pascale actively identifies as a lesbian – indeed, her former partner, Martine, refers to them both as 'goudous à cent pour cent' [one hundred per cent lesbian] (VD 123) – she, like Butler, underscores the limitations of such a label. Despite the characters' subscription to the possibility of being completely lesbian, *La Vie dure* depicts a multitude of gender identities. Whereas Catherine, according to Pascale, is 'féminine au sens traditionnel' [feminine in the traditional sense] – that is, she desires children and looks 'like a woman' – Martine and Pascale are depicted as butch lesbians (VD 16). The text might therefore be charged with reinforcing the heteronormative butch–femme dyad of lesbian couples, yet it represents this stereotype only to subvert it. Catherine's claim that she is 'the man' – ' "J'ai toujours su que c'était moi le mec, dans notre couple" ' ['I've always known that I was the guy in our relationship'] (VD 58) – contradicts the presumed nexus between femininity, femme and mothering.

While *La Vie dure* challenges the dominant portrayal of butch and femme identities, *Les Bonheurs* abandons entirely the assimilation of lesbian relationships to heterosexual standards, as the following dialogue between Anne and Michel shows:

'Mais dis, Anne, entre vous deux, comment se répartissent les rôles? Tu es l'homme ou tu es la femme?'

'Pourquoi? Tu as eu l'impression d'être pédéraste en vivant avec moi?'

'Je t'en prie …'

'Non! Eh bien, Jean non plus ne s'est pas senti pédéraste avec Sarah. Tout le monde est homme et femme à la fois. Pourquoi imaginer une complémentarité entre Sarah et moi imitant celle entre un homme et une femme? Jouer un rôle, tu vois dans la vie concrète ce que cela comporterait d'intenable et de ridicule?'

'Mais enfin, Anne, dans l'amour? Ne sois pas hypocrite, n'essaie pas de me dire que vous n'imitez pas un couple normal!' (B 188)

['So, Anne, how are the roles divided between you two? Are you the man or the woman?'

'Why? Did you feel like a homosexual while living with me?'

'Oh please …'

'No! And Jean didn't feel like a homosexual with Sarah. Everyone is both a man and a woman. Why imagine that Sarah and I complement each other in the same way as a man and a woman? Playing a role, surely you can see how unworkable and ridiculous that would be in real life?'

'Oh come on, Anne, in bed? Don't be a hypocrite, don't try and tell me that you don't copy a normal couple!']

Instead of asserting that lesbian couples are no different from heterosexual ones, *Les Bonheurs* works to legitimize same-sex relationships in their own right by challenging the very idea that they need to resemble heterosexual relationships. Anne's vision of sexual politics is more radical than Michel's belief that she and Sarah are attempting to mirror the heterosexual model. Whereas Michel cannot envisage sexual relationships without the male role or outside the gender binary, Anne rejects the gendered dynamics of heterosexual relationships as the standard against which all relationships ought to be measured. Similarly, the text suggests that gender equality does not mean that men and women must be the same:

[L]es hommes et les femmes ne pouvaient pas se rejoindre. Ils engendraient, ils coexistaient. Peut-être se rejoindraient-ils plus tard, beaucoup plus tard, quand les femmes, enfin sorties de leur condition de servantes, auraient eu tout le temps qu'il faut pour être véritablement ce qu'elles sont: les égales différenciées des hommes, sans féminisme et sans forfanterie, sans qu'il soit nécessaire d'en parler. (B 84)

[Men and women could not connect. They procreated, they coexisted. Perhaps they would connect later, much later, when women, liberated from their status as servants, had had all the time they needed to be what they really are: equals who are different from men, without feminism or bravado, without it being necessary to talk about it.]

Although *Les Bonheurs* exposes the limitations of sexual identity categories, which appears to support Butler's resistance to identity-based politics, it subscribes to a feminism that defends the existence of sexual difference. It would be a stretch to argue that *Les Bonheurs* reconciles difference and equality feminisms – indeed, this is one of just a handful of references to the feminist movement in the text – but it does at least bring these two diametrically opposed theoretical camps into dialogue, thereby challenging what has become an ever-more polarized debate in the decades since the text was published. Although *La Vie dure* also brings the traditional definition of lesbianism into question, it devotes considerably more attention to identity politics. After separating from Catherine, Pascale enters the burgeoning lesbian feminist groups and lesbian culture of the 1980s, thus alluding to the invisibility of lesbianism, its marginalization from the male-dominated gay rights movement and the paucity of lesbian social and cultural spaces.

While *Les Bonheurs* defends the notion of sexual difference, it eschews biological essentialism. Anne questions the essentialist formation of gender and sexuality when she tells her priest: ' "Il n'y a pas de prototype de comportement humain, les morales diffèrent, les usages, les coutumes" ' ['There is no prototype of human behaviour, morality is different, conventions, customs'] (B 86). Similarly, *La Vie dure* posits a constructionist view of gender roles and, moreover, rejects gender as a cornerstone of human identity: '[C]'est la répartition des rôles assignés strictement à chaque sexe qui me gêne. Ni femme féminine, ni homme manqué, je suis un être humain' [It is the division of roles according to sex that bothers me. I am neither a feminine woman, nor a failed man. I am a human being] (VD 174). Pascale makes the queer-sounding claim that it is more appropriate to talk of people rather than of men and women, thereby going beyond what queer theorists see as a reductive male–female binary. Like Anne, Pascale repudiates the pathologizing of same-sex desire: '[J]e me sentais parfaitement normale et je n'avais nulle envie de voir changer ma personnalité en quoi que ce soit' [I felt perfectly normal and had no desire to have my personality changed in any way] (VD 11). Pascale's claim to normality functions to downplay the difference between heterosexual and homosexual desire and thus renders the latter acceptable, both to the character and to readers.

By portraying mothers who at first suppress their sexuality, *Les Bonheurs* and *La Vie dure* expose how mothering is conceived as a heterosexual prerogative. Ultimately, however, they challenge this conception by eventually allowing the mothers to assume their sexuality. In addition, the texts refer to the possibility of lesbian-headed families. Although they cannot be said to embrace alternative family forms, their allusions to lesbian families are notable given that both texts are set well before same-sex parenting emerged as a political and social issue in France. In this period, since homosexuality itself was still taboo, the challenges unique to homosexuals who were also parents were necessarily fringe issues. This might explain why the aspects of these texts that are arguably the most transgressive relate to lesbian love and desire, rather than lesbian mothering. The text to which I now turn, Mallet's *Le Choix de la reine*, tackles the struggle to be an openly lesbian mother in the context of the mother–daughter relationship.

The Mother–Daughter Relationship

In *The Reproduction of Mothering* (1978), Nancy Chodorow postulates that the mother–daughter relationship is and will remain conflictual as long as gender is a crucial marker of identity and women are primarily responsible for childcare.[23] This, Chodorow argues, is because girls continue to identify with the mother post-Oedipally due to their shared anatomy and therefore fluctuate between the desire to identify with and the need to separate from the mother. Chodorow further argues that '[j]ust as the object-relations during the prepubertal period repeat elements of the

23   Chodorow, *The Reproduction of Mothering*, 135–6.

preoedipal period, the object-relations of puberty and adolescence re-semble those of the oedipal situation.'[24] The onset of puberty thus initi-ates a second period of mother–daughter conflict.

The mother–daughter relationship, as Marianne Hirsch demonstrates in her influential *The Mother/Daughter Plot* (1989), has traditionally been silenced by or submerged in the conventional plot structure of Western literature. Citing the myth of Oedipus as the 'classic and paradigmatic story of individual development in Western civilization', Hirsch shows how this plot structure obfuscates the mother–daughter relationship by portraying women only as instruments of or obstacles to the formation of male subjectivity.[25] The voices of mothers and daughters, as Hirsch's book illustrates, gradually emerged in nineteenth- and twentieth-century texts, both in fiction and in feminist and psychoanalytic theory. Today, the mother–daughter relationship is a recurrent theme of women's writing in France and across the West.[26] Recent scholarship makes the point that this body of literature is, with growing frequency, privileging the perspectives of mothers themselves.[27]

The novel to which I now turn, Mallet's *Le Choix de la reine*, follows this trend but is unique in that it portrays a relationship between a lesbian mother and heterosexual daughter. This novel is one of only two texts in this study's corpus – the other being Hélène de Monferrand's *Les Enfants d'Héloïse* [*Héloïse's Children*] (1997) – that gives more than a secondary role to the child of a lesbian mother. It thus testifies to the diverse ways in which the mother–daughter relationship is being envisaged in contemporary French women's writing. Unlike François's and Dumont's characters, who have lesbian relationships while at high school, Mallet's protagonist, Elena, apparently feels no desire for other women until after her daughter's birth. She also becomes a mother in the early 1990s, much later than François's and Dumont's characters. Nonetheless, the reconciliation of lesbianism and

24   Chodorow, *The Reproduction of Mothering*, 138.
25   Hirsch, *The Mother/Daughter Plot*, 1.
26   See Adalgisa Giorgio, ed., *Writing Mothers and Daughters: Renegotiating the Mother in Western European Narratives by Women* (New York: Berghahn, 2002).
27   Rye, *Narratives of Mothering*, 15.

mothering is far from easy in this novel – a testament to the entrenchment of the equation of parenting with heterosexuality.

In *Le Choix de la reine*, Marion upholds the norm of heterosexual motherhood by denouncing her mother's homosexuality and affair with Louise. Although Marion's immediate reaction stems in part from shock and the humiliation of finding her mother and her teacher in bed together, her equation of opposite-sex attraction with normality – ' "Je suis normale, moi! J'aime les garçons, comme grand-mère!" ' ['*I'm* normal! I like boys, like my grandmother!'] (CDLR 27) – and the language with which she insults Elena – ' "une barge de ton espèce" ' ['a nutter like you'] (CDLR 26) – affirm the normative status of heterosexuality. Marion's reaction compels Elena to choose between her daughter and her lover – that is, between mothering and her sexuality. In a gesture suggestive of the supposed irreconcilability of lesbianism with mothering, Elena opts to repress her sexuality, informing Louise that she can love no woman save her daughter:

> Tu n'as pas encore compris que Marion est l'unique amour de ma vie, ma seule priorité! Je suis désolée de te dire les choses aussi froidement, Louise, mais toi et moi, ce n'est rien de plus qu'un présent … qui ne se conjuguera jamais au futur. (CDLR 10)

> [You still haven't understood that Marion is the love of my life, my sole priority! I'm sorry to be so cold with you, Louise, but you and I are nothing more than a present … which will never become a future.]

By dedicating herself to her child at the expense of her own desire, Elena arguably reinforces not only the incompatibility of mothering with lesbianism but the incompatibility of mothering with sexual desire in general. Indeed, the most enduring example of mothering in the West is that of the Virgin Mary, a figure both maternal and asexual. By temporarily renouncing her affair, Elena exhibits the selflessness, and self-lessness, expected of mothers by patriarchal society and epitomized by the Virgin Mary. Nevertheless, in conversation with her own mother, Marinette, she scolds herself for thinking only of herself and her own desires:

> 'Je n'arrête pas de culpabiliser.'

> 'Bah! C'est exactement ce que tu m'as dit le jour de ton divorce.'

'Là, c'est différent. Il n'est pas question de choix avec Marion. C'est mon enfant, mon amour de toujours. Je dois la protéger. Elle n'a pas à souffrir de la stupidité de sa mère.'

'Je te trouve très sévère avec toi, Elena. Être amoureuse n'a rien de stupide.'

'Je ne suis pas amoureuse, maman, c'est justement ça qui me rend furieuse! Je n'ai pensé qu'à moi, à mon plaisir.' (CDLR 13)

['I can't stop feeling guilty.'

'Bah! That's exactly what you said on the day you got divorced.'

'This is different. It's not a matter of choice with Marion. She's my child, my life-long love. I have to protect her. She shouldn't suffer because of her mother's stupidity.'

'You're being very harsh on yourself, Elena. There's nothing stupid about being in love.'

'I'm not in love, Mum, that's exactly why I'm furious! I only thought about myself, about my pleasure.']

While it should be remembered that Elena's guilt, like Marion's outburst, is an in-the-heat-of-the-moment response to the sudden mother–daughter crisis, Elena unquestioningly endorses the traditional image of motherhood. For instance, she accepts the taken-for-grantedness of maternal love, its unchangeability and its superiority over love for another, here her former husband. In addition, she has internalized the dominant view of mothering as a role precluding sexual relationships with anyone other than the child's father. Elena's belief that her pursuit of affairs could cause Marion to suffer reinforces the widespread view that changes to the family structure during childhood are detrimental to children, and points to the harsh judgements often made about parents who, irrespective of their orientation, enter a relationship with someone other than the mother or father of their children. According to Louise, Elena's shame at being a lesbian in part fuels Marion's reaction: '"Elena … ça fait des années que tu n'assumes pas ta vie, tes sentiments et ta sexualité. Comment veux-tu que ta fille t'accepte telle que tu es, si tu continues de te taire?"' ['Elena … for years you have not come to terms with your life, feelings and sexuality. How do you expect your daughter to accept you as you are if you remain silent?'] (CDLR 10). The fact that Marion's reaction is certainly worsened by Elena's self-censorship suggests how important it is that parents are open with their children about their sexuality – a point that is also frequently made about adopted children and those conceived via fertility treatment.

Unlike François, who suggests that difference could be a source of empowerment, Mallet seems to want to normalize lesbianism and lesbian mother–heterosexual daughter relationships. In the quotation above, Marinette looks beyond gender and sees Elena and Louise's affair as harmless love, thus downplaying the difference between heterosexual and homosexual relationships; indeed, the fact that it is a same-sex relationship is not even alluded to. Similarly, when Marinette declares that ' "[d]e quelque bord qu'elle soit, une femme reste une femme" ' ['whichever side she is on, a woman is still a woman'], she emphasizes what lesbian and heterosexual women have in common – that is, their gender – rather than what distinguishes them (CDLR 15). Surprisingly, the grandmother is more accepting of homosexuality than are her daughter and granddaughter. The novel thus challenges the expectation that the elderly are generally more conservative and therefore less tolerant of sexual minorities than the younger generation. The grandmother, as the following quotation shows, acts not as a mouthpiece for compulsory heterosexuality but as a voice of sexual progressivism:

'Je ne te reconnais plus, ma petite fille … Cette violence … à ton âge … pour une chose aussi … aussi …'

'Banale? Ordinaire? Courante? C'est ça que tu penses?'

'N'exagère pas, Marion! De nos jours, l'homosexualité n'est plus …'

'Je m'en balance, moi, de l'époque à laquelle on vit! Pour moi, les choses sont claires: je n'avais déjà pas de père et aujourd'hui, je n'ai plus de mère!' (CDLR 29)

['I don't recognize you any more, my girl … Such anger … at your age … for something so … so …'

'Trivial? Ordinary? Common? Is that what you think?'

'Don't exaggerate, Marion! Nowadays, homosexuality is no longer …'

'I don't care what era we're living in. For me, everything's clear: I already had no father, and today I no longer have a mother!']

In contrast with Marion's conservative stance on homosexuality, Marinette takes a modern, 'it's-no-big-deal' view of homosexuality and therefore represents the all-important theme of acceptance of a homosexual child. Since Marinette is aware of her daughter's lesbianism from the beginning, the novel does not tackle, and thus deproblematizes, Elena's coming out to her mother. Why the novel presents this unlikely contrast between an older woman's open-mindedness and a teenager's volatile intolerance is an interesting question. It is perhaps an allusion to the pressure on young people to conform to and reinforce heterosexuality and to their frequent desire to blend in with their peers. Alternatively, it could be a suggestion that if the elderly, who grew up at a time when homosexual acts were fiercely repressed, can throw off heteronormative ideas and accept homosexuality and homosexual parents, then it should be easy for others to do so.

The novel therefore depicts Marinette as an embodiment of tolerance and the stereotypical wisdom that accompanies old age. It is instructive, at this point, to draw on Cristina Herrera's analysis of the grandmother's mediation of the heterosexual mother–lesbian daughter conflict in Chicana lesbian writing. Herrera argues that the grandmother, as an older, wiser woman, recognizes the adverse consequences of heteronormative discourse and protects her granddaughter in the mother's stead.[28] While *Le Choix de la reine* diverts from Herrera's model in that it is the granddaughter or, rather, the granddaughter's shock that compels her to spread heteronormative discourse, when Elena's sexuality is revealed both daughter and granddaughter turn immediately to Marinette for advice and support. Marinette is cast as the mediator of the mother–daughter conflict and ultimately facilitates their reconciliation and Marion's acceptance of Elena's sexuality.

In addition to Elena's sexuality and relationship, the second force behind the novel's mother–daughter conflict is the absence of Marion's father. Like Anne's husband in *Les Bonheurs*, he represents the patriarchal tradition of controlling women's mothering and sexuality. Using Marion as leverage and presenting Elena with an ultimatum, to choose between him and Raphaëlle, the father initially coerces her into rejecting Raphaëlle,

28 Cristina Herrera, '"The Girls Our Mothers Warned Us About": Rejection, Redemption, and the Lesbian Daughter in Carla Trujillo's *What Night Brings*', *Women's Studies: An Interdisciplinary Journal* 39/1 (2009), 18–36 (20–1).

thus compelling Elena to repress her sexuality. Marion's identification with her father further resonates with psychoanalytic theories of the mother–daughter relationship. Chodorow argues that because the mother is usually the primary carer and the sole object through which an infant first experiences the world, daughters see the father as a symbol of freedom from dependence on the mother and, therefore, seek to identify with him.[29] Comparably, Marion seeks to identify with her estranged father because she is disillusioned with her mother. Marion's wish that her father be present and her aversion to Elena's lesbianism communicate her desire to sever the mother–daughter bond. Indeed, she tells Elena in the novel's opening scene: '"Tu n'es plus ma mère"' ['You're not my mother any more'] (CDLR 9). She reinforces this rejection by moving in with her grandmother. If, however, Marion's aversion to Elena's lesbianism is an expression not of homophobia per se but of her distress because it is her mother's sexuality that is in question, this implies a closeness between Elena and Marion. The novel thus points to the psychologically complex relationships between mothers and daughters, as well as the impact that sexuality has on them. Chodorow's description of the daughter's relationship to the mother during the pubertal and prepubertal phases offers an explanation for Marion's ambivalence towards Elena: '[The daughter tries] to merge herself with anyone other than the mother, all the while expressing her feelings of dependency on and primary identification with this mother'.[30] By actively disidentifying from Elena and bonding with Marinette, Marion's identity is founded on what Elena is not. In this way, Marion necessarily defers to the authority of the mother. Marion's identification with Marinette resonates with Chodorow's view that adolescent girls may idolize another woman or family member in order to separate from the mother.

While Marion quickly comes to terms with her mother's homosexuality, the novel portrays and normalizes the often problematic relationship between a child and a parent's partner. At one point, Elena reflects: 'Consciente du rejet naturel que Marion alimentait, non plus à l'égard de son homosexualité, mais envers sa compagne, Elena s'inquiétait'

29   Chodorow, *The Reproduction of Mothering*, 121.
30   Chodorow, *The Reproduction of Mothering*, 137.

[Elena was worried by the natural rejection that Marion was deliberately harbouring, no longer towards her homosexuality, but towards her partner] (CDLR 86). In this respect, the novel divorces the mother–daughter conflict from Elena's sexuality, since children are often hostile to a parent's new partner, irrespective of gender. Again, then, Mallet seems to downplay differences between heterosexual and lesbian mothers. The novel presents the mother's lover as the daughter's rival for the mother's devotion and love. When Marion is persuading Marinette to let her move in, Marion resentfully states: ' "[E]lle a d'autres idées en tête en ce moment que de se préoccuper de moi. Alors, c'est oui ou c'est non?" ' ['She has other things on her mind at the moment than worrying about me. So is it a yes or a no?'] (CDLR 25). Thus, although Marion insists on enforcing a separation between her and Elena, her resentment towards Elena implies a subconscious and, at this precise moment, denied wish to be close to the mother, following Chodorow's model of the mother–daughter relationship.

Luce Irigaray's mother–daughter dialogue in *Et l'une ne bouge pas sans l'autre* [*And the One Doesn't Stir without the Other*] (1979) further exemplifies the daughter's fluctuation between coveting the mother's affection and forging an identity distinct from that of the mother:

> And if you lead me back again and again to this blind assimilation of you – but who are you? – if you turn your face from me, giving yourself to me in an already inanimate form, abandoning me to competent men to undo my/your paralysis, I'll turn to my father. I'll leave you for someone who seems more alive than you.[31]

The parenthetical question 'but who are you?' suggests an estrangement between mother and daughter that is later supported by the words: 'Farewell, Mother, I shall never become your likeness.'[32] Similarly, Marion's commitment to heterosexuality ensures that she does not become her mother's likeness. Indeed, her disidentification from Elena is born of a fear that she too will become a lesbian – a theory of genetically acquired homosexuality that the novel ultimately refutes:

31 Luce Irigaray, 'And the One Doesn't Stir without the Other', trans. Hélène Vivienne Wenzel, *Signs: Journal of Women in Culture and Society* 7/1 (1981), 60–7 (62).
32 Irigaray, 'And the One Doesn't Stir without the Other', 62.

'Marion, ce n'est pas parce que je suis homosexuelle que tu l'es! Regarde ta grand-mère! Elle ne l'est pas.'

'Ça saute une génération?'

'Non, ma chérie, ce n'est pas génétique.'

'C'est quoi?'

'C'est … alchimique …' (CDLR 84)

['Marion, the fact that I'm homosexual doesn't mean you are! Look at your grand-mother! She isn't.'

'Does it skip a generation?'

'No, sweetheart, it's not genetic.'

'What causes it?'

'It's … a kind of alchemy.']

While the novel thus advocates a constructionist view of sexuality, the word 'alchimique' [a kind of alchemy] connotes something loosely scientific. *Le Choix de la reine* thus engages with the contemporary debate on the existence of what is popularly dubbed the 'gay gene' and appears to bridge the constructionist–essentialist divide among feminist and queer thinkers on sexual development. Indeed, Elena goes on to describe sexuality as a cooking recipe, suggesting a multitude of 'ingredients' that are neither purely social nor purely biological.

Marion's self-inflicted separation from Elena – moving in with Marinette and transferring to a new school – is her way of avoiding the stigma attached to having a lesbian mother. Indeed, her fear of and attempt to escape this stigma enable the novel to reconfigure the acts of closeting and eventual coming out that are typically thought of only in relation to homosexuals themselves. Elena's sexuality, then, affects her daughter's sense of self, positioning it in a liminal space between normativity and otherness: as a heterosexual, Marion adheres, on the one hand, to the normative assimilation of gender and sexuality; and yet, being the daughter of a lesbian mother engenders a self-imposed marginalization. While the novel thus acknowledges the difficulties that adolescents may face as children of gay and lesbian parents, it does not present them as unresolvable, and it challenges Marion's assumption – one shared by opponents of same-sex parenting – that gay- and lesbian-parented children, because their families divert from gender norms, have trouble building positive peer relationships. Indeed, Marion's romantic relationship with her classmate Tristan, who, incidentally, encourages Marion and Elena's reconciliation, implies that, in line with recent research findings, gay- and lesbian-parented children are in fact no more likely than those raised in heterosexual families to experience bullying.[33]

Although the novel's mother–daughter relationship has a transgressive lesbian facet, its representation of lesbian mothering is politically limited. The lesbian mother–heterosexual daughter conflict becomes a subplot when Raphaëlle reappears, with the result that the novel reverts to an unoriginal focus on a love triangle between the protagonist, the protagonist's lover and the protagonist's former partner. As Diana Holmes shows in *Romance and Readership in Twentieth-Century France* (2006), women's writing, while not reducible to love stories, is often concerned with romance.[34] Central to the romance is the 'question of whether and how the two primary characters will achieve, or fail to achieve, a lasting union with each other'.[35] In a slight reformulation of Holmes's definition, central to this novel is the question of which two of the three lovers will achieve a lasting union with each other. By positioning the lesbian mother in this context, the novel could be said to rely on clichés in order to make lesbian mothering acceptable. Significantly, *Le Choix de la reine* challenges the traditional heterosexism of the romance, but this should be viewed as part of a literary context in which empowering models of lesbian love have been increasing since the second half of the twentieth century. This novel might be best understood,

---

33 See Henny M. W. Bos and Frank van Balen, 'Children in Planned Lesbian Families: Stigmatisation, Psychological Adjustment and Protective Factors', *Culture, Health & Sexuality: An International Journal for Research, Invention and Care* 10/3 (2008), 221–36; Jennifer L. Wainright and Charlotte J. Patterson, 'Peer Relations among Adolescents with Female Same-Sex Parents', *Developmental Psychology* 44/1 (2008), 117–26.

34 Diana Holmes, *Romance and Readership in Twentieth-Century France: Love Stories* (Oxford: Oxford University Press, 2006), 12.

35 Holmes, *Romance and Readership in Twentieth-Century France*, 6.

then, as a broadly typical example of popular French women's romance fiction. For Holmes, the popular and the literary differ 'in the degree of resolution they provide': popular romance 'provide[s] an imaginary experience of needs happily fulfilled, whereas "literary" novels may explore needs and desires in their tension with reality, and without offering solutions'.[36] In keeping with Holmes's distinction, *Le Choix de la reine* ends with closure, with Elena and Raphaëlle reunited after a long period of separation. Because Elena chooses Raphaëlle over Louise, the novel recycles stereotypes about the enduring, unsurpassable love for a companion presumed to have long ago disappeared for good. A more positive, reader-response-based position on the novel's ending might, however, emphasize the 'sense of optimism' that it invokes in readers, which is a source of the pleasure of popular fiction.[37] Elena and Raphaëlle's unwavering love restores the reader's faith in relationships in an era when break-ups and divorce are fast becoming the norm. Because the novel reverts to focusing on a love triangle, it ends at what is arguably its most subversive moment, when Raphaëlle moves in with Elena and Marion, thus forming a lesbian step-parent family. The novel thus sets up but leaves the lesbian family narrative undeveloped and the relationship between the daughter and her lesbian mother's partner largely unexplored. This could, however, be interpreted more optimistically as a refusal to dictate a fixed model of the lesbian step-parent family. Moreover, the novel empowers lesbian mothers through the resolution of its mother–daughter conflict, and the happy ending suggests that the future for these characters will not be problematic.

What seems to matter most to Mallet, though, is the empowerment of a range of female identities. The novel's depiction of a multitude of female identities – the mother, the daughter, the older woman and Elena's two lovers – and its relative lack of male characters work to give a voice to what Irigaray calls a 'genealogy' of women, the recognition of which, she contends, is imperative if we are to deconstruct patriarchy: 'It is also necessary […] for us to assert that there is a genealogy of women. There is a genealogy of women within our family: on our mothers' side we have mothers;

36   Holmes, *Romance and Readership in Twentieth-Century France*, 129.
37   Holmes, 'The Comfortable Reader', 288.

grandmothers and great-grandmothers, and daughters'.[38] According to Irigaray, the dominance of the father–son line and the proportionate disregard in legal and political terms of female genealogies are instrumental in maintaining patriarchy. The absence of the paternal line from the novel works to foreground that between its mothers and daughters. Mallet does not, however, succumb to naive essentialism by axing men from the plot. Although few, if any, references are made to Elena's father, she is mistaken for her boss's daughter when she visits him in hospital, and he says half-jokingly, half-seriously: '"[C]e serait assez plausible … si on arrive à se tutoyer!"' ['It would be fairly credible … if we could address each other less formally'] (CDLR 193). This misunderstanding demonstrates that perceptions still rely on the patriarchal lineage that the novel seems to dismiss. Moreover, the absence of Marion's father does not lead to her wholesale resentment of men, as evidenced by the romance that blossoms between her and Tristan. The prominence of female roles in *Le Choix de la reine* thus answers Irigaray's call to defend a female specificity while not elevating the feminine to a position of superiority over the masculine. The novel culminates in the peaceful coexistence of a plurality of identities – of different ages, genders and sexualities – that are diverse in nature but equal in value. This also seems to recall Irigaray's and Cixous's opposition to patriarchal ideals of women as a fixed, homogeneous group.

Le Choix de la reine partially challenges the dominant portrayal of mother–daughter relationships. By casting the protagonist as a lesbian, the novel contributes in a unique way to the changing configuration of the mother–daughter relationship in contemporary French women's writing. That said, the origins of the mother–daughter conflict in this novel, such as the mother's fear of pursuing a relationship with a new partner and the daughter's antipathy towards a prospective step-parent, are potentially applicable to all mother–daughter conflicts, regardless of family form. In this way, *Le Choix de la reine* seeks to normalize lesbianism, lesbian mothering and the alternative mother–daughter relationships that result from non-traditional family forms. However, the novel declines to fully explore the

---

38   Luce Irigaray, 'The Bodily Encounter with the Mother', trans. David Macey, in Margaret Whitford, ed., *The Irigaray Reader* (Oxford: Blackwell, 1991), 34–46 (44).

implications of these families because it masks the transgressive lesbian mother–heterosexual daughter relationship behind a somewhat clichéd focus on the love triangle between the protagonist and her two lovers.

Concluding Thoughts

By ultimately challenging the taken-for-granted nexus between mothering and heterosexuality, the works by François, Dumont and Mallet inscribe the passage from lesbianism or mothering to lesbian mothering. An important commonality of these texts is that they anticipate the increasing visibility of same-sex families in the 2000s by hypothesizing a parental role for the mother's lover. In *Les Bonheurs* and *La Vie dure*, both Sarah and Pascale envisage the creation of a lesbian family. *Le Choix de la reine* ends with Raphaëlle moving in with Elena and Marion, thus forming a lesbian step-parent family. Despite this, the transgressive potential of these texts is limited in this respect, since the possibility of a lesbian family is never truly embraced or is embraced only at the end of the text. Importantly, though, the texts expose the norms of the family and the challenges facing lesbian mothers in the period before same-sex parenting became a political issue. All three texts feature characters who act as mouthpieces for the heteronormative discourses that drive the mother-characters to initially suppress their sexuality: the mothers' husbands in *Les Bonheurs* and *La Vie dure*, the protagonist's priest in *Les Bonheurs* and the protagonist's daughter in *Le Choix de la reine*. Furthermore, all three texts empower lesbian characters and readers, either by normalizing lesbianism (Mallet) or through queer-sounding critique (François and Dumont).

Arguably, the representation of lesbianism in *Les Bonheurs* is ahead of its time. Although published well before queer lives became a mainstream issue, and four decades before *Le Choix de la reine* and *La Vie dure*, *Les Bonheurs*, in portraying characters who elude categorization as entirely heterosexual or lesbian, shows a nuanced awareness of the limits of sexual labels that has only recently started to be recognized. François's work also stands out for its clever interweaving of experimental form and subversive theme, whereas the texts by Mallet and Dumont are written in a highly transparent style.

Overall, these texts should be seen as reminders of the existence of lesbian parenting prior to its politicization and theorization and as precursors to the widening of family structures that France has witnessed in the first decades of the twenty-first century. Whereas the works of François, Dumont and Mallet at first present lesbianism and mothering as irreconcilable opposites by depicting mothers who must seemingly choose between the lesbian and maternal dimensions of their lives, the reconciliation of these dimensions in Hélène de Monferrand's novels, while not without its problems, is never depicted in either/or terms.

CHAPTER 3

Between Tradition and Transgression*

In *Of Woman Born* (1976), Adrienne Rich distinguishes between two definitions of motherhood: the potentially empowering experiences of pregnancy, childbirth and childcare; and the patriarchal institution, which ensures that these experiences, and all women, remain under male control.[1] This institution posits three fundamental assumptions about motherhood: firstly, motherhood is women's sole or primary function; secondly, mothers love their children absolutely; and thirdly, child-rearing comes instinctively, and therefore easily, to women. Rich's testimony exemplifies the anxiety and guilt felt by many mothers at not meeting these expectations:

> I was haunted by the stereotype of the mother whose love is 'unconditional'; and by the visual and literary images of motherhood as a single-minded identity. If I knew parts of myself existed that would never cohere to those images, weren't those parts then abnormal, monstrous?[2]

Feminists have endeavoured to challenge the assumptions of institutional motherhood and normalize the idea that women's feelings for their children are often to some degree ambivalent. Maternal ambivalence, to paraphrase Rozsika Parker's definition, describes the love- and hate-based emotions and impulses that women experience in relation to their

---

*   An earlier version of this chapter has already appeared in publication: Robert Payne, 'Lesbianism and Maternal Ambivalence in Hélène de Monferrand's *Les Amies d'Héloïse* (1990) and *Les Enfants d'Héloïse* (1997)', *Revue critique de fixxion française contemporaine* 12 (2016), 120–9.

1   Rich, *Of Woman Born*, 13.

2   Rich, *Of Woman Born*, 23.

children.[3] Because maternal love is thought to be absolute, ambivalence is often equated with bad mothering and, because women are expected to be good mothers, with deviant femininity.

As a wealth of literary criticism has established, maternal ambivalence is a recurring theme of literary works by twentieth- and twenty-first-century French women writers. In Geneviève Brisac's *Week-end de chasse à la mère* [*Losing Eugenio*] (1996), for example, the mother ultimately loses custody of her son but is nonetheless able to manage her ambivalence.[4] Other writers portray unmanageable, and highly controversial, cases of ambivalence. In Véronique Olmi's *Bord de mer* [*Beside the Sea*] (2001) and Laurence Tardieu's *Le Jugement de Léa* [*The Judgement of Léa*] (2004), ambivalence results in infanticide.[5]

The relative absence of lesbian mothers from French literature means that most literary and critical works consider ambivalence in heterosexual contexts. In this chapter, however, I examine two rare texts – Hélène de Monferrand's *Les Amies d'Héloïse* [*Héloïse's Friends*] (1990) and *Les Enfants d'Héloïse* [*Héloïse's Children*] (1997) – that explore manageable ambivalence in the context of lesbian mothering.[6] With Jocelyne François and Mireille Best, Monferrand is one of only a few twentieth-century French writers who is openly lesbian and whose oeuvre consistently focuses on lesbian characters and themes. She won the prestigious Prix Goncourt for best debut novel in 1990 and has been credited with bringing lesbianism and lesbian writing into the mainstream. Jennifer Waelti-Walters, for instance, writes that with Monferrand's accreditation with the Goncourt 'official, public space began to open up for a variety of "normal" human experiences to be attributed to lesbian characters who neither died at the end of the

3   Rozsika Parker, *Torn in Two: The Experience of Maternal Ambivalence* (London: Virago, 1995), 1.

4   See Rye, *Narratives of Mothering*, 101–9; Geneviève Brisac, *Week-end de chasse à la mère* (Paris: Éditions de l'Olivier, 1996).

5   See Edwards, 'Babykillers'.

6   Hélène de Monferrand, *Les Amies d'Héloïse*, Le Livre de Poche (Paris: Fallois, 1990); Hélène de Monferrand, *Les Enfants d'Héloïse* (Paris: La Cerisaie, 2002 [1997]); subsequent references to these works are provided as in-text citations in the following forms: (ADH p.), (EDH p.).

novel, nor were dead before it started'.[7] Similarly, Lucille Cairns states that Monferrand 'has portrayed a lesbian society within, but not antagonistic to or marginalized by, mainstream society that is literarily unprecedented in French literature'.[8]

Arguably, Monferrand's interest in the family is second only to her interest in lesbianism. *Les Amies d'Héloïse* and *Les Enfants d'Héloïse* are the first and third volumes of a trilogy depicting the fortunes of two main aristocratic families. They contain a large cast of characters belonging to several generations, as well as friends. *Les Amies d'Héloïse* is an epistolary novel set between 1964 and 1980. It follows the lives of a number of hetero-sexual and lesbian women, centring on the love triangle between Héloïse de Marèges, Erika von Tauberg and Suzanne Lacombe. Twenty-nine-year-old Erika seduces 15-year-old Héloïse, who then falls for Erika's former lover, Suzanne, who is almost 50. Humiliated and jealous, Erika shoots Héloïse and flees to Germany. Soon after, Suzanne learns that she has a brain tumour and commits suicide. Grief-stricken, Héloïse marries, has three children – a boy followed by twin girls – and is widowed prior to the birth of her daughters. She and Erika are subsequently reunited after a ten-year separ-ation. Set between 1981 and 1990, *Les Enfants d'Héloïse* picks up where *Les Amies d'Héloïse* leaves off. In *Les Enfants d'Héloïse*, Monferrand replaces the epistolary form with a third-person narrative told from multiple points of view. Héloïse pursues her relationship with Erika while raising her son, Anne, and her daughters, Mélanie and Suzanne. It is only when Mélanie finds Suzanne Lacombe's diary that the children learn of their mother's sexuality and relationship with Erika. The mother–child relationship and the role of a lesbian lover in the family are thus this novel's central themes. By casting Mélanie as a lesbian, Monferrand also returns to the exploration of adolescent lesbianism that she began in *Les Amies d'Héloïse*. Combined, the two novels cover a chronologically ordered twenty-five-year period (if the second volume, *Journal de Suzanne* [*Suzanne's Diary*] (1991), which is not analysed in this study for the simple reason that it does not portray a lesbian mother, is taken into account, the trilogy encompasses more than

7   Waelti-Walters, *Damned Women*, 5.
8   Cairns, *Lesbian Desire in Post-1968 French Literature*, 312.

half a century).[9] Central to Monferrand's work, then, is an overarching concern with tradition and transmission that is in keeping with her characters' aristocratic backgrounds.

Tradition is central to Monferrand's work on a literary as well as thematic level. Intertextual references to French literary classics, most notably Jean-Jacques Rousseau's *Julie, ou la Nouvelle Héloïse* [*Julie, or the New Héloïse*] (1761) and Choderlos de Laclos's *Les Liaisons dangereuses* [*Dangerous Liaisons*] (1782), abound in Monferrand's work.[10] The protagonist's name recalls the title of Rousseau's novel, which itself draws inspiration from the twelfth-century exchange of letters between Heloise and Abelard. In Rousseau's novel, the protagonist falls in love with her tutor; in Monferrand's, Héloïse's lover Suzanne is a teacher. There are obvious parallels between Monferrand's plot and the representation of a morally depraved aristocracy in *Les Liaisons dangereuses*; Héloïse's manipulation of Erika and Suzanne is even compared with that of the womanizing Valmont. The use of the epistolary form in *Les Amies d'Héloïse* cements the link between this novel and these eighteenth-century epistolary classics. The shift to a third-person narrative told from multiple points of view in *Les Enfants d'Héloïse* suggests the author's interest in varying literary form (it is worth noting too that *Journal de Suzanne* is, as its title makes clear, written in the form of a diary) and allows her to explore the themes of lesbianism and the family from diverse perspectives.

Monferrand's style is classical and traditionalist. In an interview with *Lesbia* magazine, Monferrand stated that clarity, rather than pretentiousness, was the most important characteristic of her writing; that she did not have 'the typically French phobia' of repeating words; and that she hated literary works that break the rules on tense use, which she claimed to respect 'scrupulously'.[11] She then concluded that '[t]he French language

9   See Hélène de Monferrand, *Journal de Suzanne* (Paris: Fallois, 1991).

10   Jean-Jacques Rousseau, *Julie, ou la Nouvelle Héloïse*, Le Livre de Poche (Paris: Librairie Générale Française, 2002 [1761]); Choderlos de Laclos, *Les Liaisons dangereuses*, Le Livre de Poche (Paris: Librairie Générale Française, 2002 [1782]).

11   Fanny Follet and Hélène de Monferrand, 'La Trilogie d'Hélène vingt ans après', *Lesbia* (2010), <https://fr.calameo.com/read/0030409913326df5f2847>, accessed 26 January 2019.

is our tool and we must respect it and all its specificities that make up its charm. Besides, what's more pleasurable than a colloquial verb, even a slang one, conjugated in the imperfect subjunctive?'.[12] Monferrand is opposed to linguistic change and committed to preserving the conventions of the French language in her own work.

I want to explore the relationship between tradition and transgression in Monferrand's novels. I begin with a formal analysis of the novels, focusing on how Monferrand aligns herself with classic epistolary works but, at the same time, transgresses norms of gender and sexuality. I then turn to the portrayal of maternal ambivalence in the novels.

Monferrand and the Literary Canon

In her introduction to *Writing the Female Voice: Essays on Epistolary Literature* (1989), Elizabeth Goldsmith remarks that '[t]he association of women's writing with the love-letter genre has been perhaps one of the most tenacious of gender–genre connections in the history of literature'.[13] This connection dates back to the sixteenth century, when the letter began to be regarded as a literary form. Yet, as Katherine Jensen points out, because women in the early modern period were rarely permitted to publish, they largely practised the genre 'as a social art while men [...] exercised it socially *and* literarily'.[14] The first epistolary texts were therefore written by men attempting to replicate the style of women's letters. For Jensen, this appropriation of women's epistolary writing suggests a concern about female power.[15] The first epistolary texts took the form of instructive

---

12   Follet and Monferrand, 'La Trilogie d'Hélène vingt ans après'.

13   Elizabeth C. Goldsmith, ed., *Writing the Female Voice: Essays on Epistolary Literature* (London: Pinter, 1989), viii.

14   Katherine A. Jensen, 'Male Models of Feminine Epistolarity; or, How to Write Like a Woman in Seventeenth-Century France', in Elizabeth C. Goldsmith, ed., *Writing the Female Voice: Essays on Epistolary Literature* (London: Pinter, 1989), 25–45 (28).

15   Jensen, 'Male Models of Feminine Epistolarity', 28.

manuals that taught the user to write effective letters. In her illumin-
ating study of these collections, Jensen argues that male authors sought to
consolidate men's power not through the wholesale exclusion of female-
authored letters but by including them as tokens that positioned women
in non-literary, private spaces and that represented them as sexually sub-
ordinate and, in particular, as constant and willing sufferers of unrecipro-
cated desire. Goldsmith therefore theorizes an interesting paradox about
the relationship between women and epistolary writing: 'The one genre
with which women have been persistently connected has specialized in
narrowing the range of possible inflections for feminine expression'.[16] The
popularity of the epistolary novel reached its peak with the publication
of Rousseau's *La Nouvelle Héloïse* and Laclos's *Les Liaisons dangereuses* in
the late eighteenth century. The use of this form in *Les Amies d'Héloïse*
and its similarities to the works by Rousseau and Laclos are undoubtedly
an attempt by the author to position her work within, and perhaps even
to revive, this tradition.

  To some extent, Monferrand challenges contemporary assumptions
about what writing a letter involves. A letter is commonly understood as
a means of communicating fairly ordinary information and sentiment
between two parties in lieu of a face-to-face conversation. In *Les Amies
d'Héloïse*, however, some letters include details of notable historical events,
extracts from lesbian poetry and transcriptions of entire conversations. By
representing the letter as a site of intellectual and philosophical, as well as
sentimental, discussion, the novel reflects the tradition among artists of
using the letter as a space for debate – a tradition that Monferrand might
be said to be reclaiming. Some letters, in contrast, contain just a few words.
At times, letter writing is portrayed almost as a reflex for Monferrand's
characters in times of crisis. When, for example, Héloïse advises her best
friend, Claire, to avoid becoming pregnant before finishing university,
Claire simply responds: 'Trop tard' [Too late] (ADH 198). Following
her first sexual encounter with Héloïse, Erika writes to Suzanne: 'C'est
fait. Stop. Ouf. Stop. Tout va bien' [It is done. Stop. Phew. Stop. All is
well] (ADH 32). These letters closely resemble dialogue and thus blur the

16   Goldsmith, *Writing the Female Voice*, xii.

boundaries between writing and speech. The final letter imitates the style of a telegram – 'stop' being the word used to end a sentence in telegram messages. These examples show the diversity and instability of the letter in *Les Amies d'Héloïse*.

This sense of instability is reinforced by the novel's representation of time. Although time remains linear in *Les Amies d'Héloïse*, with each chapter devoted to one calendar year, the novel distorts chronology by varying the time intervals between letters. Communication between Héloïse and Claire is, at times, almost daily. Sometimes, however, the gaps between letters are greater, which, because communication by letter often breaks down, arguably increases the realism of the characters' correspondence. The chapter dedicated to the year 1969, for instance, ends with a letter from Héloïse to Claire sent from Stockholm on 9 August. The next chapter begins with another letter from Héloïse to Claire sent from Vienna on 18 January 1970. On 9 August, it is evident that the two will soon meet, as Héloïse states at the end of her letter that her mother is looking forward to seeing Claire and the children, but it is unclear what happens during the intervening six months or why Héloïse moves to Vienna.

Given the association between women and letter writing, the use of the epistolary form in *Les Amies d'Héloïse* could be said to reinforce norms of femininity. It is therefore particularly significant that Monferrand uses it in a lesbian novel that inherently challenges the norm of female heterosexuality.[17] It also portrays female characters who assume high-powered roles in a traditionally male public sphere: Erika skilfully manages her father's lucrative company; Suzanne is a high school history teacher; and Héloïse reads history and pharmaceutical studies at university before going on to run her own pharmacy. Moreover, Monferrand reverses the patriarchal tradition of silencing women by giving overwhelming precedence to female perspectives. Although men feature in the novel, usually, like the women, in positions of social and economic power – for instance, Héloïse's father is an ambassador, and Erika's is a renowned entrepreneur – only the female

---

17   Natalie Edwards makes a similar point about Linda Lê's use of the epistolary form in *À l'enfant que je n'aurai pas* [*To the Child I Will Never Have*] (2011) to recount the narrator's rejection of mothering. See Edwards, *Voicing Voluntary Childlessness*, 81.

characters write letters. The range of voices and absence of an omniscient authorial or narrative voice, which, as Elizabeth MacArthur demonstrates, are defining characteristics of the epistolary genre, function to resist the patriarchal view of women as a fixed and homogeneous group.[18]

Although Monferrand therefore questions norms of gender and sexuality, importantly she does not ignore the challenges of being a lesbian in a heteronormative society. *Les Amies d'Héloïse* exposes the dominant idea that heterosexuality is the natural end result of female sexual development, as exemplified by Claire's response to Héloïse's admission that she has had sex with Erika:

> Bien sûr, je sais que ces choses-là existent; on dit même qu'à notre âge c'est fréquent et que ça ne dure pas, mais je suis vraiment étonnée […]. Moi, je n'ai jamais eu envie, et puis je ne vois pas très bien ce qu'on peut faire dans le lit d'une dame. (ADH 33)

> [Of course, I know that such things exist; it is even said that at our age it is common and that it does not last, but I am really surprised […]. I have never wanted to, and also I do not really see what one can do in bed with a woman.]

Although Claire is generally an enlightened, tolerant character, here she represents the heteronormative view that sex between women is not really possible and the long-held belief that lesbianism is merely a phase of adolescence. Even Erika expresses worry that Héloïse will succumb to the 'tentation de mener une vie normale' [temptation to lead a normal life] (ADH 69). The novel also recognizes the normative status of heterosexuality and pressure to conform. Despite the strong solidarity between the heterosexual and lesbian characters, coming out to anyone outside the immediate social circle is unthinkable, as is publicly acting on same-sex attraction, as Erika laments in her diary:

> Si je n'étais pas une femme, je pourrais montrer mon intérêt. Au lieu de ça je me laisse conter fleurette par des hommes qu'il me faut ensuite écarter habilement. De toute façon, je laisse tomber. Dans ce milieu, dans ce pays, c'est sans avenir. (ADH 19)

18   Elizabeth J. MacArthur, *Extravagant Narratives: Closure and Dynamics in the Epistolary Form* (Princeton, NJ: Princeton University Press, 1990), 9.

[If I were not a woman, I could show my interest. Instead, I let myself be wooed by men that I must then skilfully brush off. In any case, I will let it go. In these circles, in this country, there is no future in it.]

These obstacles aside, however, lesbianism is broadly unproblematic in *Les Amies d'Héloïse*. Although the characters must be discreet about their relationships in public, they are open with and accepted by their friends and family, and Héloïse's remark that ' "[j]e ne vais pas parler de ma vie sexuelle à tout le monde, quand même!" ' ['I'm hardly going to talk about my sex life with everyone!'] suggests some scepticism about the need to publicly come out (ADH 387). Héloïse even claims that she has never suffered discrimination because of her sexuality. While this is not the experience of all lesbians, it is aspirational and, in this sense, empowering to lesbian readers.

Unlike in classic epistolary novels, in *Les Amies d'Héloïse* the female characters enjoy and exercise control over their sexual relationships. Monferrand challenges the stereotype that lesbians are less interested in sex than in love and do not engage in the promiscuity commonly associated with gay men. Erika admits that she can no longer count how many sexual partners she has had. Héloïse sees her relationship with Erika as sexual, rather than romantic; she grows bored when Erika becomes clingy, and cheats on her with Suzanne. The characters thus resist conventional and purportedly moral long-term, monogamous relationships. Furthermore, the novel portrays sex as a game primarily controlled by its young lesbian protagonist: finding a boyfriend is dismissed as 'facile' [easy]; finding another female lover is 'difficile et donc valorisant' [difficult and therefore rewarding]; seducing Suzanne is described as 'un excellent exercice' [an excellent exercise]; and staying loyal to Erika is unappealing because Héloïse 'ne [s]'amuse plus' [is no longer having fun] (ADH 103). Finally, the hierarchical dynamics of sexual relationships are embraced, rather than denounced as disempowering, thus challenging the idea that lesbian relationships are inherently egalitarian. The *tu* [informal 'you'] and *vous* [formal 'you'] forms are employed to ritualize the power relations between the protagonist and her lovers, as the following passage from a letter from Héloïse to Claire makes clear:

[J]e suis bien contente que les précautions prises à l'époque de ma minorité nous aient conduites à ne jamais nous tutoyer. Tu ne peux pas savoir le supplément de sensualité qu'apporte cette pratique. Mes parents le savent bien, je parie. J'aimais aussi l'inégalité du rapport avec Suzanne. C'était le maître et l'élève … autre chose … (ADH 442)

[I am quite pleased that the precautions that I took when I was a teenager led us to never say *tu* to each other. You would not believe how much extra sensuality this practice brings. I bet my parents know. I also liked the inequality of the relationship with Suzanne. It was a teacher–pupil thing … it was something else …]

For Héloïse, the ritualized *vouvoiement* [using the formal 'you'] is a source of sexual pleasure and arguably communicates her emotional detachment from Erika. The skewed *tu–vous* distribution between Héloïse and Suzanne – Suzanne says *tu* to Héloïse, but Héloïse addresses Suzanne in the *vous* form – evidences the sexually gratifying power relations of their affair. Monferrand thus deproblematizes her young heroine's presumed sexual exploitation by her older lovers. Unexpectedly, it is Héloïse who toys with Erika and entices Suzanne into bed and who occupies the role of seducer in her sexual relationships.

Les Amies d'Héloïse further differs from classic epistolary novels in its portrayal of despair and revolt. In her article on contemporary women's epistolary novels, Elizabeth Campbell succinctly describes how the treatment of these themes has changed since the seventeenth and eighteenth centuries:

In the epistolary novels of the seventeenth and eighteenth centuries we are more likely to find despair as the letter writer either feels herself succumbing to the temptation of her seducer, or, having been seduced and abandoned, bewails her fate to another. In contemporary epistolary novels we are still likely to find despair, but more often we see women moving away from despair to revolt.[19]

Although contemporary epistolary novels therefore retain the despairing female characters common in those in the past, they also permit them to rebel against lovers who mistreat them. In keeping with this model, Héloïse, Erika and Suzanne all go through periods of despair that they

19   Elizabeth Campbell, 'Re-visions, Re-flections, Re-creations: Epistolarity in Novels by Contemporary Women', *Twentieth Century Literature* 41/3 (1995), 332–48 (337).

turn into revolt. When Erika learns that Héloïse is sleeping with Suzanne, she shoots Héloïse in a fit of jealousy. Suzanne ends her own life, which is undeniably tragic, but it is also a form of revolt in the sense that she takes control of her own destiny. Indeed, the matter-of-fact tone in which Suzanne explains her suicide suggests that it is not an act of despair but a rational choice: '[J]e suis obligée de me tuer car j'ai une tumeur au cerveau. [...] Je dois profiter de ce que je suis parfaitement saine d'esprit pour m'évader' [I have to kill myself because I have a brain tumour. [...] I need to escape while I am still completely sound of mind] (ADH 276). Because Suzanne's suicide is motivated by illness, rather than unrequited love or desire, *Les Amies d'Héloïse* departs from classic epistolary novels in which love is portrayed as a curse. This is a rare tragedy in a novel that, overall, presents lesbian love as unproblematic. Indeed, Suzanne's final letter to Héloïse portrays love positively:

> Pourtant, il faut que tu saches qu'on survit toujours à la mort de l'autre: je le sais, je l'ai fait. Et je répondrai maintenant à une question que tu m'as posée autrefois: combien de fois j'ai aimé: trois fois, et c'est bien assez dans une vie. C'est toi que j'ai le plus aimée. (ADH 277)

> [However, you should know that people always survive the death of a lover. I know, I have done it. And now I will answer a question that you once asked me: how many times have I been in love? Three times, and that is enough for one life. You are the one whom I have loved the most.]

Suzanne's pragmatism about love challenges still pervasive stereotypes of women in love as helpless and passive, and this is rendered more powerful by the context of the character's imminent suicide. The uplifting portrayal of lesbian love arguably lessens the severity of the tragedy; love is not the cause of death but is perhaps what enables Suzanne to face it with a degree of optimism. In this respect, *Les Amies d'Héloïse* follows the turn in contemporary epistolary novels, and in French lesbian writing, towards the portrayal of strong female characters.

Unlike in the epistolary novels of the seventeenth and eighteenth centuries, Héloïse and Erika do not bemoan their lack of fortune. The novel thus resists contemporary claims that women are inherently more emotionally expressive and receptive than men and, as a result, need to talk about their feelings. Indeed, it is telling that Héloïse, the novel's central character and the one who writes the most letters, ceases all correspondence in the immediate aftermath of Suzanne's death. Similarly, Erika stops writing letters altogether after she and Héloïse break up and chooses instead to write exclusively in the more private writing space of her diary. In this way, writing – or, more precisely, writing selectively or declining to write – becomes symbolic of the characters' emotions. Although Erika updates her diary more regularly following the break-up, she struggles to come to terms with it. After a thorough critique of her own appearance, she writes: 'Le mental maintenant. Non, je ne suis pas prête encore à examiner ça' [Now the mind. No, I am not ready to look at that yet] (ADH 174). Four days later, she writes: 'Je ne rêve plus d'ELLES, toutes les deux ensemble. Oh merde, ça me fait mal, ça me fait encore mal de l'évoquer' [I no longer dream of THEM together. Damn, it hurts, it still hurts to think about it] (ADH 174–5). Although the diary serves as a means of expression, perhaps even salvation, following a painful separation, ironically Erika remains unable to confront her feelings, especially where Héloïse and Suzanne are concerned. While *Les Amies d'Héloïse* therefore maintains the suffering female characters that were typical of classic epistolary novels, the novel departs from this model in having the protagonists refuse to write their despair and share it with others.

The characters' tendency to write selectively is equally evident in their treatment of sex. Given the foregrounding of lesbian desire and love in Monferrand's work, it is significant, and perhaps surprising, that neither of the *Héloïse* novels contains a description of lesbian sex. Although they make it plain that sex takes place, they refuse to eroticize the act by avoiding explicit descriptions. For example, in the letter cited above in which Erika informs Suzanne that she has slept with Héloïse, '[c]'est fait' [it is done] signifies sex, but 'ouf' [phew] connotes relief, rather than sexual satisfaction. Another technique that Monferrand uses to avoid eroticizing lesbianism is to replace the explicit details of lesbian sex with ellipses, as in the following passage in which Héloïse relates her encounter with one of her other lovers, Melitta:

> [J]e lui ai dit: 'Montrez-moi votre chambre.' […] Après, elle m'a dit: 'Tu es complètement folle de t'être mariée, tu n'es pas faite pour ça du tout.'

'Mais non, ne crois pas ça. Ça marchait assez bien.'

'Allons donc! mieux que ça?', puis […].

J'ai repris: 'Toi aussi tu étais mariée, après tout.' (ADH 343)

['Show me your bedroom,' I said. […] Afterwards, she said: 'You were completely mad to get married, you're not made for it at all.'

'No, don't think that. It was all right.'

'Yeah right! Better than this?', then […].

I continued: 'You were married too, after all.']

The bracketed ellipses indicate Héloïse's omission of details that she is unwilling to disclose. The fourth occurrence of 'ça' [this] pre-empts Melitta's instigation of a second sexual act, but the form that it takes is left unsaid. It is easy to see why this could frustrate lesbian readers trying to come to terms with and understand their sexuality through literature: the fact that Héloïse stops short of an overt affirmation of her sexuality through a description of her experience with another woman appears to equate lesbian sex with the unspeakable. However, the lack of description of sex in the novel chimes with some feminists' arguments about the potentially useful role of the unsaid in the valorization of female sexuality. According to Hélène Cixous and Luce Irigaray, for instance, female sexuality cannot and should not be defined within the confines of phallocentric language.[20] Cixous and Irigaray argue that defining female sexuality follows the patriarchal tradition of restricting it to fixed codes. By omitting the details of sex, *Les Amies d'Héloïse* sidesteps this danger while still representing sexually active lesbian characters.

Instead of describing sex graphically, the novel talks about it euphemistically, as exemplified by the references to 'la chambre' [the bedroom] and 'ça' [it] in the quotation above. Héloïse's coming out to Claire further exhibits Monferrand's use of euphemism: '[H]ier soir je me suis retrouvée dans un lit avec Erika von Tauberg, et j'ai aimé ça' [Last night, I found myself in bed with Erika von Tauberg, and I liked it] (ADH 32). Being

---

20   Cixous, 'Le Rire de la Méduse', 39; Irigaray, *Ce sexe qui n'en est pas un*, 93.

in a bed together means euphemistically that Héloïse and Erika have sex. Soon after, Héloïse provides Claire with more context:

> Nous avons décidé de prendre un bain avant de sortir dîner, et c'est là que tout s'est joué. Je me suis retrouvée dans ses bras d'abord, puis sur un lit au milieu d'un tas de serviettes-éponges. Je ne sais pas comment c'est arrivé; et ce qu'elle a fait, ce que nous avons fait toute la nuit, je ne peux pas le raconter. (ADH 35)

> [We decided to take a bath before going out for dinner, and that is when it all happened. I found myself in her arms first, then on a bed covered in towels. I do not know how it happened, and what she did, what we did all night, I cannot recount it.]

The phrases 'tout s'est joué' [it all happened] and 'c'est arrivé' [it happened] indicate that 'it' happened, but the details remain unclear. Héloïse's refusal to share the details suggests a degree of embarrassment, and perhaps fear of rejection, that evidences her lack of sexual experience. Alternatively, 'je ne peux pas' [I cannot] might, following Cixous, be said to signify Héloïse's inability to communicate female sexual experience using traditional linguistic codes. On the other hand, the euphemistic description of sex enables lesbian readers to construct and fantasize about what is left unsaid for themselves, rather than it being imposed on them. In this light, the subtle inscription of sex is empowering and liberating for lesbian readers.

The use of euphemism extends to sexuality. Significantly, the words 'lesbienne' [lesbian] and 'lesbianisme' [lesbianism] do not appear in *Les Amies d'Héloïse* and appear only rarely in *Les Enfants d'Héloïse*. It is tempting to criticize this omission as an unintended endorsement of the taboo on lesbianism, but it is equally a powerful reflection of its invisibility in the 1960s and 1970s. Rather than labelling the characters as lesbians, Monferrand uses imprecise but connotative substitute phrases, such as 'les filles dans mon genre' [girls like me] (ADH 248), or ellipses, such as when Lise, Erika's colleague, responds to her coming out: ' "Vous voulez dire que … vous ne les [les hommes] aimez pas … pas du tout? … même pour …" ' ['You mean … you don't like them [men] … at all? … Even for …'] (ADH 245). However, just as not describing lesbian sex does not amount to precluding lesbian sex, refusing to name lesbianism does not amount to refusing lesbianism: *Les Amies d'Héloïse* and *Les Enfants d'Héloïse* are irrefutably lesbian novels in which lesbianism is broadly problem-free. The unsaid is a consistent aesthetic approach by the author to handling sex and sexuality.

Just as language is essential to Monferrand's literary project, then, so too is literature. As we have seen, Monferrand draws overtly on the classic epistolary novels of Rousseau and Laclos. By aligning herself with the most prolific epistolary novelists to come out of France, Monferrand positions herself within a literary elite. In doing so, she is attempting to claim a place for lesbian identities and texts in an established, highly acclaimed French literary canon. Clearly, attempting to make lesbianism count is valuable. However, this method is also objectionable: why, for instance, should lesbian writing seek legitimacy through a traditionally androcentric literary canon? Can it not be legitimate in its own right? Yet, by positioning herself within this canon, Monferrand seems to move away from the notion of lesbianism as something ontologically different or radical. As Cairns states, this 'functions to legitimate [her] literary status and […] to suggest more common ground between homosexual and heterosexual dynamics than is normatively held to exist'.[21] In other words, the relationship between Monferrand and the classic epistolary novels of the eighteenth century normalizes lesbianism and lesbian writing. Paradoxically, then, Monferrand's recourse to tradition is in fact integral to her transgressive literary project.

Monferrand also deploys intertextual references to lesbian-themed novels and texts in both *Les Amies d'Héloïse* and *Les Enfants d'Héloïse*. According to Waelti-Walters, Monferrand is the first lesbian author to make reference to other lesbian authors, which underlines both the uniqueness of her work and the literary need for it, since this surely helps to break the 'story of serial isolation' that is the history of lesbians in French novels.[22] The references to other lesbian-themed texts create a distinctly lesbian space sought by readers and one character in particular: Héloïse's daughter, Mélanie. For Mélanie, the burgeoning desire for other women is at first an isolating experience – an isolation that is perhaps compounded by Héloïse's discretion regarding her own lesbianism – before she gradually

21   Cairns, *Lesbian Desire in Post-1968 French Literature*, 313.
22   Waelti-Walters, *Damned Women*, 212.

comes to terms with her sexuality by discovering and identifying with lesbian characters from the French literary canon, especially those in the works of Émile Zola and Jeanne Galzy. Through these intertextual references, Monferrand might be said to trace the development of, and to position her own work within, a lesbian literary landscape and, in doing so, to legitimize the treatment of same-sex desire. Mélanie first learns about lesbian desire by reading Zola:

> Donc cela existait et c'était tellement horrible que même Zola en était écœuré. Donc elle n'était pas seule et c'était rassurant. Enfin, rassurant? Dans la mesure où cela prouvait qu'elle n'était pas folle, c'est tout. Elle était tarée, et après tout quoi d'étonnant? On prétend toujours que les nobles sont dégénérés, et elle l'était, ce qui constituait une excuse. (EDH 340)

> [So it did exist and it was so horrible that even Zola was sickened by it. So she was not alone and that was reassuring. Well, reassuring? In the sense that it proved that she was not mad, that was all. She was defective, and after all that was not surprising! People always claim that the nobility are degenerate, and she was one of them, which gave her an excuse.]

Although reading Zola proves to Mélanie that she is not alone in experiencing same-sex desire, and therefore not mad, Zola's alignment of lesbianism with depravity is of little reassurance to her. Her interpretation of Galzy is considerably more positive, however: '[O]n n'était plus du tout dans les sous-entendus effrayants de Zola' [It was quite unlike Zola's frightening undertones]; 'Oui, les héroïnes de Galzy se cachaient, mais elles n'avaient pas l'air de se sentir malades ou coupables' [True, Galzy's heroines hid, but they did not seem to feel ill or guilty] (EDH 375). In this way, Monferrand is overviewing the emergence of an empowering literary representation of lesbian desire and love. Whereas Zola aligns lesbianism with the unsayable, condemning it to silence – 'Ce restaurant bon marché de Pigalle [...] avait quelque chose d'étrange à cause, justement, du ton allusif de l'auteur' [This cheap restaurant in Pigalle had a strange quality, precisely because of the author's allusive tone] – Galzy's depiction is more overt (EDH 339). The abundance of intertextual references in the novels allows Monferrand to reappropriate the predominantly male literary canon in order to make female and lesbian identities count.

Héloïse and Mélanie also share a desire to inscribe their sexuality in writing. Interestingly, Monferrand thus fictionalizes both lesbianism and the process of writing about lesbianism. In her first novel, one of Héloïse's letters to Claire includes a love poem of her own creation, which describes the physical side of her relationship with Erika:

> Et le frémissement de ses mains immobiles
> Qui me faisaient gémir et me faisaient ployer …
> J'ai connu sa douceur dans un plaisir farouche
> Et sa brutalité dans un soupir léger. (ADH 94)

> [And the quivering of her still hands
> That made me moan and yield …
> I felt her sweetness as a wild pleasure
> And her brutality as a light sigh.]

Héloïse deploys nouns and adjectives oxymoronically: the stillness of the lover's hands contradicts their quivering, and her gentle sigh contrasts with her brutality, which is also dichotomized with her gentleness in the previous line. In *Les Enfants d'Héloïse*, Anne, Mélanie, Suzanne and their cousins begin work on a story entitled *Le Feuilleton* [*The Serial Novel*], which initially focuses on the Thirty Years' War. As the others lose interest, Mélanie begins to use the story as a space in which she can come to terms with her lesbianism: '[*Le Feuilleton*] lui servait de point de départ à des rêveries imprécises sur les gens, la vie en général, et surtout les attirances secrètes qu'elle ressentait pour certaines élèves à qui elle n'avait, la plupart du temps, jamais parlé' [*The Serial Novel* was her starting point for vague musings on people, life in general and in particular the secret attractions that she felt for certain (female) pupils to whom she had, most of the time, never spoken] (EDH 242). By fictionalizing both lesbian desire and its literary construction, the novels underline the importance of writing as a medium of subversion, specifically the creation of a space for the inscription of non-normative gender and sexual identities. For Mélanie, writing becomes a means to affirm a lesbian identity safely: 'Dans ses livres elle se transformerait en homme et décrirait des femmes, des âmes de femme, des corps de femme, ce qui serait une manière de les aimer que personne ne pourrait critiquer' [In her books, she would become a man and describe women, women's souls, women's

bodies, which would be a way of loving them that no one could criticize]
(EDH 341). Undoubtedly, it is problematic that Mélanie cannot assume
her lesbianism openly. Yet, at the same time, she is empowered by and
enjoys the process of writing about her sexuality.

While Monferrand's self-alignment with an elite and largely male
literary canon might put off some readers, she arguably positions herself
within the canon only to reclaim it for lesbians. This is most apparent in
her use of the epistolary form in *Les Amies d'Héloïse*, in which the female
characters, in sharp contrast with those in classic epistolary novels, are
sexually autonomous and fulfilled. Monferrand challenges the idea that
lesbians are uninterested in sex through Héloïse, who pursues her relationships primarily for sexual, rather than romantic, gratification. Monferrand
is, then, rewriting ideas about women received through literature. I now
turn to the portrayal of the concept that is perhaps the most integral to
ideas about femininity: motherhood.

Lesbianism and Maternal Ambivalence

Mélanie's initial reluctance to assume her sexuality recalls Héloïse's decision not to tell her children about her relationship with Erika. Although
this seems, at first glance, to imply that lesbianism and mothering are irreconcilable, Héloïse affirms that '"[l]es enfants […] n'ont pas besoin de
connaître la vie privée des adultes"' ['children don't need to know about
the private lives of adults'] (EDH 15). Héloïse's discretion regarding her
relationship therefore has more to do with her own relationship with her
children than it does with her sexuality. Indeed, at the beginning of *Les
Enfants d'Héloïse* the relationship between the protagonist and her children is described as follows:

> Héloïse était une mère distante, curieusement intimidée par des enfants qu'elle traitait
> comme des adultes miniatures. Toute son attitude semblait dire: 'Vous êtes assez
> sympathiques, mais vous ne m'intéresserez vraiment que quand vous serez grands.'
> Tout comportement enfantin – qu'elle qualifiait plutôt d'infantile – l'agaçait, et les
> enfants étaient suffisamment intuitifs pour le sentir. (EDH 11)

[Héloïse was a distant mother, curiously intimidated by children, whom she treated like miniature adults. Her whole attitude seemed to say: 'You're quite nice, but you'll only really interest me when you're grown up.' All child-like behaviour – which she described as childish – irritated her, and the children were intuitive enough to sense it.]

On the surface, this description appears to reinforce the heteronormative idea that lesbians make bad or disinterested mothers. Indeed, Héloïse herself voices regret at having children – '"Mais pourquoi ai-je fait ces gosses? Pourquoi?"' ['Why did I have these kids? Why?'] (ADH 448) – and even describes herself as a bad mother: 'Voilà comment je suis devenue une bonne maîtresse, tout en restant une bien mauvaise mère' [That is how I became a good mistress and, at the same time, remained a really bad mother] (ADH 450). Problematically, this quotation seems to uphold the stereotype that gay and lesbian parents prioritize their sexual relationships over their children's welfare.

On the other hand, these statements might be more positively interpreted as testaments to the imperfect nature of maternal love and as attempts to go against the romanticized grand narrative of motherhood. Héloïse discredits her confessions of bad mothering by repeatedly acting to ensure the safety of her children. For example, she seeks the help of her lover to prevent a near miscarriage during her second pregnancy, which underlines her concern for her twin daughters' wellbeing. When, to give a second example, Héloïse leaves her husband – a 'gamin névrosé' [neurotic kid] (ADH 339) – she considers but decides against abandoning her infant son: 'Voilà comment j'ai quitté le domicile conjugal. Et moi qui ai toujours proclamé que je n'aimais ni les enfants, ni les animaux, ni les malades, j'ai laissé le malade (imaginaire) et le chat, mais j'ai quand même pris l'enfant' [That is how I left the marital home. I who have always claimed not to like children, animals or sick people, I left the (imaginary) invalid and the cat, but I still took the child] (ADH 337). The humorous juxtaposition of the child with the cat and the husband works to trivialize the urge to abandon the child. In *Les Enfants d'Héloïse*, the protagonist recalls the night when she left her husband:

Elle avait songé très lucidement à laisser le bébé à son père mais à la réflexion ne s'en était pas accordé le droit. Non parce qu'on l'aurait mal jugée, ça elle s'en fichait complètement, mais parce qu'elle s'était sentie tout à coup responsable de lui. [...]

'En somme, c'est cette nuit-là [...] que j'ai commencé à l'aimer. Il était temps! Peut-être que je suis normale, finalement? Une mère d'ancien régime, en somme, comme les décrivent Ariès et Badinter.' (EDH 122)

[She had given serious thought to leaving the baby with his father but had, on reflection, decided that she did not have the right. Not because people would have thought badly of her, she could not care less about that, but because she had suddenly felt responsible for him. [...] 'In short, that was the night [...] I started to love him. And about time too! Perhaps I am normal, after all? A mother from the Ancien Regime, in short, as described by Ariès and Badinter.']

Héloïse's feelings for her son challenge the patriarchal understanding of maternal love as absolute and natural and exemplify Parker's conception of ambivalence. For Parker, ambivalence is not simply mixed feelings but refers to the coexistence of contradictory emotions and impulses towards the same person. As Parker puts it, '[t]he positive and negative components sit side by side and remain in opposition.'[23] Ambivalence, in other words, is not an oscillation between love and hate but describes the state of experiencing these feelings simultaneously; neither love nor hate ever ceases entirely. In this passage, Héloïse's dislike of Anne – the urge to abandon him – is juxtaposed with her love and sense of responsibility for him. Her reference to the love that she has for her son nuances her assertion in *Les Amies d'Héloïse* that she hates children; she is unapologetically a distant mother, but she does not mistreat her children. Furthermore, the protagonist's indifference to the potential criticisms of others normalizes maternal ambivalence, although her tentative declaration of normality betrays some anxiety at not meeting the expectation that women love their children absolutely. It is notable too that the novel refers to influential intellectuals who question the notion of maternal instinct and contend that maternal love is historically variable, as Héloïse notes. Héloïse's admission that she started to love Anne when she left her husband suggests that maternal love, especially in an unloving marriage, is not necessarily instinctive but established gradually. Instead of labelling Héloïse as a neglectful mother, the novel thus seems to underline the mutability of maternal love and range of patterns of childcare across

23   Parker, *Torn in Two*, 6.

social classes. For instance, the class of women to which Héloïse belongs, the aristocracy, traditionally handed over the task of nurturing their children to wet nurses and nannies. The reference to the Ancien Regime recalls Monferrand's taste for tradition. The evolution of mothering and the variability of maternal experience among different social classes and historical contexts suggest that maternal norms are constructed, rather than inherent, and that maternal experience is not reducible to a patriarchal ideal. Héloïse's case alludes to the difficulty of being a distant mother in the modern era when mothering is often seen as a hands-on role and when mothers who contravene this expectation are often judged harshly.

Although Monferrand therefore deproblematizes maternal ambivalence, she concedes that it is taboo. Erika and Anne de Marèges, Héloïse's mother, worry about Héloïse's lack of maternal fibre, leading Anne to give her daughter a copy of Élisabeth Badinter's *L'Amour en plus* [*The Myth of Motherhood*] (1980). This could be read as an endorsement of maternal ambivalence, given Badinter's contention that maternal instinct is relative. Indeed, Anne's and Erika's concerns are satirized. Maintaining the relationship between Héloïse and her children becomes a sort of game between her, Anne and Erika. When Héloïse plans to send the children to their grandmother's in Vienna for a month, Anne and Erika unsuccessfully attempt to foil the plan. The fact that the plan fails legitimizes the protagonist's desire not to always be around her children. While *Les Enfants d'Héloïse* therefore alludes to attempts by society to 'cure' ambivalence, it does not allow the norms of institutional motherhood to be re-established.

Héloïse's experience of mothering is, then, characteristic of feminist theories of maternal ambivalence. Indeed, she displays the will to protect her children alongside a wish to be rid of them. While this undoubtedly conveys Héloïse's need for a life beyond motherhood, it does not vindicate her confessions of bad mothering. On the contrary, Parker argues that the dialogue between the simultaneous feelings of love and resentment encourages women to reflect on their mothering and to try to know and understand their children. Parker's notional theorization of a non-ambivalent mother elucidates this point:

> Perhaps this becomes clearer if we invent a hypothetical mother who does not experience ambivalence but regards her child only with hostile feelings, or conversely

only with untroubled love. In neither case will she find it necessary to dwell on her relationship with her child or to focus her feelings on her child's response to herself because she will not know what is missing. It is the troubling co-existence of love and hate that propels a mother into thinking about what goes on between herself and her child.[24]

Put simply, the coexistence of love and hostility can in fact improve women's mothering. According to Parker, then, 'ambivalence itself is emphatically not the problem; the issue is how a mother manages the guilt and anxiety ambivalence provokes'.[25] Far from being a neglectful mother, then, Héloïse is reflecting on her feelings of love and resentment vis-à-vis her children, voicing – often unashamedly – her ambivalence. Further, Parker distinguishes between manageable and unmanageable ambivalence.[26] Monferrand deploys humour to manage the negative emotions that Héloïse harbours in relation to her children, as evidenced by the ironic comparison cited earlier between the child, the cat and her hypochondriac of a husband. This enables the novels to subvert their heroine's declarations that she is a bad mother who dislikes children. While they thus explore maternal ambivalence from a lesbian perspective, the novels do not imply that lesbianism causes ambivalence or that lesbian mothers are less able than heterosexual mothers to manage it. Admittedly, *Les Amies d'Héloïse* depicts a stark contrast between its ambivalent lesbian heroine and her heterosexual best friend, who intends to have seven children and 'veu[t] tout simplement avoir le plus longtemps possible des enfants à la maison' [quite simply wants to have children in the house for as long as possible] (ADH 451). The maternal experiences of the novels' other heterosexual women are, however, less idyllic. Erika's half-sister, Manuela, is trapped in an unhappy marriage and, in *Les Enfants d'Héloïse*, becomes pregnant with another man's child. Monferrand thus suggests that mothering is hard to varying degrees but that the difficulties of mothering do not necessarily have any relation to the mother's sexuality. This is equally applicable to other aspects of the novel. For instance,

24   Parker, *Torn in Two*, 7.
25   Parker, *Torn in Two*, 6.
26   Parker, *Torn in Two*, 6.

neither the women's gender nor their sexuality has any bearing on their success in the public sphere – Monferrand's women are all well-educated professionals – or on their political views. Indeed, Monferrand challenges the typical association between gay and lesbian activism and the political left by creating characters who, on subjects other than sex, are socially conservative, as exemplified by Héloïse's defence of the traditional education system whereby lower-achieving pupils sit at the back of the classroom.

The novels' portrayal of mothering, then, bears some resemblance to Rich's theory of a lesbian continuum – that is to say, 'a range […] of woman-identified experience; not simply the fact that a woman has had or consciously desired genital sexual experience with another woman'.[27] According to Rich, sexuality cannot be reduced to a binary of heterosexual or homosexual desire, just as mothering, for Monferrand, is not reducible to a simple question of good or bad. By synthesizing Rich's lesbian continuum with the maternal experiences of Héloïse and her friends, it could be argued that Monferrand's work goes beyond the parochiality of binary logic. On many levels, Monferrand distorts the reader's assumptions: her women are not oppressed; Héloïse is not a stereotypically doting mother; and despite the novel's obvious acceptance of homosexuality, politically the characters occupy the positions of those who have traditionally opposed the extension of rights to LGBT+ people. Monferrand's novels also expose the limitations of accepted sexual identity categories. Héloïse disrupts the conventional definition of lesbianism by engaging in and, crucially, enjoying sex with men. As Héloïse comments on her brief marriage to François: 'Un échec, oui, mais pas au lit. À la fin de leur mariage c'était même la seule chose qui marchait et ils se réconciliaient souvent sur l'oreiller' [A failure, yes, but not in bed. At the end of their marriage, it was even the only thing still working, and they would often make up in bed] (EDH 196). Following her husband's death, Héloïse also has a one-off heterosexual encounter with another man whom she describes as 'un garçon superbe' [a gorgeous boy] (ADH 336). Héloïse's decidedly non-binary sexuality nods towards Hélène Cixous's concept of 'other bisexuality' – that is, the recognition that everyone is, to some degree, both male and female and that, by extension,

27   Rich, 'Compulsory Heterosexuality and Lesbian Existence', 648.

everyone's desire extends beyond the heterosexual–homosexual binary.[28] While it is tempting, then, to regard Héloïse as bisexual, as Cairns points out her assessment of sex with François, which she describes as 'assez bien' [quite good] (ADH 332), is markedly less enthusiastic than her immediate attraction to women, such as Melitta: '[D]ès que je l'ai vue, je me suis sue incapable de résister' [As soon as I saw her, I knew I just could not resist her] (ADH 343).[29] In addition, there is the unambiguous statement that '[m]algré tout Héloïse avait fini par conclure qu'elle n'était pas fondamentalement bisexuelle' [despite everything, Héloïse had come to the conclusion that she was not fundamentally bisexual], which suggests that, ultimately, the protagonist is a lesbian (EDH 196). Nonetheless, the novels undoubtedly question the presumed fixity of sexual desire and suggest that traditional sexual identity categories fail to account for the nuances of sexual desire and practices.

The novels' recognition of the flaws of maternal love nods towards Andrea O'Reilly's theory of feminist mothering.[30] Building on Rich's distinction between the experience and institution of motherhood, O'Reilly argues that maternal experience can only empower women if the institution of motherhood is broken. Central to maternal empowerment is the possibility that mothers have a sense of self that is separable from mothering. By reconciling mothering with her desire to have a love life and embracing, even mocking, imperfect maternal love, Monferrand's heroine can be said to resist institutional motherhood. *Les Enfants d'Héloïse* utilizes the perspectives of Héloïse's children to further normalize maternal ambivalence and to challenge the assumption that imperfect maternal love is damaging to children. While Suzanne doubts whether Héloïse loves them, the possible absence of maternal love is remarkably deproblematized:

> 'Maman? Ça dépend. Elle ne s'intéresse pas à nous. Peut-être qu'elle ne nous aime pas? Quand on y réfléchit c'est son droit. Pourquoi les parents seraient-ils obligés d'aimer leurs enfants?'

---

28   Cixous, 'The Laugh of the Medusa', 884.
29   Cairns, *Lesbian Desire in Post-1968 French Literature*, 323.
30   For an overview of O'Reilly's sizeable contribution to feminist work on mothering, see Chapter 1.

'Maman nous aime!'

'Qu'est-ce qui te le prouve? À mon avis elle nous aime bien, oui … et de nous trois elle préfère Anne.' (EDH 246)

['Mum? It depends. She isn't interested in us. Perhaps she doesn't love us? When you think about it, it's her right. Why should parents be obliged to love their children?'

'Mum loves us!'

'How do you know? I think she likes us … and of the three of us, Anne is her favourite.']

Suzanne's acceptance of, even complete indifference to, maternal ambivalence further challenges the normative stereotype that women love their children absolutely. Through her distinction between love and like, the novel raises the important question of what it means to love one's child and encourages the reader to reflect on the fine line between these two degrees of affection, just as Parker encourages us to consider the proximity of love and hate. Moreover, Suzanne challenges the modern but widespread expectation that women love all their children equally by suggesting that Héloïse loves Anne more than she does her daughters. Indeed, Héloïse confirms her daughter's belief in conversation with Erika: ' "Moi je ne suis pas une bonne mère. J'ai des préférences, mais elles varient. En ce moment, j'ai un petit faible pour Anne" ' [*I'm* not a good mother. I have favourites, but they vary. At the moment, I have a soft spot for Anne'] (EDH 155). As well as her habitual self-denigration as a bad mother, Héloïse again exposes the mutability and flawed nature of mother-love and can be said to be continuing the aristocratic tradition of favouring the first-born son. Indeed, his name, which is almost always a female name today, is a reference to the few male members of the former French nobility called Anne.

Anne, for his part, adores Héloïse and is unquestioningly loyal to her. When his paternal grandmother, whom he cannot abide, mistakenly tells him that Héloïse killed his father, he immediately concludes: '[S]i Maman avait tué Papa, elle avait une excellente raison' [If Mum did kill Dad, she had a very good reason] (EDH 67). Thus, Anne's love for his mother seems to be unconditional, as Héloïse realizes when Anne informs her of his grandmother's accusation: 'Qu'avait-elle fait pour mériter un amour aussi inconditionnel? Et qu'auraient pensé les filles dans la même situation?' [What had she done to deserve such unconditional love? And what would the girls have thought in the same situation?] (EDH 291). Just as the children reveal the variability of maternal love, Héloïse alludes to the different degrees to which children love their parents. *Les Enfants d'Héloïse* thus goes beyond representing maternal ambivalence to a portrayal of the shared ambivalence that mothers and children experience in relation to each other, thus revealing the intricate dynamics of relationships in the family. Suzanne, for instance, states that she loves her grandmother, Lise – a friend of the family – and Anne more than she does Héloïse. Mélanie, on the other hand, prefers Erika to her mother.

Mélanie's identification with Erika is particularly strong, and she says that Erika might be the person whom she loves most in the world. Indeed, for Mélanie, Erika 'était quelqu'un de mystérieux qui la fascinait totalement, depuis toujours. Plus exactement depuis le soir, à l'âge de quatre ans, où elle l'avait vue pour la première fois, ce dont elle se souvenait très bien' [was someone mysterious whom she had always found completely fascinating. More precisely since the evening when, at the age of four, she had seen her for the first time, which she remembered very well] (EDH 54). Mélanie attempts to maintain her attachment to Erika by opting to spend one Christmas in Le Cernix because, in previous years, Erika has spent a few days there. As Mélanie enters puberty, her attachment to Erika becomes increasingly sexual. While the novel could thus be said to reinforce a model of genetically acquired homosexuality, Suzanne neatly challenges this view when her sister confides in her:

> [J]e peux fournir quantité d'autres explications aussi simples. L'atmosphère, des choses presque invisibles entre Maman et Erika que tu as captées sans t'en apercevoir. Peut-être même es-tu un peu amoureuse d'Erika, je le croirais volontiers, d'autant plus que tu m'as avoué qu'elle te troublait. Bref tu as fait ton Œdipe à l'envers. (EDH 390)

> [I can think of lots of other equally simple explanations. The atmosphere, almost invisible things between Mum and Erika that you picked up without realizing. Perhaps you're even a bit in love with Erika. It wouldn't surprise me, especially because you admitted to me that you were attracted to her. In short, you resolved your Oedipus complex in reverse.]

Suzanne postulates sexuality as psychologically and socially conditioned rather than biologically determined. Moreover, her reference to the Oedipal configuration reapplies, perhaps mockingly, Freudian psycho-analysis to non-heterosexual kinship structures. Mélanie, Suzanne claims, has induced mother–daughter separation by finding a new love-object in the form of another woman. Importantly, though, this is remarkably deproblematized by Suzanne, suggesting Monferrand's rebuttal of psychoanalytic theories of development.

Whereas Mélanie's attachment to Erika therefore becomes progressively sexual, the role that Erika covets and forges with Héloïse's children is parental. By building a positive relationship with Héloïse's children, Erika hopes to ensure her partner's long-term commitment to her: 'En admettant qu'Héloïse tombât un jour amoureuse de quelqu'un d'autre, elle hésiterait certainement à détruire l'équilibre familial, même s'il s'agissait en l'espèce d'une famille hors normes' [Supposing that one day Héloïse fell in love with someone else, she would certainly think twice about disrupting the family, even if the family was, in this case, out of the ordinary] (EDH 17). Although Erika's motive for coveting the parental role is thus not entirely selfless, she nonetheless envisions the possibility of two women parenting together. Similarly, Anne de Marèges encourages Erika to move into the apartment block where Héloïse and her children live with a view to providing the children with a 'normal' family environment. Héloïse ironically wonders, however, whether her mother realizes how far her daughter's family goes against the norm. Significantly, Erika's gender and sexuality are regarded as unimportant here: what matters is that she is emotionally invested in the children. While *Les Enfants d'Héloïse* thus acknowledges lesbian-headed families, it ultimately forecloses the possibility of publicly declaring this family configuration in a social and cultural context in which gay and lesbian parenting is invisible and taboo. Nonetheless, Héloïse and Erika actively subvert norms of the family, as their conversation about Héloïse's plan to send Mélanie and Suzanne to boarding school illustrates:

'Il est vrai que ça ne me regarde pas.'

'Mais si, ça vous regarde! Vous vous souvenez de ce qu'a dit Lise, il n'y a pas longtemps, à propos des enfants et de nous?'

'Je ne crois pas.'

'Mais si, elle a dit que vous faisiez la mère et moi le père. Que toute notre attitude …'

'Elle plaisantait.'

'Pas tout à fait. Il y a beaucoup de vrai dans cette remarque. Le père que je suis pensait qu'il fallait les séparer à l'école primaire, même si elles en pleuraient, et qu'il est bon de les mettre en pension maintenant, ce qui ne leur déplaît pas. Vous, vous jouez le rôle de la mère classique: vous vous tordez les mains en vous lamentant.' (EDH 154–5)

['It's true that it's none of my business.'

'But it is! Do you remember what Lise said, not long ago, about the children and us?'

'I don't think so.'

'You know, she said that you were the mother and I the father. That our whole attitude …'

'She was joking.'

'Not entirely. There is a lot of truth to this remark. As the father, I thought it was necessary to separate them at primary school, even if it made them cry, and that it's right to send them to boarding school now, which they're not unhappy about. You're playing the role of the typical mother: you're wringing your hands and moaning.']

Although the relationships between Héloïse, Erika and the children are ironically assimilated to a heteronormative mother–father–child triangulation, it is not insignificant that Monferrand's novel portrays a lesbian family, of sorts, prior to the emergence of same-sex parenting as a cultural, political and social issue during the French debates on civil partnerships in 1999. Indeed, *Les Enfants d'Héloïse* is a reminder that, although same-sex families have gained visibility in the twenty-first century, and especially in the run-up to the legalization of same-sex marriage in 2013, such families are not as recent a cultural phenomenon as is commonly believed, and the texts studied in this chapter and the preceding one attest to the existence of lesbian mothers long before then. Lesbian mothers have, of course, existed for as long as heterosexual mothers in cases where women, like Héloïse, have children in a heterosexual partnership before or while assuming a lesbian identity. Although *Les Enfants d'Héloïse* thus paves the way for a lesbian step-parent family, its characters never truly embrace this mode of kinship. While Erika lives a floor below Héloïse

and the children, she never moves in with them and is never entirely in-
corporated into the family. Most importantly, Erika is never introduced
to the children as Héloïse's partner, although the children eventually dis-
cover the nature of the relationship between Héloïse and Erika.

At first glance, Monferrand appears to reinforce the supposed irreconcilability of lesbianism and mothering, yet the portrayal of Héloïse –
an ambivalent lesbian mother who unapologetically prioritizes her sexual
relationships over motherhood – serves to debunk grand narratives of
femininity and motherhood. In particular, the *Héloïse* novels challenge,
notably through humour, the common belief that women love their children absolutely and instinctively. Moreover, Monferrand alludes to the
complex relationships in the family by portraying not only maternal ambivalence but the differing degrees to which children love their parents.

Concluding Thoughts

While Monferrand's recourse to a classical literary genre and style may
appear out of place in a novel that transgresses norms of gender and
sexuality, this is in fact integral to her literary project: to normalize and
create a space for lesbianism within the mainstream. In Monferrand's
novels, lesbianism is remarkably unproblematic: it is no barrier to
the characters' place in traditionally male-dominated spheres or to
their relationships with other, heterosexual women. Indeed, there is
a striking solidarity between heterosexual and lesbian women in these
novels. It is, perhaps, unrealistic not to devote more attention to the
obstacles facing lesbians, particularly in the era in which the novels
are set, and one might reasonably wonder how easily lesbians with less
socioeconomic privilege than Monferrand's characters might integrate
into the mainstream. Nevertheless, Monferrand's work deserves credit
for creating a fictional world in which sexuality, so often a subject that
generates conflict, is not a source of division. In this sense, her presen-
tation of lesbianism as ordinary is valuable and empowering for lesbian
readers.

This empowerment extends to lesbian mothers. Monferrand rejects the patriarchal view of maternal love as absolute and natural, while also challenging the link between lesbianism and neglectful mothering. On the face of it, Héloïse upholds this normative equation. However, on closer inspection Héloïse's relationship with her children is marked by ambivalence rather than neglect. By portraying Erika in a quasi-parental role to Héloïse's children, *Les Enfants d'Héloïse* can, to some extent, be said to anticipate the increasing visibility of same-sex families in twenty-first-century France. Ultimately, however, the fact that Erika never truly assumes this role indicates the continuing ideological commonplace of the heterosexual nuclear family in the social and cultural context of the plot. The texts to which I now turn are premised on the possibility of an openly lesbian family. Whereas in Chapters 2 and 3 I have focused on lesbian mothers who have children in heterosexual relationships, in Chapters 4 and 5 I turn to representations of planned lesbian families, and in these texts the family is reimagined to a greater extent than we have seen thus far.

CHAPTER 4

Planned Lesbian Families

In *Mothering Queerly, Queering Motherhood* (2013), Shelley Park coins the term 'monomaternalism' to refer to the 'ideological assumption that a child can have only one real mother'.[1] According to Park, this assumption stems in part from the equation of mothering with participation in a series of biological acts that includes pregnancy, childbirth and lactation. Because these acts are said to create a unique bond with the child, the biological mother is thought to be better suited to raising the child than other caregivers. Monomaternalism thus functions to naturalize the nuclear family and to obfuscate and stigmatize alternative family forms, such as adoptive, blended, lesbian and polygamous families.[2]

The increasing visibility of these families has, however, prompted legal changes that challenge the monomaternalist assumption. In France, same-sex adoption was legalized in 2013, and the terms 'mother' and 'father' were replaced by the gender-neutral term 'parent' in the legal documents relating to adoption.[3] In April 2015, in six separate cases the courts of appeal in Aix-en-Provence and Versailles permitted six non-biological mothers to adopt the children of their same-sex spouse.[4] Although this had been legal since 2013, the adoption requests were initially refused on the grounds that the children were conceived abroad via fertility treatment, which at the time was only open to heterosexual couples in France. In 2019, the National Assembly voted to make fertility treatment available to lesbian and single

---

1   Park, *Mothering Queerly, Queering Motherhood*, 3.
2   Park, *Mothering Queerly, Queering Motherhood*, 6.
3   Gross, *Parent ou homo*, 78.
4   Catherine Mallaval, 'Adoption pour tous: les juges récalcitrants prennent une claque', *Libération* (16 April 2015), <http://next.liberation.fr/vous/2015/04/16/adoption-pour-tous-les-juges-recalcitrants-prennent-une-claque_1243918>, accessed 15 February 2019.

women. These changes point to an emerging view that a monomaternalist legal framework is not necessarily in children's best interests and does not account for the diversity of contemporary family practices.

Recognizing the range of contemporary family forms requires not only a reformed legal system but also an alternative, non-biologistic theory of the family. In 'Is Kinship Always Already Heterosexual?' (2002), Judith Butler defines kinship as a 'set of practices' that 'emerge to address fundamental forms of human dependency, which may include birth, child-rearing, relations of emotional dependency and support, generational ties, illness, dying, and death (to name a few)'.[5] For Butler, then, kinship is based on social, rather than biological, relationships. This view is derived from the theory of gender that she put forward in *Gender Trouble* (1990). Just as gender is 'performatively constituted by the very "expressions" that are said to be its results', kinship is constructed by the practices that are assumed to stem from blood ties.[6] Similarly, maternal identity is, or at least can be, produced by the care-giving role that is usually thought to be the effect of being a mother.

In this chapter, I examine texts that portray lesbian couples who plan to become parents together and that thus reflect the emergence of family forms built on social as well as biological ties. I focus on five texts: Éliane Girard's *Mais qui va garder le chat?* [*But Who's Going to Look After the Cat?*] (2005); Laurence Cinq-Fraix's *Family Pride* (2006); Brigitte Célier's *Maman, Mamour, ses deux mamans: Grandir dans une famille homoparentale* [*Maman, Mamour – Her Two Mums: Growing Up in a Same-Sex Family*] (2008); Myriam Blanc's *Elles eurent beaucoup d'enfants … et se marièrent: Histoire d'une famille homoparentale* [*The Women Had Lots of Children … and Got Married: The Story of a Same-Sex Family*] (2012); and Claire Bénard's *Prince Charmante: Que fait-on quand on tombe amoureuse d'une femme?* [*Princess Charming: What Do You Do When You Fall in Love with a Woman?*] (2013).[7] Apart from

---

5   Butler, 'Is Kinship Always Already Heterosexual?', 14–15.
6   Butler, *Gender Trouble*, 34.
7   Éliane Girard, *Mais qui va garder le chat?* (Paris: JC Lattès, 2005); Laurence Cinq-Fraix, *Family Pride* (Paris: Philippe Rey, 2006); Brigitte Célier, *Maman, Mamour, ses deux mamans: Grandir dans une famille homoparentale* (Paris: Anne Carrière, 2008); Myriam Blanc, *Elles eurent beaucoup d'enfants … et se marièrent: Histoire*

Bénard, these authors primarily focus on the characters' journeys to motherhood, rather than on their romantic or sexual relationships. As Blanc wryly puts it: 'Mon livre est scandaleusement dépourvu de détails croustillants, et, par exemple, vous n'apprendrez rien sur la manière dont on fait l'amour entre filles. Juste comment on fait des bébés ...' [There is a scandalous lack of raunchy details in my book, so you will not, for example, learn anything about how girls make love. Just how we make babies ...] (HFH 52).

Significantly, all these texts were written and are set in the period between the creation of civil partnerships in 1999 and the legalization of same-sex marriage and adoption in 2013. At this time, the law made no provision for same-sex families, for while civil partnerships granted certain legal benefits to same-sex couples, those benefits did not include parental rights. Consequently, non-biological parents had no automatic right to contact with their children if they separated from the biological parent. There were, however, ongoing calls to extend parenting rights to same-sex couples throughout this period, most notably from the Socialist Party in the 2007 presidential election. It is in this context of legal precarity and political debate, then, that the texts explore the journey to same-sex parenthood, and this in itself encourages us to read them as politically meaningful cultural objects. Indeed, publishing a text on this topic at this moment strongly suggests a desire on the writer's part to give visibility to this emerging social phenomenon and her belief in the role of literature as a vehicle of social and political change.

Although the texts are, then, similar in terms of themes and context, they differ greatly in form and genre. Girard's *Mais qui va garder le chat?* and Cinq-Fraix's *Family Pride* are novels. In *Mais qui va garder le chat?*, Cécile, the future biological mother, and her new partner, Fanny, decide to

---

d'une famille homoparentale, new edn (Marseille: Le bec en l'air, 2012 [2005]); Claire Bénard, *Prince Charmante: Que fait-on quand on tombe amoureuse d'une femme?* (Paris: La Boîte à Pandore, 2013); subsequent references to these works are provided as in-text citations in the following forms: (MQV p.), (FP p.), (MM p.), (HFH p.), (PC p.).

create a child via medically unassisted artificial insemination with a known donor – a process that Fanny humorously calls 'la procréation "seringue et pot de yaourt"' ['syringe-and-yogurt-pot' procreation] (MQV 136). The donor offers to provide the couple with his sperm but will take no part in the child's upbringing. In *Family Pride*, the narrator, Cécile, and her partner, Anna, enter a co-parenting arrangement with a gay couple, Éric and Benoît. Anna and Éric are the biological parents, and Cécile and Benoît the non-biological parents. By giving the role of narrator to the non-biological mother, Cinq-Fraix legitimizes the performative notion of mothering that the character embodies.

Célier's *Maman, Mamour* and Blanc's *Elles eurent beaucoup d'enfants* are autobiographical, retrospective accounts of the journey to and experience of same-sex parenthood. Interestingly, both texts are structured not chronologically but thematically, with chapters addressing topics such as conception, sexuality and the role of the father. This structure enables the authors to shift attention away from their attempts at textual self-reconstruction in order to focus on making their personal experiences useful to readers. In *Maman, Mamour*, the reader learns that the narrator and her partner, Dominique, the biological mother, had their daughter, Géraldine, in 1985 in a co-parenting arrangement with their gay friend, Christian. The parents planned to have two children simultaneously – one from each mother – but had to abandon this plan when Christian discovered that he had contracted HIV. He passed away before Géraldine was born. In Blanc's *Elles eurent beaucoup d'enfants*, the narrator and her partner, Astrid, have two daughters conceived in Belgium via artificial insemination with different, unknown sperm donors. Blanc is the biological mother of their eldest daughter, and Astrid the biological mother of their youngest. This text is the expanded edition of a 2005 work entitled *Et elles eurent beaucoup d'enfants … Histoire d'une famille homoparentale* [*And the Women Had Lots of Children … The Story of a Same-Sex Family*], which Blanc was asked to update following François Hollande's election in 2012 on a manifesto that promised to legalize same-sex marriage. Although these texts have a clear political function, then, they are also literary, storytelling projects. Interestingly, Blanc claims that while writing the book she would refer to it as 'mon roman' [my novel], and she has expressed some regret that journalists have overlooked the literary intention behind it.[8] Concerning the genre of her book, she has also stated:

> What I wanted to create was a sort of 'non-fictional novel', if this expression means anything. The idea was to transform us – my family and me – into characters from a novel. Honestly, I am quite pleased with this idea. I find it quite effective. If you seem like a nice character from a novel, a human one, not a caricature from a fairy-tale [...], people will identify with you more easily, which is nice from a literary point of view, but also very effective from an activist point of view.[9]

Whether or not the 'non-fictional novel' exists, Blanc's use of this term testifies to her desire to write, as she puts it, 'more than an account'.[10] Given the simplistic but powerful association of autobiography with truth, and the political weight that this lends to autobiography, it is interesting that Blanc regards the novelistic elements of the text as politically effective. *Maman, Mamour* includes extracts from another text entitled *Chères parents* [*Dear (Female) Parents*], which Célier gave to her daughter on her twentieth birthday and in which she tells the story of her daughter's life. In a sense, then, the reader is in fact reading two texts: an intertext initially intended for personal use and the text written for the public. The extracts from the intertext often touch on the issues discussed in the main body, suggesting that this literary technique serves to substantiate the text's political message.

According to Philippe Lejeune's taxonomy of literary genres, Bénard's *Prince Charmante* is an autobiographical novel.[11] The words 'témoignage et document' [account and document] on the front cover indicate that the plot is based on real events. The text is a classic example of autobiographical

---

8   Myriam Blanc, '*Et elles eurent beaucoup d'enfants ... Histoire d'une famille homoparentale*: témoignage ou "roman vrai"?', unpublished paper given at 'LGBT and Parenting: An Emerging Theme?', Institute of Modern Languages Research, University of London, 19 October 2018.

9   Blanc, '*Et elles eurent beaucoup d'enfants ... Histoire d'une famille homoparentale*: témoignage ou "roman vrai"?'.

10 Blanc, '*Et elles eurent beaucoup d'enfants ... Histoire d'une famille homoparentale*: témoignage ou "roman vrai"?'.

11 For more on Lejeune's taxonomy, see Chapter 2.

writing in that it is a chronological, first-person account of the author-protagonist's life that opens with her childhood. However, the plot is punctuated by short, italicized extracts in which an omniscient narrator – who, the reader understands, is in fact the author-protagonist speaking with the benefit of hindsight – comments on the plot. The shift between these two points of view suggests that identity is a negotiation between past, present and future, rather than a journey towards a finite goal. The protagonist, Zélie, has two daughters in a heterosexual marriage before beginning an affair with Alice. Towards the end of the text, Zélie, Alice and the children move in together, and the couple travel to Barcelona to receive fertility treatment. The text ends during the third trimester of Zélie's pregnancy.

In this chapter, I analyse these texts concurrently in an issue-based discussion. I begin by examining the portrayal of lesbian characters coming to terms with their desire to have children. I then discuss the texts' varied representations on the role of the father in planned lesbian families. Finally, I discuss the construction of maternal identity in the texts, particularly in the absence of a culturally all-important biological connection to a child.

Coming to Terms with Lesbian Mothering

The process of coming to terms with lesbian mothering is underlined by the titles of these texts. Cinq-Fraix's title juxtaposes two normatively dichotomized notions – family and homosexuality – the word 'pride' being strongly associated with the LGBT+ rights movement. Similarly, *Elles eurent beaucoup d'enfants* combines norms of femininity – marriage and motherhood – with a reference to non-normative family forms and recalls the traditional closing line of a fairy tale: 'Ils se marièrent et eurent beaucoup d'enfants' [And they lived happily ever after]. Blanc thus lays claim to the traditionally heterosexual values of parenting and the family and simultaneously indicates how the text departs from the normative family model. Like Blanc's, Célier's title is a play on words: 'mamour', the term that Géraldine uses to address Célier, is a combination of the words 'maman' [mum] and 'amour' [love], which symbolizes the greater importance of love relative to biology and parental sexuality in matters of the family. The word 'mamour' also recalls the expression 'se faire des mamours' [to cuddle] and therefore connotes the care-giving that is central to the text's understanding of mothering and the writer's maternal identity. Bénard's ungrammatical title (the 'e' at the end of the word 'charmante' [charming] denotes that the prince is female) works to place the text in opposition to the dominant models of sexuality and gender relations embodied by the fairy-tale prince. The overtly transgressive titles of these texts, then, oblige the reader to acknowledge the existence of same-sex relationships and families.

This demand for recognition resurfaces in the autobiographies of Célier and Blanc. In the first chapter of *Maman, Mamour*, Célier makes the bold and empowering statement that '[q]ue l'on soit d'accord ou que l'on s'y oppose avec force, l'homoparentalité existe, on est bien obligé de l'admettre. Progressivement devenue sujet de nombreuses discussions, cette réalité n'est plus à discuter' [whether one agrees with or is strongly opposed to it, same-sex parenting exists, one has no choice but to admit it. This reality, which has progressively become the subject of numerous debates, is now indisputable] (MM 12–13). Such demands for recognition were understandable and valuable at a time when same-sex families had no legal status. In addition, Célier and Blanc aim to address the ignorance and prejudice towards same-sex families. Célier expresses her hope that her readers feel 'un peu moins de perplexité et un peu plus de sympathie' [a little less confusion and a little more kindness] for these families (MM 15), while Blanc states in *Elles eurent beaucoup d'enfants*: 'Comme un peu de pédagogie ne nuit pas, ce livre se veut [...] une sorte de manuel de l'homoparentalité heureuse, à destination tout particulièrement de nos amis les hétéros' [Since there is no harm in a bit of pedagogy, this book is intended to be a sort of handbook of happy same-sex parenting that is particularly aimed at our straight friends] (HFH 52). Blanc's tone is light, but the words 'pédagogie' [pedagogy] and 'manuel' [handbook] suggest that the author considers her text to be useful to readers. These passages suggest a need to convince potentially sceptical heterosexual readers, as well as same-sex couples considering parenthood, that same-sex families provide a healthy environment for children. Although Célier and Blanc resist the generalizability of their experiences, the texts necessarily give some indication of how lesbian couples plan for and experience parenting. In this respect, the autobiographical nature of these texts lends political weight to their positive representations of same-sex families. Despite the less than straightforward relationship between autobiography and truth, it is difficult to dismiss the positive portrayals of same-sex families as strategic narrative choices, and readers may well interpret the texts as signs that same-sex families can work.

These texts fulfil not only the didactic purpose of informing a heteronormative French readership about same-sex parenting but also the authors' need to come to terms with their own marginal existence. A section in *Elles eurent beaucoup d'enfants* entitled 'Suis-je vraiment une femme?' [Am I Really a Woman?] describes the author's initial disquiet about but eventual indifference to the normative disassociation of lesbianism and femininity. Furthermore, the insights into the authors' personal experiences are sometimes highly poignant. In a section that contrasts sharply with the ironic, light-hearted tone of most of the text, Blanc describes a miscarriage that she suffered before becoming pregnant with her eldest daughter. In *Maman, Mamour*, Célier tells the reader that a hospitalized Christian formally recognized Géraldine as his child just two days before he died. The inclusion of these passages works to create a sense of plot and depict the authors as relatable characters, which encourages readers to sympathize with their political messages. The blend of didactic and personal narrative allows the authors to create a space for their own experiences while addressing the broader matter of the legal, political and social obstacles facing same-sex parents in France. This hybridity legitimizes both the authors' own experiences and the social phenomenon that they represent.

In the texts by Girard, Cinq-Fraix and Bénard, the characters' sense of legitimacy as lesbian mothers is underpinned by their experiences of coming out. *Prince Charmante* revolves around the protagonist's journey from homophobe to homosexual. Before meeting Alice, Zélie upholds the normative status of heterosexuality and expresses uneasiness with homosexuality and especially lesbianism:

[J]'ai mes p'tites réticences aussi, hein, comme tout le monde, c'est normal, non, non, ce n'est pas de l'homophobie, c'est juste que … quand deux filles s'embrassent, je fais semblant d'être cool, mais je suis pas très à l'aise quand même … Hein? (PC 107)

[I have small reservations too, right, like everyone, it's normal, no, no, it's not homophobia, it's just that … when two girls kiss, I pretend to be cool, but I'm a bit uncomfortable all the same … Yeah?]

The awkwardness of Zélie's claim that she is not homophobic betrays her intolerance, and this may well be a response to homosexuality with which lesbian readers are familiar. Similar responses re-emerge throughout the text, for instance when Zélie's colleague comes out to her as gay:

'Ah ben tu sais, pas d'souci; l'homosexualité c'est pas un problème pour moi …'

Complètement con comme réplique. Comme si on disait 'l'hétérosexualité, c'est pas un problème pour moi.' (PC 131)

['Oh well, you know, no worries; I've got no problem with homosexuality …'

What a bloody stupid response. As if you would say 'I've got no problem with heterosexuality.']

Zélie's view that '[t]ant que ça ne se passe pas sous son nez, tout va bien' [as long as it's not right under your nose, it's fine] exemplifies the pressure on LGBT+ people to mask their identity behind a heteronormative façade (PC 148). These passages would make for uncomfortable reading for lesbian audiences were it not for the promise of a lesbian love story made by the title. With this assurance, the lesbian reader is free to laugh at the irony of these instances of homophobia and can ultimately feel empowered when the protagonist falls in love and has a child with another woman.

In *Mais qui va garder le chat?*, the characters' experiences of coming out are reported retrospectively, rather than embedded into the plot, which has the effect of foregrounding the couple's journey to parenthood. Although this is not a coming out novel, then, it describes experiences of this process ranging from relatively unproblematic to disastrous. Cécile remains closeted from her colleagues, but her parents are very accepting of her sexuality; they have welcomed Cécile's former girlfriends into the family and loan her money so that she and Fanny can buy a house. The fact that

Cécile considers herself fortunate to have such tolerant parents, however, shows that homosexuality could still be a source of family conflict in the late twentieth century. Indeed, Fanny tells us that she struggled to come out to her mother, who believed that her daughter's lesbianism was a phase that would pass with marriage and motherhood, reflecting the view that lesbianism is only possible in the absence of a natural and preferred heterosexuality. The reader is told that the parents of Cécile's former partner, Magali, had no inclination of their daughter's sexuality, and their reaction led to a loss of contact and to Magali becoming depressed. Although contact was gradually re-established, Magali's sexuality remains an undiscussed topic. Furthermore, the novel alludes to the challenge of assuming lesbian relationships:

> On avait vécu comme deux adolescentes. La société, la famille, nous y avait poussées. Se cacher, ne pas dire, inventer, monter des bateaux: des restes d'enfance. Adultes, on apprend à dire, à affirmer, à s'imposer. Magali et moi, étions 'dans le placard' dès le palier de notre appartement. À l'extérieur, à part pour nos amis, nous étions deux bonnes copines. Point. (MQV 38)

> [We had lived like two teenagers. Society and our families had driven us to do so. Hiding, not saying, inventing, coming up with cock and bull stories: the remains of childhood. As adults, we learn to speak up, to assert ourselves, to impose ourselves. Magali and I were 'in the closet' as soon as we set foot out of our apartment. Outside, to everyone but our friends, we were two close friends. Full stop.]

Despite the growing social and cultural acceptance of homosexuality, Cécile and Magali represent the difficulty, even in the early 2000s, of publicly affirming a lesbian relationship and the need to hide it behind a mask of platonic friendship. A scene in which Magali and her new girlfriend are sexually harassed by a homophobic mob and receive no sympathy from the police further reinforces the novel's exposure of the difficulty of being openly lesbian.

As in *Mais qui va garder le chat?*, in *Family Pride* the characters' experiences of coming out are contrasting and described retrospectively. In one scene, Cécile wonders how she became a lesbian, reflecting the heteronormative assumption that people are heterosexual by default and that homosexuality needs to be explained. We are told that Cécile came out to her parents only after she and Anna had been together for two years. On the surface, her parents take the news well – ' "Tu restes notre fille et l'important c'est que tu sois heureuse" ' ['You're still our daughter and the important thing is that you're happy'] (FP 21) – but Cécile later learns that 'la pilule avait eu du mal à passer et qu'elle leur restait encore un peu aujourd'hui en travers de la gorge' [the pill had been difficult to swallow and that a bit of it was still stuck in their throats] (FP 21). Anna came out to her mother aged 14 and suffered no negative repercussions: 'Disons même qu'une fois le choc passé […] [sa mère] en retirait une certaine fierté. Son seul regret peut-être: celui de ne jamais pouvoir être grand-mère' [Once the shock had worn off, her mother even took a certain pride in it. Perhaps her only regret was that she would never become a grandmother] (FP 27). The novel therefore alludes to the potential stigma attached to having a lesbian daughter, which, importantly, is reinterpreted as a source of pride. The novels by Girard and Cinq-Fraix illustrate the range of coming out experiences that gays and lesbians go through and the diversity of positions on homosexuality today: homosexuality is accepted by many people, yet it remains a potential source of family conflict. While the positive responses to the characters' coming out represent the important theme of acceptance of a gay or lesbian child, the negative reactions are a reminder of the continued pressure to conform to heterosexuality. Taken together, the characters act as representatives of the ambiguous status of homosexuality in the twenty-first century.

Although Anna's mother's regret that she will never have grandchildren would seem to uphold the assumed incompatibility of lesbianism with parenting, it should be remembered that, as Petra Nordqvist argues, it is understandable that some of the older generation view homosexuality as irreconcilable with parenting because they grew up at a time – in Anna's mother's case, probably the 1950s – when gay and lesbian parents were largely invisible and homosexuality itself was taboo.[12] On the other hand, Nordqvist suggests that motherhood, the role traditionally regarded

12   Petra Nordqvist, ' "I've Redeemed Myself by Being a 1950s 'Housewife' "': Parent– Grandparent Relationships in the Context of Lesbian Childbirth', *Journal of Family Issues* 36/4 (2015), 480–500 (488).

as the most natural for women, can enable a lesbian daughter to 'render her lesbian life intelligible to her own mother (and father) and slot back into a liveable life'.[13] Similarly, Cathy Herbrand shows that the child can function as a 'reconciliation factor' between parents and lesbian daughters that enables parents to overcome their rejection of their daughter's homosexuality.[14] To some extent, this is the case for Anna's mother, who embraces the news that her daughter is starting a family. In *Mais qui va garder le chat?*, however, the reaction of Cécile's parents is ironically compared with the Apocalypse. This suggests that, in the eyes of some grandparents, for a lesbian daughter to become a mother is an additional transgression that works to further distance her from the norm. Indeed, as Cinq-Fraix's narrator notes ironically: 'Homosexuels passe encore, mais parents, faut quand même pas exagérer' [Being homosexual is one thing, but parents? Don't push it] (FP 14).

In Girard's *Mais qui va garder le chat?*, Cécile and Fanny must first look beyond their own heteronormative reservations before opting into parenthood. Cécile tells us that for a long time she saw her sexuality as preclusive to motherhood. She believed that children need a mother and father, and that 'c'est égoïste de mettre au monde un enfant dans une situation déjà hors norme' [it is selfish to bring a child into a situation that is already unusual] (MQV 40). These passages foreshadow the arguments used by opponents of same-sex marriage and adoption in the 2012–13 Manif pour Tous. By initially portraying Cécile as a character with doubts about same-sex families, Girard persuades more conservative readers to identify with the character before encouraging them to reform their opinions alongside her. A further, arguably problematic, concession to conservative readers is the representation of a female character who feels a strong and supposedly feminine desire to have children:

13   Nordqvist, ' "I've Redeemed Myself by Being a 1950s 'Housewife' " ', 490.
14   Cathy Herbrand, 'Les rendre grands-parents: l'enjeu des relations intergénérationnelles au sein de coparentalités gaies et lesbiennes en Belgique', in Jérôme Courduriès and Agnès Fine, eds, *Homosexualité et parenté* (Paris: Armand Colin, 2014), 175–88 (180).

Je crois que si je n'en [des enfants] ai pas je le regretterai toute ma vie. Tu sais quand je vois Louise, Benjamin, Paolo ou Garance, tous ces petits enfants que nos copines ont conçus ou adoptés, je me sens jalouse. Je me sens stérile, égoïste, ma vie me paraît vide. (MQV 74)

[I think if I don't have any [children], I'll regret it for the rest of my life. You know when I see Louise, Benjamin, Paolo or Garance, all these little children that our friends have conceived or adopted, I feel jealous. I feel sterile, selfish, my life feels empty.]

Although this passage makes the important point that lesbians want children as much as heterosexual women, the use of negative adjectives such as 'jalouse' [jealous], 'stérile' [sterile], 'égoïste' [selfish] and 'vide' [empty] reduces the character to the patriarchal stereotype of the woman for whom motherhood is the only means of fulfilment. The reference to jealousy evokes Freud's claim that maternal desire is the expression of 'penis envy', while the notions of sterility and emptiness suggest his broader conception of female sexuality as a lack. The character's self-description as selfish recalls the patriarchal belief that it is a woman's duty to have children. This passage is, however, a singular blemish on the novel's overwhelmingly positive representation of same-sex families. Indeed, the presence of other children raised by same-sex parents serves to reinforce Cécile's legitimacy as a future lesbian mother. The concessions to conservative readers might, then, reveal something about what was marketable and palatable to an early twenty-first-century readership.

In Cinq-Fraix's *Family Pride*, the narrator, who is also named Cécile, must resolve her own anxieties about having a child. She has no desire to be the birth mother or to travel to Belgium to receive fertility treatment. As in *Mais qui va garder le chat?*, Cinq-Fraix's Cécile must look beyond the equation of lesbianism with childlessness before opting into parenthood. Reflecting on her partner's proposal that they become parents, Cécile wonders:

Est-ce qu'on en avait le droit? Si indigent soit-il, l'état actuel de mes connaissances scientifiques et juridiques me permettait d'affirmer sereinement que l'homosexualité n'est plus une pathologie ni un délit. Jusqu'ici tout va bien. Et puis après, naturellement, tout se complique. Comme si cette reconnaissance enfin admise m'empêchait d'aller plus loin. Comme beaucoup de mes congénères, j'ai toujours vécu avec cette idée profondément ancrée que le fait d'être homosexuel interdit d'avoir des enfants. Une

idée partagée unanimement par mes non-congénères. Le beau consensus. Moi, ça
m'arrangeait plutôt puisque je ne voulais pas d'enfant. Mais enfin, on peut s'interroger,
non? Pourquoi ce déni de maternité ou de paternité concernant les homosexuels?
En quoi serai[en]t-ils inaptes à être parents? (FP 106–7)

[Did we have the right to? However poor it may be, the current state of my scientific
and legal knowledge enabled me to calmly assert that homosexuality is no longer a
pathology or a crime. All good up to now. And then, of course, everything gets complicated. As if this overdue recognition were preventing me from going further. Like
many of my counterparts, I have always lived with the deeply engrained idea that
being homosexual makes it forbidden to have children. An idea that is unanimously
shared by my non-counterparts. A nice consensus. I didn't really mind because I didn't
want children. But then again, we can wonder, can't we? Why deny motherhood or
fatherhood to homosexuals? What would make them unfit to be parents?]

This passage represents the internalization of a counter-movement to liberation that compels LGBT+ people to settle for the rights that they now
have and trivializes their continued demands for equality. Cécile's recognition that homosexuality no longer carries the stigma that it once did
prevents her from 'going further' – that is to say, from aspiring to become
a parent. The novel thus regards same-sex parenting as a transgression,
rather than as a reinsertion of same-sex relationships into the normative
model. While Cécile therefore has doubts about her legitimacy as a potential parent, she immediately challenges the heterosexual monopoly
on parenting and dissociates lesbianism from unfit parenting. Having
children, Cécile suggests, is not a right but a capacity: 'Il ne s'agit pas de
revendiquer le droit d'avoir des enfants et d'obtenir la permission de les
faire. Nonobstant une stérilité, une femme peut toujours procréer' [It is
not about demanding the right to have children and obtaining permission to make them. Unless she is infertile, a woman can always procreate]
(FP 107). Cécile's rapid change of attitude towards same-sex parenting
empowers lesbian readers and works to legitimize the social and cultural phenomenon that she represents – namely, the growing demands of
homosexuals to start a family.

   Although the protagonist therefore reconciles lesbianism and
mothering, the novel reveals how the prospect of a lesbian family can be
negatively welcomed by the extended family. Cécile's brother reacts angrily
to her and Anna's plan to start a family:

'Calme-toi, Franck. On est homosexuelles, ça ne veut pas forcément dire qu'on est stériles.'

'Arrête tes conneries, Cécile. Qu'est-ce que vous allez faire?'

'Comment ça, "qu'est-ce que vous allez faire"?'

'Pour l'enfant! Il va s'en prendre plein la tête ce môme …'

'Parce que tu crois qu'on n'y a pas réfléchi.'

'T'aurais pu nous en parler, quand même.'

'Eh bien, non. Tu m'en as parlé, toi, quand tu as décidé de faire un enfant avec Corinne?'

'Arrête, ce n'est pas du tout pareil.' (FP 189–90)

['Calm down, Franck. We're homosexual, that doesn't necessarily mean we're infertile.'

'Stop fooling around, Cécile. What are you going to do?'

'What do you mean "what are you going to do"?'

'About the child! The kid's going to have a rough time.'

'You think we haven't thought about that?'

'Even so, you could've talked to us about it.'

'Er, no! Did *you* talk to me about it when you decided to have a child with Corinne?'

'Pack it in, that's totally different.']

In this conversation, the characters represent two opposing positions on same-sex families. Cécile resists three common heteronormative and homophobic arguments used to oppose or preclude same-sex parenting: firstly, that homosexuality is synonymous with infertility; secondly, that children raised by homosexuals will somehow suffer; and finally, this passage reveals a heteronormative double standard, which Éric Garnier refers to as the heterosexual right to a child.[15] Detractors of same-sex parenting frequently claim that no one has the right to a child. Garnier argues that, in fact, these detractors defend heterosexual couples' right to have a family, since this is 'natural', but deny this right to homosexual

---

15   Garnier, *L'Homoparentalité en France*, 36.

couples. For Franck, whereas Cécile and Anna require permission to have children, for him and Corinne that permission is taken for granted.

The initial reservations of the lesbian characters at the prospect of becoming parents represent the dilemma faced by would-be same-sex parents in a society in which homosexuality has traditionally been thought to preclude parenthood. By portraying lesbian characters who ultimately come to terms with their desire to have children, the texts legitimize same-sex families and give a voice to the same-sex parents whom they represent. As well as recognizing their legitimacy as parents, same-sex couples must decide how they will create their families. Specifically, would-be lesbian parents have an important decision to make about what role men will have in their immediate family: some couples decide to parent alone, in which case the male role is purely biological; others decide that they want their child to grow up with one or more fathers.

Mothering with(out) a Father

The consensus that children grow up best when surrounded by a mother and father is often used to oppose same-sex families.[16] In France, this consensus is defended by two major discourses: religion and psychoanalysis. Although a secular country, France is still greatly influenced by Catholicism, and the Church campaigned against same-sex marriage on the grounds that the creation and rearing of children by a man and woman is natural, ergo unchangeable and untouchable.[17] The website of the French Catholic Church features a section dedicated to the same-sex marriage debate, which defends sexual difference as the foundation of

16   See Gross, *Parent ou homo*, 175–84.
17   On the role of religion in defending the mother- and father-headed family, see Céline Béraud, 'Un front commun des religions contre le mariage pour tous?', *Contemporary French Civilization* 39/3 (2014), 335–49; Odile Fillod, 'L'invention de la "théorie du genre": Le mariage blanc du Vatican et de la science', *Contemporary French Civilization* 39/3 (2014), 321–33.

the family: 'Traditional marriage is the social consecration of man and woman in preparation for the creation of a family. We believe that there is a good that is specific to this union – a social good that originates in sexual difference'.[18] The role of Christianity in opposing same-sex marriage is common across the West and was, perhaps, to be expected in a traditionally catholic country such as France. However, the influence of psychoanalysis in the debates on same-sex families is unique to the French case. Camille Robcis demonstrates how French left- and right-wing deputies frequently drew on some of the most complex ideas of psychoanalysis and structural anthropology, specifically in the works of Jacques Lacan and Claude Lévi-Strauss, to promote what she calls 'familialism' – that is, the normative heterosexual family.[19] As was discussed in Chapter 1, Freudian psychoanalytic theory holds that the resolution of the Oedipus complex depends on the mother–father–child triangulation. In Freudian thinking, the father ensures the infant's separation from its mother and its formation of a gendered identity. Psychoanalysis has faced sharp criticism from scholars working on same-sex parenting. Park, for instance, contends that another mother is just as capable as a father of preventing the fusion between infant and biological mother.[20] Martine Gross, who shares Park's view, convincingly argues that psychoanalysis falsely assumes that children grow up in isolation from wider society and from a broader network of social relations.[21] Gross maintains that children, regardless of their parents' gender, come to understand sexual difference because of the gendering of society.

Gross's distinction between two-parent and multiparent same-sex families provides insights into the rationale behind same-sex couples' chosen family form:

18   Xavier Lacroix, '"Une mesure discriminatoire pour l'enfant"', (7 January 2013) <http://www.eglise.catholique.fr/actualites/dossiers/dossiers-2013/le-mariage-pour-tous/359669-une-mesure-discriminatoire-pour-lenfant/>, accessed 2 February 2017.
19   Robcis, *The Law of Kinship*, 2.
20   Park, *Mothering Queerly, Queering Motherhood*, 10.
21   Gross, *Parent ou homo*, 178–9.

According to the two-parent family model, a child primarily needs to be raised in a single household by two people who love them and each other. In this configuration, the 'conjugal' couple and the 'parent' couple are one and the same. Parents will have to choose between adoption, artificial insemination with a known or unknown donor, or surrogacy. According to the multiparent family model, it is in the child's interests to grow up with a mother and father. In this case, parents will have to choose between a co-parenting arrangement or, for lesbians, its lighter version with a known donor–identified genitor.[22]

Gross suggests that the choice between these two forms of parenting is made according to what, in the minds of the couple, is best for the child. Virginie Descoutures, however, counter-argues that although the distinction between two-parent and multiparent families is pertinent from an ethnographic standpoint, Gross's interpretation of the reasons for which couples choose one configuration or the other is reductive and rests on the normative discourse of the best interests of the child:

> Reducing the reasons for choosing from two very different family configurations to a matter of the child's interests seems to me to mask the primary difference between two models: whereas for some lesbians the presence of a father is indispensable, for others it is not.[23]

Descoutures contends that Gross's categorization of same-sex families might be explained not simply with reference to the number of parents but in terms of the configuration's adherence to or transgression of the gender binary. She further proposes that this choice could instead depend on the legal and practical options available to the couple.[24] For instance, in the period before fertility treatment was made available to all women, wealthy lesbian couples and those living close to the Belgian or Spanish borders might have been more likely to opt for fertility treatment. From a gender studies perspective, Descoutures's analysis is more intriguing because it pertains to the importance of sexual difference. Whereas multiparent lesbian families preserve the male–female binary, albeit with the addition of a second mother and/or second father, two-parent lesbian

22   Gross, *Qu'est-ce que l'homoparentalité?*, 91–2.
23   Descoutures, *Les Mères lesbiennes*, 97.
24   Descoutures, *Les Mères lesbiennes*, 98–9.

families go beyond it by leaving out the male role. As Gross herself points out, the lack of opposition to heterosexual adoptive and blended families suggests that the argument that children grow up best when surrounded by a mother and father is not a defence of the status of biological parents but an assumption that children develop optimally in an environment of sexual alterity.[25] Conservatives therefore regard same-sex parenting as a step towards the erasure of the male–female binary. While the words 'mother' and 'father' have been erased from the French adoption regulations and replaced by the gender-neutral term 'parent', this amendment serves not to degender individuals but to account for children with two parents of the same gender.

Taken together, the texts reveal the differing positions on the role of the father and therefore intervene in the debate on the widely assumed superiority of the mother-and-father-headed family. *Family Pride* depicts a multiparent family comprising two mothers and two fathers. The lesbian couple in *Maman, Mamour* planned to raise their daughter in a co-parenting arrangement but had to raise her without her father. In the texts by Girard and Blanc, the lesbian couples decide to parent on their own. Whereas Girard's couple choose a known sperm donor, Blanc and her partner opt to conceive their daughters with different, anonymous donors. In *Prince Charmante*, Zélie has two daughters in a heterosexual marriage and conceives a child that she will raise with Alice. Alice is therefore a step-parent and a future non-biological primary carer. Even this small corpus of texts thus illustrates the range of circumstances in which same-sex families are created, and the range of family forms problematizes a singular, essentializing notion of the same-sex family.

In *Family Pride*, Anna embodies a slightly orthodox stance on the importance of having mixed-sex parents by insisting that her and Cécile's child needs a father:

> Tu sais, sous mes airs libérés, je reste quand même assez 'tradi'. Je ne peux pas envisager un enfant sans père, c'est comme ça. Je n'arrive pas à m'affranchir des schémas, des histoires de référents, tout ça. Je voudrais un papa. Un papa présent. Mais un enfant surtout, né de notre désir à nous. Tu comprends? (FP 105–6)

25   Gross, *Parent ou homo*, 176.

[You know, underneath my liberal appearance, I'm really quite old-fashioned. I just can't imagine a child with a father. I can't free myself from norms, that stuff about models, all that. I would like a father. A present father. But most of all a child born of *our* desire. Do you understand?]

Although Anna can only envisage a family based on the mother–father–child triangulation, her awareness that this is a conservative view, which she herself concedes is 'tradi' [old-fashioned], works to soften its political implications. The choice of a multiparent family is not portrayed as prescriptive but simply as a matter of what feels right for Anna and her partner.

In *Maman, Mamour*, Célier also alludes to the importance of the mother–father–child triangulation by making plain that, despite his absence, Christian has had a profound psychological influence on Géraldine and that this has helped her immensely. Like Anna, however, she avoids claiming that co-parenting arrangements are the right way for same-sex couples to become parents:

[C]'est sans difficulté que je peux imaginer qu'un enfant ait plus qu'un seul père ou qu'il ait deux mères et pas de père, ou deux pères et pas de mère. Si je ne me sens ni désireuse ni autorisée à donner mon avis sur toutes ces situations et autres choix, je suis en revanche convaincue qu'il est incontestablement important que les parents soient clairs sur leur identité et sereins quant à leur choix de vie. (MM 68)

[I can easily imagine a child with more than one father or with two mothers and no father, or with two fathers and no mother. Although I do not feel inclined or permitted to give my opinion on all these situations and alternative choices, I am convinced that it is unquestionably important that parents are clear about their own identity and at ease with their life choices.]

Like *Family Pride, Maman, Mamour* underlines the need for the parents to be comfortable with their choice of family form. Rather than favouring one configuration over another, Célier underscores the diversity among same-sex families, thus making a queer-sounding claim that same-sex families are not reducible to one homogeneous group. Célier demonstrates this more explicitly in her first chapter, in which she describes the various configurations of same-sex families.

In *Family Pride*, Cécile, Anna, Éric and Benoît decide that their child's time will be spent equally between the two couples. In this respect, the novel reflects Gross's point that co-parenting arrangements closely resemble those of a post-divorce family.[26] Gross makes a further point that in multiparent families, as in post-divorce families, family life extends beyond a single household: 'In multiparent families, family life is formed within a network rather than within a unit. Holidays, weekends, parties and birthdays are as much opportunities to establish how the network functions'.[27] The transgressive potential of multiparent families lies not in terms of the gender binary – for, as has been noted, the mother–father–child triangulation remains intact in multiparent configurations – but in its enlarging of the family unit. In *Maman, Mamour*, Célier tells us that Géraldine has developed positive relationships with her paternal extended family, underlining the size of the family unit resulting from co-parenting arrangements. While it is suggested that parents only come in twos – for we are told that Géraldine uses the phrase 'mes parents' [my parents] to refer collectively to Célier and Dominique or to Dominique and Christian but rarely to Célier, Dominique and Christian – Célier affirms that 'dans la tête de Géraldine, Papa, Maman et Mamour ont cohabité sans grande difficulté' [in Géraldine's head, Mum, Dad and *Mamour* have coexisted without much difficulty] (MM 86). In *Family Pride*, the parents collectively buy a disused printing shop and convert it into two neighbouring apartments, so that each couple can live virtually separate lives while always being near to the child. This arrangement reflects the common belief that a fixed location provides the child with greater stability. Further, it exemplifies the creativity, ingenuity and thought that often go into forming same-sex families, which seems to be a statement about how committed same-sex parents are to ensuring the best interests of their children, as well as how much they want them. It also testifies to the novel ways in which parenting is being done in the contemporary West and, interestingly, is reminiscent of family groupings in parts of the world where members of the extended family play a greater role in child-rearing. The set-up in *Family Pride*, then,

26   Gross, *Qu'est-ce que l'homoparentalité?*, 103.
27   Gross, *Qu'est-ce que l'homoparentalité?*, 104.

exposes the normative status of the heterosexual nuclear family in the West and the fact that this is different from much of the world.

While Cécile and Anna are adamant in their belief that their child needs a father, *Family Pride* presents the potential disadvantages of co-parenting arrangements. Cécile expresses her concern about her lack of legal protection if relations between the couples break down. Anna voices the same anxiety:

> 'Si je meurs par exemple,' poursuit Anna, 'Eh bien je tiens à ce que Cécile puisse continuer d'assumer le rôle qu'elle va avoir auprès de cet enfant. J'irai même plus loin: je voudrais qu'elle soit la mère de cet enfant. Ce n'est pas moi qui décide, c'est sûr. Mais j'aimerais que ce soit écrit quelque part.' (FP 163)

> ['If I die, for example,' Anna went on, 'I want Cécile to be able to continue to assume the role that she's going to have in relation to this child. I'd even go further: I'd like her to be this child's mother. It's not my decision, of course. But I'd like that written somewhere.']

The couple's anxiety can be read as a critique of the French system of filiation, which offered no legal protection to co-parents in the immediate post-PACS context in which this novel is set.

While relations between Cinq-Fraix's couples never become hostile, the friendship that forms during their journey to parenthood regresses to cordiality. Dividing the child's time equally between the two couples becomes problematic when Anna refuses to let Éric and Benoît take Angèle on a ten-day holiday, as she cannot bear to be separated from her newly born daughter. This is perhaps another concession to conservative readers, who may take reassurance from seeing a biological mother who is so attached to her child. In Célier's *Maman, Mamour*, Brigitte and Dominique thought it essential that the father of their child was a friend, so that their child, especially if it turned out to be a boy, could later envisage his or her conception as an affective act. This suggests a surprisingly traditional outlook on gender and the family. By creating a child with a friend, the couple presumably hoped to avoid the kind of conflict depicted in *Family Pride*. Ultimately, however, Brigitte and Dominique's decision to opt for a co-parenting arrangement was motivated by their desire to create a child as naturally as possible: '[N]ous souhaitons que ce soit le plus naturellement du monde que les petites graines se rencontrent' [We want the little grains to join together in the most natural way possible] (MM 19). Although this sounds like a claim to equal rights with heterosexual couples, we might ask why it matters that the child is created as naturally as possible, especially for a family based on a social rather than biologistic definition of parenting. Although *Family Pride* and *Maman, Mamour* are, then, progressive in many ways, they make certain concessions to potentially conservative readers that, it might be argued, chime with the defence of sexual difference that is at the core of multiparent family forms.

The texts by Girard, Blanc and Bénard undermine the assumption that children thrive only when surrounded by a man and woman. In *Prince Charmante*, Zélie and Alice give no thought to incorporating a father into their family. There is a potential link between their rejection of the presumed necessity of a father and the reluctance of Zélie's ex-husband, the father of her two daughters, to undertake responsibility for childcare or any domestic tasks. Indeed, this father's lack of commitment, which the following passage exemplifies, implies that, far from being a prerequisite of his children's healthy development, he is in fact partially expendable:

> Mon Homme fait l'homme avec les autres hommes, il va chercher du vin, mais ne fait les courses qu'en râlant; bien qu'il soit un excellent cuisinier, ne prépare pas à manger; ne met pas la table; ne fait pas le ménage; ne débarrasse pas; ne range pas la cuisine, valable pour tous les repas sans exception. (PC 100)

> [My Man does man things with other men, he goes out to buy wine, but moans about doing the shopping; although he is very good at cooking, he does not make dinner, set the table, do the housework, clear the table, tidy the kitchen – and this is the case for all meals without exception.]

This passage critiques the gendered division of domestic labour, which, despite the changes to women's status and opportunities in the last half-century, remains a primarily female role. More significantly, the fact that the husband remains unnamed – he is referred to throughout the text as 'l'Homme' [the Man] or 'mon Amour' [my Love] – works to foreground Zélie's relationship with Alice. While Zélie's marriage is, as the preceding passage suggests, conflictual and ends in divorce, the nameless-ness of the husband is neither an attempt to erase the relationship from memory nor a denial of the love that Zélie once felt for him. Rather, his anonymity foregrounds the text's central theme: desire and love between women. Similarly, Zélie's daughters are referred to as 'Fille Aînée' [Eldest Daughter] and 'Grande' [Big] or 'Cadette Chérie' [Little Dear]. This is not to indicate a conflict between the mother and her daughters; on the contrary, the ease with which Zélie eventually comes out to her children and the incorporation of Alice into the family – events that are described only in passing – suggest a harmonious relationship between mother and children. The suddenness of Zélie and Alice's decision to undergo fertility treatment, which takes place in a single, final chapter, normalizes lesbian couples' desire for a family and suggests that lesbian family planning need not be more complicated or protracted than that of would-be heterosexual parents.

Like Bénard's text, *Elles eurent beaucoup d'enfants* rejects outright the need for a present father. For Blanc and Astrid, a father would have been an intrusion into their life together, and Blanc defends their decision to bring two children into the world without a father. Blanc insists that having two mothers does not amount to suppressing the existence of sexual difference:

> Mettons bien les choses au point: pas de papa ne veut pas dire pas d'homme; il n'a jamais été question de faire croire à nos filles qu'elles ont été conçues sans intervention masculine (bien qu'Assia, par un bel hasard, soit née le jour de l'Immaculée Conception …), ni que les hommes n'existent pas. (HFH 81)

> [Let's get things straight: no dad does not mean no man; it has never been about making our daughters believe that they were conceived without male intervention (even though Assia, as luck would have it, was born on the day of the Immaculate Conception …) or that men do not exist.]

Like Gross, who points out the unfeasibility of a same-sex couple pretending to have conceived naturally, Blanc rebukes the stereotype that same-sex parents deny the existence of sexual difference and lie, or need to lie, to their children about their origins.[28] Moreover, Blanc's allusion to the Immaculate Conception, which in Catholic dogma refers to the conception of the Virgin Mary, is a humorous reminder of the

---

28   Gross, *Parent ou homo*, 180.

ideological centrality throughout Christendom of a mother who, like Blanc and Astrid, gave birth to a child conceived by non-conventional means. *Elles eurent beaucoup d'enfants* stands out among the texts treated in this chapter for its engagement with psychoanalytic theories of child development and sexuality. In line with many scholars of same-sex parenting, Blanc argues that another mother is just as capable as a father of preventing mother–child fusion. Moreover, she condemns the homophobia of modern psychoanalysts who oppose same-sex parenting on the grounds that homosexuality is the result of childhood trauma and that children of same-sex parents cannot understand where they come from.

Although the couple reject the indispensability of a father, their interactions with people attest to the entrenchment of the heterosexual family and sexual union. While awaiting the birth of Assia, for example, Blanc ironically remarks that 'c'est moi qui fai[s] l'homme puisque c'est Astrid qui est enceinte' [I am the man because it is Astrid who is pregnant] (HFH 64). The text thus reveals two founding principles of Western kinship: firstly, the heterosexual couple is the standard frame of reference for thinking about affective relationships. Because pregnancy is an exclusively female experience, Astrid, as the baby's carrier, is assumed to be 'the woman' in her relationship. Within the dominant Western framework of affectivity, Blanc must, therefore, occupy the male position. The implication is that Astrid, as 'the woman', is also the baby's mother and Blanc, as 'the man', its father. As such, the second founding principle of Western kinship postulates that children have only two parents and only one of each gender. Blanc voices her frustration at the deep-seatedness of this heteronormative and monomaternalist (and monopaternalist) model of kinship – 'Mais pourquoi faudrait-il à tout prix un homme dans cette affaire?' [But why must there absolutely be a man in this business?] (HFH 65) – and resists it by deploying humour and irony: '[S]i seulement j'avais un peu moins l'air d'une femme. Je ferais presque tapette comme mec, tiens' [If only I looked a little less like a woman. If I were a guy, I could almost pass as a fairy'] (HFH 64). Blanc and Astrid are, then, at ease with their sexuality and parental roles; the problem for them is the ignorance of others surrounding their relationship and family. Instead of seeking to legitimize lesbian relationships through their assimilation to the heteronormative model, the text does so by challenging that model's authority and, as such, redresses the traditional power imbalance across the heterosexual–homosexual binary. Like Blanc's text, those by Girard and Bénard criticize the heteronormative and monomaternalist discourses prevalent in Western societies. *Prince Charmante* exposes the 'everyday heterosexism' with which homosexuals have to contend. When, for example, Zélie visits a pharmacy to purchase medicine for Alice, the pharmacist assumes that Zélie's *amie* [girlfriend] – '[l]e mot neutre par excellence' [the neutral word *par excellence*] due to its unvoiced feminine inflection – is a man (PC 319). In *Mais qui va garder le chat?*, Cécile's boss assumes that Cécile will be a single mother when he learns that she is pregnant and has no male partner. The boss's heteronormative assumption is, as Cécile reflects, also a monomaternalist one: 'Jean-René n'a même pas imaginé qu'on pouvait être deux. Deux femmes' [Jean-René did not even imagine that there might be two of us. Two women] (MQV 202). As for Blanc and Astrid, a problem for Cécile is the ignorance surrounding same-sex parenting in wider society.

Of the texts analysed in this chapter, Girard's *Mais qui va garder le chat?* deliberates most extensively over the need for a father. Cécile and Fanny ultimately conclude that having two committed parents, regardless of their gender, is what counts in terms of the child's development: ' "Fanny et moi ne sommes pas encore tout à fait d'accord sur la nécessité d'un père présent […]. D'un côté ça paraît évident, dans un autre sens on se demande si deux parents ce n'est pas suffisant" ' ['Fanny and I don't entirely agree on the need for a present father […]. On the one hand, it seems obvious; on the other hand, we're wondering if two parents aren't enough'] (MQV 110). It is telling that Cécile's claim about the obvious need for a paternal figure remains unsubstantiated, for this exposes the heteronormativity engrained in this remark. Gilles, Cécile and Fanny's sperm donor, refers to himself as ' "un père qui n'en est pas un" ' ['a father who is not one'] (MQV 113) and states: ' "[J]e veux bien endosser le rôle de père biologique mais je ne veux pas être papa" ' ['I'm happy to take on the role of a biological father, but I don't want to be a dad'] (MQV 115). In the same way, Cécile's response to Gilles's offer to donate his sperm carefully distinguishes between biological fathering and the novel's redefinition of fathering as a social role: ' "[I]l faut que tu [Gilles] réfléchisses. Si on fait un enfant ensemble, il sera de toi mais pas à toi. Tu comprends?"' ['You need to think. If we make a child together, it'll come from you, but it won't be yours'] (MQV 114). Cécile's strict definition of Gilles's role exhibits her and Fanny's reluctance to admit a third party into their family. As in *Prince Charmante* and *Elles eurent beaucoup d'enfants*, a care-giving father is regarded by the couple as intrusive and superfluous.

The couple must negotiate the reservations of their family and friends about their plan to raise a fatherless child. These characters represent a society in which the family is founded on the heteronormative and monomaternalist assumption that children have only two parents and only one of each gender. Cécile's former partner, Magali, contends that the child will suffer without the presence of a father. Fanny's father brands his daughter a false father, and Cécile's mother, unable to envisage a family without a father, presumes that Fanny, as the non-biological mother, will act as the child's father and that Cécile, as the birth mother, is the real mother. Like Blanc in *Elles eurent beaucoup d'enfants*, Cécile resists the assimilation of her family to the heteronormative and monomaternalist framework epitomized by Magali and the couple's parents: ' "Non Fanny n'est pas un papa, ça se voit non?"' ['No, Fanny isn't a father, isn't it obvious?'] (MQV 148).

Collectively, the texts offer a range of positions on the role of the father. Although none of the texts advocate one family form over another, those by Cinq-Fraix and Célier suggest the importance of the father's role in child development, while for Girard, Blanc and Bénard the father is unnecessary and an intrusion in the lives of the couple. Moreover, factors such as the use of a sperm donor, whether the donor is anonymous (Blanc, Bénard) or known (Girard), the death of a parent (Célier) and the existence of a past heterosexual relationship (Bénard) show that the presence or absence of a father is not the only point of difference between lesbian families. The range of family forms portrayed in these texts makes it hard to talk about a fixed notion of the same-sex family, especially when set in opposition to a singular notion of the heterosexual family. If the various positions on the role of the father pertain to the ideologically powerful mother–father–child triangulation, the presence of a non-biological mother in the family interrogates the normative biologistic model of the family.

Mothering with(out) Biology

The family has traditionally denoted a system of biological relationships rather than a network founded on mutual care-giving. In *Maman, Mamour*, Célier reveals the biologistic, monomaternalist assumption that underpins the normative definition of the family in the West:

> Il y a aussi tous ceux qui nous ont connues après la naissance et qui (se) demandent laquelle est la vraie mère. Cette curiosité, simplement naturelle pour certains, suggère pour d'autres l'idée qu'ils en imaginent une fausse, ou plus exactement que, pour eux, comme pour beaucoup, seule la filiation biologique est à considérer comme incontestable. (MM 93)

> [There are also all those who met us after the birth and who ask (themselves) which of us is the real mother. This curiosity, which is simply natural for some, suggests for others the idea that they imagine that there could be a fake mother, or more specifically that, for them, as for many people, only biological filiation can be considered to be indisputable.]

Célier argues that claims about real mothering presuppose the existence of false mothers, where 'real' is synonymous with the biological aspects of mothering. The resultant equation of functional mothering with falsity excludes non-biological mothers from the family. While these texts thus recognize the heteronormative and monomaternalist discourses that lesbian mothers face, they ultimately challenge these forces by redefining filiation and the family in terms of care-giving. Célier openly calls for the formal recognition of parent–child relationships built on affectivity, arguing that this would merely be an extension of existing adoption laws:

> Hier, avec l'adoption, un lien juridique a remplacé un lien biologique. Ne pourrait-on une nouvelle fois modifier la loi et reconnaître un autre lien, de type contractuel par exemple, qui avaliserait un lien parental déjà vécu d'un point de vue affectif et de plus en plus reconnu d'un point de vue social? (MM 193)

> [Previously, with adoption, a legal link replaced a biological one. Could we not modify the law again and recognize another link, a contractual link for example, that would guarantee a parental link that already exists in practice from an emotional point of view and that is increasingly recognized socially?]

Géraldine defines Célier as her 'second' mother, since she has always clearly identified as her mother 'celle qui l'a portée dans son ventre et lui a donné le sein' [the woman who carried her in her tummy and breastfed her] (MM 86). Although this seems to privilege a biologistic definition of mothering, neither Géraldine nor her parents have ever reduced Célier to the status of an aunt, godmother or friend. While Célier is a second mother, then, she is in no way of secondary importance, as she says: 'Ma compagne me considère depuis toujours et sans aucune hésitation comme mère de sa fille, à part entière' [My partner has always and without a moment's hesitation regarded me as her daughter's full mother] (MM 89). While Célier's self-identification as Géraldine's mother is unproblematic, some of her family and friends demonstrate the attachment to the biologistic definition of mothering that *Maman, Mamour*, like all the texts treated in this chapter, endeavours to challenge:

> Pensant à l'enfant que je souhaitais avoir mais que je n'ai donc jamais 'porté', une amie m'a dit un jour qu'elle imaginait quel renoncement avait dû être le mien. Certes, ma situation n'a pas toujours été confortable. Le statut social de co-parent étant inexistant, j'ai dû progressivement inventer et légitimer ma place aux yeux de beaucoup, mais je sens si profondément Géraldine être 'ma fille', et pas seulement 'comme ma fille', que le sentiment d'avoir renoncé à avoir un enfant m'est totalement étranger. (MM 91)

> [Thinking about the child that I wished to have but that I never 'carried', a friend once said to me that she was imagining what I had given up. Admittedly, my situation has not always been comfortable. As the social status of co-parent does not exist, I have had to progressively invent and legitimize my place in the eyes of many, but I feel so strongly that Géraldine is 'my daughter', and not only 'like my daughter', that the feeling of having given up on having a child is one with which I am completely unfamiliar.]

Célier's friend assumes that being the co-mother requires a sort of sacrifice. The implication, here, is that being the biological mother is superior to being the co-mother. Célier, however, neatly deproblematizes this by equalizing the status of biological mothering and its performative, care-giving function. In this way, she dismisses monomaternalist ideas about 'real' mothering and, as she puts it, gradually invents and legitimizes her identity as Geraldine's 'real' mother. Moreover, Célier uncouples maternal feeling from biology, thereby challenging the assumption that

this is natural and demonstrates that it can, rather, stem from caring for
a child.

Mais qui va garder le chat? queers the established definitions of 'mother'
and 'father' by positing that a parent's identification as one or the other is
not predetermined by his or her biological sex. The novel's fictional psychologist specializing in same-sex parenting questions why the paternal role
is necessarily a male one – ' "Pourquoi le rôle du père devrait-il être tenu
par un homme?" ' ['Why must the father's role be held by a man?'] – and
does not rule out the possibility that Fanny could identify as the child's
father (MQV 158–9). While this question is intended to be transgressive,
rather than a naive defence of the heterosexual family, it arguably retains
a trace of the male–female binary that is intrinsic to heteronormative kinship. Although the psychologist seeks to uncouple fathering from mascu-
linity, a more radical argument would be to collapse the gender binary by
dispensing altogether with the terms 'mother' and 'father' and referring to
all primary caregivers simply as 'parents'. The fact that she does not means
that the novel stops short of a total degendering of parenting and wholesale
overthrow of sexual difference. Just as the novel challenges the definition
of fathering as a male role, it also disrupts the nexus between gestation
and mothering, for although Fanny wishes to be a mother, she has no
desire to carry a child. Fanny's impatience with those, including her own
mother, who regard pregnancy as the only path to mothering – 'Combien
de fois va-t-il falloir que je me justifie de ne pas vouloir être enceinte tout
en ayant un désir d'enfant?' [How many times must I explain that I do not
want to be pregnant but still want a child?] – is a critique of the rigidity of
normative, biologically defined kinship (MQV 91). While the novel thus
valorizes the status of the lesbian co-mother, it seeks above all to emphasize the multitude of women's relationships to maternity. In contrast with
Fanny, Cécile covets pregnancy: ' "[J]e crois que j'ai envie de le porter cet
enfant. J'aurais peur que la grossesse me manque. J'ai envie d'être enceinte,
de l'avoir en moi, de le sentir grandir" ' ['I think I want to carry this child.
I'd fear that I'd miss being pregnant. I want to be pregnant, to have it inside
me, to feel it growing'] (MQV 112–13). *Mais qui va garder le chat?* does
not, then, trivialize the physiological elements of mothering but works to
equalize the legitimacy of biological and social family ties in a pre-equal
marriage era when filiation was defined almost entirely in biological terms.

Girard's *Mais qui va garder le chat?* exposes the impact of not having recognition, especially on the co-mother. Because this role lacks legal and social validation, Fanny struggles to construct an identity in relation to the child for which she and Cécile are planning: ' "Tu [Cécile] es la mère, c'est TON enfant et personne ne pourra le remettre en question. Mais moi? Moi? Je te pose la question?" ' ['You [Cécile] are the mother, it's YOUR children and no one can question that. But what about me? I'm asking you'] (MQV 151). The novel thus reveals, and can be said to critique, the deep-seated monomaternalism that characterizes Western kinship. Moreover, it testifies to the power of institutional recognition to create and regulate social roles, including who has the right to identify as a mother: ' "Là où ni la biologie, ni la loi ne donne de droits, les autres ne t'en donnent pas plus. Je n'existe pas par rapport à cet enfant" ' ['When biology or the law gives you no rights, others don't give you any. I don't exist in relation to this child'] (MQV 151). Collectively, these passages reveal the dominance of biology and the law in defining family ties such that no place is given to a parent's commitment and desire to have and nurture children. Cécile and Fanny understand that the latter's biological and legal estrangement from the child makes it crucial that she invents a maternal identity for herself. With no biological or legal status in relation to her child, Fanny's identity as a mother is unstable and difficult to put into words:

> Il me plaît que le père de mon enfant soit […] un beau mec. Je viens d'écrire 'le père de mon enfant' sans même y réfléchir. Une phrase absurde en soi au regard de la loi et de la société, puisque Gilles ne sera pas père et moi encore moins mère. Que serai-je alors? […] Une co-mère, comme elle [Cécile] dit? Le mot est trop moche. Un co-parent, comme on est co-équipier, co-propriétaire? Le problème est que je suis la seule à avoir l'honneur de porter ce si joli titre. Cécile est mère. Point. (MQV 117–18)

> [I am pleased that the father of my child is […] a good-looking guy. I have just written 'the father of my child' without even thinking about it. A ridiculous sentence in itself as far as the law and society are concerned, because Gilles will not be a father, and I will be even less of a mother. What will I be, then? A co-mother, as she says? The word is so ugly. A co-parent? Like a teammate[29] or co-owner? The problem is that I am the only one to have the honour of having that pretty title. Cécile is the mother. Full stop.]

29 The play on the words 'co-parent' and 'co-équipier' that relies on their common prefix is lost in translation.

It is a testament to monomaternalism that Gilles, as the sperm donor, will have a greater claim to being a parent than Fanny, despite the latter's commitment to the long-term care of the child. A co-parent, as Fanny puts it, is 'un mystère aux yeux de tous, un parent virtuel que l'on peut zapper à tout instant' [a mystery to everyone, a virtual parent that can be forgotten at any time] (MQV 118). Indeed, the excerpt from Fanny's diary demonstrates her acute awareness of her own marginal existence. Fanny's question – 'Que serai-je?' [What will I be?] – and her dissatisfaction with the social scientific terms 'co-mother' and 'co-parent' indicate the inconceivability of her role at the level of language. Put simply, the vocabulary that would facilitate Fanny's construction of a maternal identity does not exist. The novel thus reveals the centrality of language in the construction of identity – a point to which I will return in Chapter 5. The psychologist advises Cécile that Fanny, in order to feel that she has a role in the child's life, must be designated a name that the child will call her, as Célier in *Maman, Mamour* does. In Fanny's case, her maternal name remains unclear, but her own mother, the child's non-biological grandmother, decides that the child will call her 'Mamoune' (MQV 187).

Whereas Girard's and Bénard's novels neatly distinguish between biological and social mothering, Blanc's lesbian family comprises two women who have both given birth to a child and who both assume the role of co-mother. In this respect, Blanc's text goes beyond the transgressive potential of those by Girard and Bénard by allowing both for the possibility of a polymaternal family and for a family unit in which there is more than one biological mother. Despite this, Blanc frequently affirms that her family has no basis in biology: 'Biologie, pas biologie, mes deux filles ont la même immense place dans mon cœur depuis qu'elles sont nées, et même avant' [Biology or not, my two daughters have had the same huge place in my heart since they were born, and even before] (HFH 42). Furthermore, Blanc questions the need for biological ties. When she discusses her and Astrid's decision to use different sperm donors for each daughter, she asks rhetorically: 'Pourquoi créer un lien biologique entre nos enfants, alors que de toute évidence notre famille n'est en rien fondée sur la biologie?' [Why create a biological link between our daughters when clearly our family is in no way based on biology?] (HFH 96). Unlike Cécile and Fanny in *Mais qui va garder le chat?*, Blanc and Astrid do not find it necessary to provide their children with a clear filiation. By downplaying the biological in favour of the functional, Blanc's text reimagines the basis of kinship ties. As it is for the mothers in Girard's and Bénard's texts, mothering, for Blanc and Astrid, is a set of performative acts – that is, a care-giving role – and only secondarily a biological function.

The need to establish a relationship with a child in the absence of a biological connection concerns not only the non-biological mother but also her side of the extended family. By giving a voice to the couples' own parents, the novels by Girard and Cinq-Fraix give some indication of this process. The large cast of characters in *Mais qui va garder le chat?* and *Family Pride* reveals the impact of same-sex parenting beyond the parenting couple, and the characters act as mouthpieces for the interests and positions of the many members of the extended family. Studies suggest that grandparents, in both heterosexual and homosexual families, attach considerable importance to being biologically connected to their grandchildren, both in France and across the West.[30] The emerging scholarship on grandparent–grandchild relationships in same-sex families is concerned, then, with the extent to which they transcend biological ties and demonstrate, on the whole, that grandparents are more likely, at least at the moment, to reinforce the normative biologistic definition of the family.

Collectively, the texts illustrate the potentially conflict-inducing repercussions of becoming a lesbian mother. In line with the social scientific literature just outlined, *Mais qui va garder le chat?* and *Family Pride* suggest

---

30   See Megan Fulcher, Raymond W. Chan, Barbara Raboy, and Charlotte J. Patterson, 'Contact with Grandparents among Children Conceived via Donor Insemination by Lesbian and Heterosexual Mothers', *Parenting: Science and Practice* 2/1 (2002), 61–76; Martine Gross, 'Être grand-parent dans un contexte homoparental en France: Chassez le biologique par la porte, il revient par la fenêtre', *Recherches féministes* 22/2 (2009), 69–76; Herbrand, 'Les rendre grands-parents', 188; Danielle Julien, Marie-France Bureau, and Annie Leblond de Brumath, 'Grand-parentalité et homoparentalité au Québec: Nouvelles dispositions législatives et proximité des liens en fonction de la composition familiale', in Benoît Schneider, Marie-Claude Mietkiewicz and Sylvain Bouyer, eds, *Grands-parents et grands-parentalités* (Ramonville Sainte-Agne: Érès, 2005), 199–217.

that grandparents attach considerable importance to being biologically connected to their grandchildren. In *Mais qui va garder le chat?*, Fanny's parents, Gabriel and Simone, express disappointment that it is not their daughter who is pregnant. Gabriel's reasons for this are primarily dynastic: he wants the child to bear his name. As was noted earlier, he refers to Fanny as a false father, implying his subscription to gender-normative ideas about parenting. Simone, as the following exchange with Fanny demonstrates, worries that she will be considered inferior to the biological grandmother:

> 'Ce ne sera pas mon petit-enfant.'
>
> 'Si, nous allons l'élever comme un couple.'
>
> 'Mais tu n'es pas le père!'
>
> 'Non, il aura deux mères.'
>
> 'Pourquoi ce n'est pas toi la vraie mère?'
>
> 'Je ne voulais pas être enceinte et Cécile, elle, en avait très envie. Le choix s'est fait comme ça. Mais c'est mon enfant.'
>
> 'Je ne comprends rien.'
>
> 'Je sais, c'est difficile à appréhender comme situation. Mais tu seras sa grand-mère, je te le garantis.'
>
> 'Moins que l'autre, la mère de la vraie mère.' (MQV 184)
>
> ['It won't be my grandchild.'
>
> 'Yes, it will. We're going to raise it as a couple.'
>
> 'But you're not the father!'
>
> 'No, it'll have two mothers.'
>
> 'Why aren't you the real mother?'
>
> 'I didn't want to be pregnant, whereas Cécile really did. That's how we decided. But it's my child.'
>
> 'I don't get it at all.'
>
> 'I know, it's a difficult situation to understand. But you will be its grandmother, I promise.'
>
> 'Less than the other one, the mother of the real mother.']

Simone's confusion stems from her unquestioning acceptance of the heterosexual nuclear family as the cornerstone of kinship. Unlike Fanny, who is able to envisage a family comprising two mothers and no father, Simone cannot imagine a situation other than the biologically linked mother–father–child triangulation. Whereas Fanny thus underscores her and her mother's role as functional parents, Simone delegitimizes their relationship to the child because it is not grounded in biology. Indeed, as Cécile reflects: 'Le seul point [que Simone] comprenait était que ce n'était pas sa fille qui portait l'enfant, donc elle ne voyait pas très bien ce que Fanny venait faire là-dedans' [The only thing that Simone understood was that it was not her daughter who was carrying the child, so she could not really see what it had to do with Fanny] (MQV 185). Cécile's parents, who are initially delighted by the news of their daughter's pregnancy, are shocked when they learn that the couple's sperm donor will have no hand in raising the child and try to assimilate Fanny's status as a co-mother to the normative paternal role. Like Simone, then, they unquestioningly accept the biologically linked mother–father–child triangulation as the founding principle of the family and, therefore, assert that the donor, because of his biological connection to the child, is de facto a father.

In *Family Pride*, Anna's mother, Béatrice, is delighted by Cécile and her daughter's plan to become mothers via a co-parenting arrangement, yet she admits to Cécile that she is relieved to be the child's biological grandmother:

> Ça ne doit pas être évident pour [tes parents]. Tu sais, je ne sais pas comment je réagirais moi, si Anna m'apprenait que tu es enceinte. Malgré toute l'affection que je te porte, je ne serais pas précisément transportée de joie. C'est compliqué, votre histoire. (FP 193–4)
>
> [It can't be easy for your parents. You know, I don't know how *I* would react if Anna told me that you were pregnant. Despite my affection for you, I wouldn't exactly be over the moon. Your situation is complicated.]

Despite her open-mindedness, then, Béatrice gains reassurance from being able to position herself within the culturally recognized framework of biological kinship and sympathizes with Cécile's parents because they are, as non-biological grandparents, excluded from this framework.

Béatrice thus exposes the hierarchy in the kinship network. On the other hand, she demonstrates her understanding of the co-parenting arrangement – ' "[J]'ai à peu près compris comment ça marchait entre vous quatre" ' ['I more or less understand how you four are doing things'] (FP 195) – when she asks to meet the child's fathers, pointing out that they will, on occasion, cross paths.

Although several of the grandparents in *Mais qui va garder le chat?* and *Family Pride* are confused or troubled by their daughter's plan to parent, it would be hasty to conclude that these novels portray grandparents as staunch defenders of the normative status of biological kinship. Indeed, they quickly come to terms with the prospect of becoming the grandparent of a lesbian-parented child. In *Mais qui va garder le chat?*, Simone is persuaded by her best friends that she will be a grandmother to the child, despite the absence of a biological connection. In *Family Pride*, Jean-Louis and Solange, having reacted unfavourably to the revelation of Anna's pregnancy, subsequently invite Anna and Cécile for Christmas, leading to the family's reconciliation. To some degree, then, the grandparents' initial defence of the heterosexual nuclear family is an in-the-moment response to the news of their daughter's plans. With time, they are quickly able to work through the discourses that preclude same-sex families – namely, the importance of biology in the definition of family ties – and position themselves within their daughter's family. Following Gross, who argues that non-biological grandparents' capacity to relate to their grandchildren depends ultimately on the stability of their daughter's identity as a non-biological mother, the texts suggest that the non-biological grandparents are able to come to terms with their status vis-à-vis the child because the parents insist on equalizing the importance of biology and care-giving as modes of parental involvement.[31] The texts therefore contend that, ultimately, care-giving is recognized, even by the older members of the family, as a mode of parenting that is as legitimate as biology.

By representing families premised on the idea of two women parenting together, the texts interrogate the traditional, biologistic notion of the family. Ultimately, the texts redefine the family in social terms by

---

31   Gross, 'Être grand-parent dans un contexte homoparental en France', 75.

emphasizing the fact that mothering is a care-giving, as well as biological, role. What comes out most of all from these texts, however, is the importance, and difficulty, of constructing a maternal identity for non-biological mothers, as well as for members of the extended family. This challenge seems to stem from both the legal framework and the day-to-day language used to define the family. While the 2013 same-sex marriage law has done much to account for same-sex parents, the continuing lack of terms of address for non-biological parents problematizes their sense of parental identity. These terms may appear in the future, but in the meantime the multiple, nuanced definitions of motherhood found in these texts have a most vital role to play in legitimizing non-biological parenthood.

Concluding Thoughts

The texts examined in this chapter should primarily be seen as functional texts that give visibility and a voice to lesbian parents and families. They intervene in, and in some cases, even prefigure the debates on same-sex families in France in the period between the creation of civil partnerships and legalization of same-sex marriage and adoption. In particular, they contribute to rethinking the supposed importance of sexual difference in the family and the definition of the family as a system of biological ties. Although the texts grant occasional concessions to more conservative readers – such as the slightly traditional outlook on the need for a father in *Family Pride* and *Maman, Mamour* – they should be regarded as progressive contributions to the debates on the meaning of parenting and the family.

It is especially notable that some of the texts, particularly *Mais qui va garder le chat?* and *Family Pride*, give some indication of the repercussions of lesbian mothering on the extended family, as well as the parenting couple. This serves as an important reminder that the family is not reducible to parents and children – the normative focus of the nuclear family – but, rather, encapsulates a broader network of relationships. In addition, the large cast of characters in these novels offers opportunities for didactic conversations in which the characters embody the various positions on the state of the family in twenty-first-century France.

The fact that these texts focus primarily on the characters' journeys to motherhood, rather than their experience of it, is in some measure representative of where society is 'at' in terms of same-sex parenting. Given that planned same-sex families, although much discussed, are a social phenomenon still in its infancy, it is fitting that many of these texts end with or just after the birth of a child. The decision by the authors to stop writing at this point is perhaps reflective of the current lack of knowledge of what same-sex families become years after their formation.

Having examined how these texts intervene in the social debates on same-sex parenting, I now turn to their interventions in a wider theoretical debate: that on difference, and the question of its reconcilability with equality.

Difference, Sameness and Equality

The extent to which same-sex families differ from traditional family forms, and the reconcilability of difference with the demand for equality, is a point of debate among activists, parents and scholars. As we saw in Chapter 1, early social scientific studies of same-sex families found no notable differences between mixed- and same-sex-parented children in terms of social, psychological and sexual development. This consensus, known as the 'no differences' model, has since been challenged on empirical and ideological grounds. Recent research shows that the division of paid and unpaid labour is more likely to be equal in same-sex families than in heterosexual families and that children in same-sex families are more open to diversity than those in heterosexual families. This body of research is also opposed to early studies' uncritical acceptance of the heterosexual family as the standard according to which same-sex families ought to be judged.

France is often accused of failing to recognize difference due to its deep-seated attachment to universalism and the notion of an imagined republican subject. According to Domna Stanton, this originated in the construction, during the seventeenth century, of a nation state founded on the principle of 'one king, one faith, one law'.[1] This translated into opposition to certain 'others within', notably protestants, women and homosexuals, who distorted the image of the nation that France wanted to project.[2] Stanton argues that this ideal persists today and informs the notion of the republican subject, who is 'defined mythically by equality but regulated by

---

1   Domna C. Stanton, 'Contesting the Exclusive Nation and the Republican Subject: For a New Universalism and Cosmopolitanism', *Contemporary French and Francophone Studies* 17/2 (2013), 123–40 (124–5).
2   Stanton, 'Contesting the Exclusive Nation and the Republican Subject', 125.

apparatuses of assimilatory sameness over and against fractious multiplicity'.[3] Assertions of difference risk being branded as support for 'American-style' identity politics, or *communautarisme* – that is, as un-French – as was the case with the PACS and same-sex marriage laws, the latter of which was, incidentally, reframed in universalist terms as 'mariage pour tous' [marriage for all]. Republican universalism has, then, been subjected to criticism, yet one might reasonably assert that opposition to difference is a poor application of universalism, rather than a problem inherent to it: the idea that we all have the same rights does not amount to saying that we are all the same. Moreover, as Scott Gunther notes in his history of homosexuality in France, the universalist principle of French law has done much to protect homosexual citizens, particularly by decriminalizing sodomy as early as 1791.[4] Nonetheless, compared with countries where diversity is, at least to some extent, embraced, difference would seem to be a thorny issue in France.

In this chapter, I discuss issues related to equality, difference and sameness, focusing on the five texts considered in the previous chapter: Éliane Girard's *Mais qui va garder le chat?* [*But Who's Going to Look After the Cat?*] (2005); Laurence Cinq-Fraix's *Family Pride* (2006); Brigitte Célier's *Maman, Mamour, ses deux mamans: Grandir dans une famille homoparentale* [*Maman, Mamour – Her Two Mums: Growing Up in a Same-Sex Family*] (2008); Myriam Blanc's *Elles eurent beaucoup d'enfants … et se marièrent: Histoire d'une famille homoparentale* [*The Women Had Lots of Children … and Got Married: The Story of a Same-Sex Family*] (2012); and Claire Bénard's *Prince Charmante: Que fait-on quand on tombe amoureuse d'une femme?* [*Princess Charming: What Do You Do When You Fall in Love with a Woman?*] (2013).[5] I explore not only how different same-sex families are from heterosexual families but also how and why the texts utilize claims to both sameness and difference. I begin by discussing where the texts position themselves in the sameness–difference debate outlined above. I then turn to their stances on LGBT+ identity politics.

3   Stanton, 'Contesting the Exclusive Nation and the Republican Subject', 126.
4   Scott Gunther, *The Elastic Closet: A History of Homosexuality in France, 1942–Present* (Basingstoke: Palgrave Macmillan, 2009), 1–2.
5   For an overview of the plot and genre of these texts, see the introduction to Chapter 4.

The Sameness–Difference Debate

The texts represent four main positions on the sameness–difference debate: the separatist argument, the difference-as-progressive argument, the normalizing argument and the historical argument.

Today, the legalization of same-sex marriage and adoption is widely regarded as the pinnacle of heterosexual–homosexual equality. Yet for gay separatist groups of the 1970s, such as the *Front Homosexuel d'Action Révolutionnaire* [Homosexual Front for Revolutionary Action], marriage and parenting were heterosexual norms incompatible with gay liberation. Some of the characters in the texts subscribe to this position. In *Mais qui va garder le chat?*, Cécile's former partner, Magali, regards same-sex parenting as an attempt to conform to heterosexual values: ' "[J]'ai l'impression que c'est singer les hétéros d'essayer de m'insérer dans la société en construisant une famille. Perdre une partie de mon identité" ' ['I feel it's mimicking straight people to try and integrate into society by creating a family, losing a part of my identity'] (MQV 133). Similarly, for Cécile's friend, Claire, a lesbian activist: 'Procréer c'est accepter l'hétéro-centrisme [...]. Quand on est lesbienne, on doit refuser ce schéma réducteur de la famille' [To procreate is to accept heterocentrism [...]. When one is a lesbian, one must refuse this reductive model of the family] (MQV 136). Magali and Claire represent the FHAR's claim that the essence, and liberating potential, of homosexuality is its rejection of the procreative imperative of heterosexual society.

Whereas the separatist argument assumes that parenting is necessarily heteronormative, advocates of the difference-as-progressive stance postulate that raising children does not have to mean raising them in normative ways.[6] In *Elles eurent beaucoup d'enfants*, Blanc echoes this view: 'J'ai plutôt l'impression que l'homoparentalité invente quelque chose de nouveau' [I rather feel that same-sex parenting invents something new] (HFH 80). In *Mais qui va garder le chat?*, Cécile's friend, So, makes the same point: ' "Vous [Cécile et Fanny] avez aussi tout à inventer. Vous pouvez

---

6   See, for example, Park, *Mothering Queerly, Queering Motherhood*, 9.

redistribuer les rôles. C'est une certaine liberté" ' ['You [Cécile and Fanny] have to invent everything. You can reassign the roles. It's kind of liberating'] (MQV 126). Although same-sex families are thus portrayed as potential sources of freedom from restrictive gender codes, Cécile's response betrays a certain disquiet about the unconventionality of the same-sex family: ' "Et une grande responsabilité. On n'a pas des siècles d'expérience derrière nous pour nous montrer la voie" ' ['And a big responsibility. We don't have centuries of experience behind us to show us the way'] (MQV 126). The lack of models of same-sex families supports a queer notion of kinship as performative; the fact that there is no prototype of this family configuration that Cécile and Fanny can imitate exposes the constructed nature of all family types.

Although these texts thus acknowledge that same-sex families are relatively new and still uncommon, the characters aspire and lay claim to ordinariness. *Family Pride* unambiguously affirms that the daily lives of same-sex parents and their children are no different from those in heterosexual families:

> Mieux vaut le savoir: le quotidien d'un enfant de parents homosexuels ne diffère en rien de celui d'un enfant de parents hétérosexuels. […] Mieux vaut le savoir (bis): le quotidien de parents homosexuels ne diffère en rien de celui de leurs homologues hétérosexuels. (FP 245)

> [Note: the daily life of a child with homosexual parents is in no way different from that of a child with heterosexual parents. […] Note (encore): the daily lives of homosexual parents is in no way different from those of their heterosexual counterparts.]

The emphasis on the everyday makes the characters and the same-sex families that they represent seem ordinary and relatable to readers. The novel further endeavours to normalize same-sex parenting by deploying the images and language of stereotypical parental behaviour. In one scene, for instance, Cécile explains the different seasons to Angèle and tells her about their holiday plans. Scenes such as this one encourage readers to compare their experiences of childhood and parenting with those of the character, thus normalizing same-sex families, and underline the pleasure that Cécile takes from her relationship with her child: 'J'avais naturellement beaucoup de choses à lui dire et adorais nos conversations'

[Naturally, I had a lot to say to her and loved our conversations] (FP 234). The portrayal of a lesbian mother, especially a non-biological lesbian mother, who enjoys parenting is crucial given the traditional disassociation of lesbianism and mothering. In *Elles eurent beaucoup d'enfants*, Blanc writes: 'On se sent tellement des parents comme les autres qu'on en oublie parfois qu'on est différentes' [We feel so like other parents that we sometimes forget that we are different] (HFH 61); and her daughter, Augustine, states: ' "Je trouve ça tellement normal d'avoir deux mamans que je n'en parle jamais" ' ['I find having two mums so normal that I never talk about it'] (HFH 20). Furthermore, Blanc normalizes her and her partner's desire to become parents:

> Un désir d'enfant banal donc. Un vrai désir de serrer un bébé dans ses bras, de lui faire des bisous dans le cou, de l'appeler mon amour ma chérie, mon câlin ma poupette mon canard, de le faire rire aux éclats, de l'entendre dire non et gâteau et maman et papa (euh, ça non, voir plus loin), de lui apprendre à faire du tricycle et à coller des gommettes. Comme tout le monde, eh oui!, on a choisi sur un banc public les prénoms de nos premiers bébés. Comme tout le monde. Sauf que ... On a été obligées de se poser deux questions qui n'effleurent pas la plupart des gens: 1) est-ce qu'on a le droit? 2) comment? (HFH 80)

> [A common desire to have a child, then. A real desire to hold a baby tightly in one's arms, to kiss its neck, to call it love, sweetheart, darling, dear, to make it laugh aloud, to hear it say no and cake and mum and dad (oh, no, not that, see below), to teach it to ride a bike and play with stickers. Like everyone – oh yes! – we chose our first babies' names on a public bench. Like everyone. Except ... We had to ask ourselves two questions that do not cross most people's minds: 1) do we have the right? 2) how?]

As in *Family Pride*, Blanc's description of the images and language of stereotypical parental behaviour and emphasis on the common experiences of heterosexual and lesbian parents serve to present her family as just like any other. The adjective 'banal' [common] downplays the originality of same-sex couples' desire to start a family. This strategy is also used by Célier in *Maman, Mamour* with the same effect: 'Notre projet initial n'était assurément pas d'une grande originalité: nous souhaitions seulement fonder une famille' [Our initial plan was certainly not original: we just wanted to start a family] (MM 41). Yet the resurfacing of the specificity of the same-sex family in both texts testifies to the tenacity of difference. As the above passage indicates, Blanc cannot escape the terms of the sameness–difference debate, while Célier notes that '[n]e pas avoir "une famille comme les autres" n'a [...] pas toujours été simple pour Géraldine' [not having a 'family like everyone else's' has not [...] always been simple for Géraldine] (MM 105). The texts thus take a highly nuanced stance on difference: although they lay claim to ordinariness on the whole, this does not lead to a false denial of the self-evident specificity of the same-sex family.

Moreover, Blanc repeatedly affirms that her and her partner's emotional attachment to their children is no different from that of heterosexual parents:

> Malgré cette petite mais néanmoins voyante différence, nos préoccupations sont les mêmes que celles des autres parents [...]: voir nos enfants rire, jouer, apprivoiser leur corps, leur cerveau, apprendre, vivre avec les autres, les respecter et se respecter puis rire et jouer encore. Comme presque tout le monde. En tout cas dans ce domaine-là, si spécificité il y a, elle est étrangère à notre statut sexuel. (HFH 61)

> [Despite this small but nonetheless obvious difference, our concerns are the same as those of other parents [...]: to see our children laugh, play, understand their bodies, minds, learn, live with others, respect them and respect each other, then laugh and play again. Like almost everyone. In any case, if there is something unique about us in this respect, it has no connection to our sex or sexuality.]

Blanc's use of the adjective 'petit' [small] diminishes the importance of family structure relative to the emotional commitment to one's child – a strategy that can be found elsewhere in the text: '[Notre famille] ressemble à toutes les familles, à ce détail près qu'elle compte deux mères et pas de père' [Our family is like all families, aside from the small detail that it has two mothers and no father] (HFH 7). Furthermore, Blanc also uncouples the specificities of her family from her and her partner's sexuality. In doing so, she goes beyond the limits of the traditional sameness–difference debate: instead of thinking about the differences between heterosexual and same-sex families, which rests on the normative heterosexual–homosexual binary, Blanc endorses a somewhat queer view by suggesting that alterity might be reconceived in terms other than parental sexuality. This allows for a multitude of configurations of kinship that are not based on categories of gender and sexuality. Ultimately, then, Blanc contends that family structure is less important than the desire to have children and the quality of the parent–child relationship. Girard seems to share this view, for Cécile realizes that the emphasis that she has put on the configuration of her family, rather than on her desire for it, is misguided: 'Jusque-là j'avais passé plus de temps à justifier l'existence de cet enfant, de sa conception, plutôt que de valoriser le désir qui nous animait' [Until then, I had spent more time justifying this child's existence, its conception, rather than emphasizing the desire behind it] (MQV 159). This establishes common ground between heterosexual and homosexual couples given that the desire to have children in unrelated to sexuality.

Finally, the historical argument posits that same-sex families are merely one of many phenomena contributing to the gradual deconstruction of the nuclear family. Echoing Martine Gross and other advocates of the 2013 same-sex marriage law, Célier points out that cohabitation, divorce, contraception and abortion threatened the hegemony of the nuclear family long before same-sex parenting became a visible social and cultural phenomenon.[7] She sees the sameness–difference debate as a process:

> Lorsque la sexualité de ces familles ne questionnera pas plus que celle des autres, un grand pas aura été franchi vers ce que réclament les gays et les lesbiennes, le droit à la différence d'abord, le droit à l'indifférence ensuite. Restons optimistes et souhaitons qu'on n'en parle bientôt plus que de parentalité, sans obligation de préciser s'il s'agit d'homoparentalité ou d'hétéroparentalité. (MM 135)

> [When sexuality is no more an issue for these families than it is for others, a big step will have been taken towards what gays and lesbians are calling for: firstly, the right to difference, then the right to indifference. Let us remain optimistic and wish that we will soon only talk of parenting, without it being necessary to specify whether it is same-sex or heterosexual.]

For Célier, difference is inevitable and necessary in the short term, but the long-term goal must be to look beyond difference. Célier ultimately wants her and her partner's sexuality to be 'un paramètre parmi d'autres' [one factor among others], rather than the defining feature of her family (MM

---

7   Gross, *Parent ou homo*, 12–13.

44). As such, she presents sexuality as part of a spectrum of differences and, in doing so, moves beyond the reductive heterosexual–homosexual binary. For Célier, equality will only have been achieved when the sexuality of one's parents, and of oneself, is no longer a talking point.

Although the mothers in these texts accept the obvious fact that the make-up of same-sex families differs from the heteronormative model, they ultimately emphasize that their emotional attachment to their children is the same as that of a heterosexual couple. While they therefore represent several positions on the sameness–difference debate, the overall trend is towards normalization. Célier claims that same-sex families differ from heterosexual families only in their lack of legal recognition:

> Au fil des pages, le lecteur remarquera que la vie d'une famille homoparentale est presque identique à celle d'une famille traditionnelle, en ce qui concerne leur vie quotidienne tout au moins, car tel n'est pas le cas sur le plan juridique, si l'on considère notamment la protection dont bénéficient les enfants de ces familles. (MM 14)

> [As the reader turns the pages, they will notice that the life of a same-sex family is almost identical to that of a traditional family, at least as far as their daily lives are concerned, since this is not the case at a legal level, especially if one considers the protection given to children in these families.]

In this light, the normalization of lesbian mothering can be interpreted as a strategy for the acquisition of greater legal rights for same-sex couples and families. Indeed, the allusion to the legal disparities between heterosexual and same-sex families suggests that the latter's alterity derives from their othering in a heteronormative legal system and society. *Family Pride* posits the same view. When, for example, Anna and Cécile attend a haptonomy class, the instructor is shocked when Anna informs her that Cécile will attend the birth. Cécile's wry response – 'Nul doute, la situation était inédite pour elle autant que pour nous les mystères de l'haptonomie' [No doubt the situation was as new to her as the mysteries of haptonomy were to us] (FP 202) – is perhaps a humorous way of dealing with difference and the sense of otherness.

Cinq-Fraix depicts the innocence and naivety of children to further normalize same-sex families. Given that the best interests of children are central to debates on same-sex parenting, the child's perspective may well be a strategic choice by the author. In the final chapter, the narrator's daughter, Angèle, explains to her cousin, Joseph, that she has four parents:

> Toi, tu as deux parents. Moi, j'ai quatre parents. Ma maman, c'est pas Cil, c'est Anna ma maman. Mais moi, je suis aussi la fille de Cil. Tu comprends? Toi, t'es pas mon cousin, mais t'es aussi mon cousin, tu comprends? (FP 259)

> [You have two parents. I have four parents. Cil's not my mummy, Anna's my mummy. But I'm also Cil's daughter. Understand? You're not my cousin, but you also are my cousin. Understand?]

Angèle challenges the meaning of mothering by identifying Anna as her mother while identifying herself as Cécile's daughter. Similarly, Joseph simultaneously is and is not her cousin. It is interesting that this explanation of same-sex families does not lead to an unsubtle denial of biology but to a highly nuanced view of the family. Angèle understands that kinship can be a biological tie or a relationship founded on caregiving, and Joseph's albeit delayed reaction – ' "Comme ça, oui. Alors, d'accord" ' ['When you put it that way, yes, OK'] (FP 259) – emphasizes how natural this mode of kinship seems. Contrary to claims made by the Manif pour Tous about children's best interests, Angèle and Joseph are portrayed as neither adversely affected nor disturbed by their involvement with a homosexual couple. Cinq-Fraix further utilizes the child's perspective to call for greater legal parity between heterosexual and same-sex couples, most notably same-sex marriage. Until Cécile explains otherwise, Angèle mistakenly believes that same-sex couples can get married:

> Joseph a raison, mon cœur. Des filles ne peuvent pas se marier ensemble. Parce qu'elles n'ont pas le droit. Des garçons non plus, d'ailleurs, ne peuvent pas se marier ensemble. C'est comme ça, c'est la loi. Mais tu vois, Joseph, des filles peuvent être amoureuses d'autres filles. Et des garçons amoureux de garçons. Regarde Anna et moi, par exemple, on est des amoureuses. (FP 259)

> [Joseph's right, sweetheart. Girls can't marry other girls. Because they're not allowed to. Boys can't marry other boys either. That's the way it is, it's the law. But you see, Joseph, girls can love other girls. And boys can love other boys. Look at Anna and me, for example, we love each other.]

Angèle's assumption that same-sex couples can get married illustrates the injustice of a marriage law with a heterosexual bias and functions to re-iterate how natural same-sex marriage is in the eyes of a child. Cécile is quick to affirm that homosexuals' exclusion from marriage does not preclude homosexual love; the legitimacy of desire is not dependent on institutional recognition.

The normalization of lesbian mothering for the purpose of acquiring legal rights also appears in Blanc's *Elles eurent beaucoup d'enfants*:

> Reste une taraudante question: aspirons-nous vraiment à la normalité? Je n'en suis pas très sûre. Mais il s'agit d'une boutade, évidemment, car si nous désirons convoler, ce n'est pas pour un motif de conformité [...]. Ce n'est pas non plus pour nous donner une preuve d'amour dont nous n'avons nulle nécessité, ni nous jurer une fidélité éternelle. La vraie, sinon la seule, raison de nos noces, c'est qu'ensuite nous pourrons – enfin! – adopter nos filles. (HFH 39)

> [There remains an annoying question: do we really aspire to normality? I'm not too sure. But it's a joke, obviously, because our desire to get married is not about wanting to conform [...]. Nor is it to give each other proof of our love, of which we have no need. Nor to swear eternal fidelity to each other. The real, the only, reason to get married is that we will then – finally! – be able to adopt our daughters.]

Blanc's insistence on the need for equal marriage is not a defence of the institution per se; marriage is not, she suggests, proof of fidelity or love. Rather, the appeal of marriage is the right that it will grant Blanc and her partner to adopt their non-biological daughters. In this sense, Blanc seems to support Shelley Park's position on institutional recognition: 'There is no doubt that cooperative mothering would be facilitated by transformed public policies. However, as queer theory has taught us, kinship need not (and should not) be dependent on state recognition.'[8] Although Park thus calls for the recognition of queer families at an institutional level, she contends that state recognition is not the only legitimate mode of kinship. For the same reason, Judith Butler cautions against the conflation of equality with state-endorsed modes of kinship.[9] For Butler, the focus on marriage risks reinforcing marriage as a norm, thus ostracizing

---

8   Park, *Mothering Queerly, Queering Motherhood*, 8.
9   Butler, 'Is Kinship Always Already Heterosexual?', 26.

a multitude of families created outside marriage, and accepts uncritically the state's power to confer legitimacy. It may, in Butler's view, be possible to acquire legitimacy without state mediation: 'Are there not other ways of feeling possible, intelligible, even real, apart from the sphere of state recognition? And should there not be other ways?'.[10] That said, Butler maintains that state recognition is politically valuable.[11] Unlike Park and Butler, Blanc does not go as far as challenging the state's authority to determine what constitutes a relationship, but she certainly considers marriage to be little more than a means to an end – namely, her and her partner's legal protection and the wellbeing of their daughters. Indeed, *Elles eurent beaucoup d'enfants* inverts the rhetoric of the best interests of the child, which is often used to oppose same-sex parenting, to call for the legal enshrinement of modes of kinship founded on care-giving rather than biology. Blanc recalls her daughters' distress at not being able to use their non-biological mother's surname. At the same time, Blanc demonstrates an acute, quasi-Butlerian awareness of the limitations of legal rights: '[I]l faudra sans doute plus qu'une loi pour faire évoluer les dogmes bien-pensants' [It will probably take more than a law to change narrow-minded dogma] (HFH 45). This suggests that the text itself, as part of a body of cultural representations of same-sex parenting, has a role to play in the ideological change to which Blanc refers. Literature has the power to inscribe marginalized realities and, as a result, to foster acceptance and tolerance. This quotation, then, is perhaps a statement about the importance of social and cultural visibility to the cause of same-sex parents – a point to which I will return below.

The texts also intervene in the controversial debate on fertility treatment. In France, fertility treatment has only been available to lesbian couples since 2019, so the texts were written in the context of the ongoing calls for this change to France's strict bioethics laws. In *Mais qui va garder le chat?* and *Family Pride*, the characters point out the impracticalities of arranging and financing fertility treatment abroad, thus revealing the need for the recent change to the law. *Elles eurent beaucoup d'enfants* reveals the potential

---

10   Butler, 'Is Kinship Always Already Heterosexual?', 26.
11   Butler, 'Is Kinship Always Already Heterosexual?', 28.

costs of artificial insemination with an anonymous donor, and Blanc criticizes the limitations of same-sex marriage legislation, one of which was lesbians' continued exclusion from access to fertility treatment. The bill, Blanc argues, stopped short of an overhaul of the French system of filiation:

> À l'évidence, Madame Taubira n'a pas l'intention de saisir la chance historique qui lui est offerte de devenir celle qui réformera de fond en comble le droit français de la famille. Dommage pour elle. Pas de procréation médicalement assistée (PMA): dommage pour les lesbiennes qui devront continuer à arpenter l'Europe pour faire des enfants. Pas de gestation pour autrui (GPA): dommage pour les couples de gays et les hétéros infertiles à qui on ne fait même pas l'aumône d'un débat sur le sujet. Pas de présomption de parentalité ni d'adoption pour les concubins et les pacsé(e)s: dommage pour nous. (HFH 39)

> [Plainly, Mrs Taubira has no intention of seizing the historic opportunity presented to her to become the one to reform French family law from top to bottom. Too bad for her. No fertility treatment: too bad for the lesbians who will have to continue going all over Europe to have children. No surrogacy: too bad for gay male couples and infertile straight people who are not even being given a debate on the subject. No presumption of parenthood or adoption for civil partners: too bad for us.]

Blanc exposes the limitations of the same-sex marriage law: although a big step towards equality, it reinforced the dominance of heterosexuality by prohibiting all but one of the means – adoption – through which same-sex couples can become parents. Like the PACS, which stopped short of extending parental rights to same-sex couples, the marriage law's potential to enforce complete legal parity between heterosexual and homosexual couples was curtailed to satisfy the more conservative deputies in the National Assembly. In addition, the marriage law failed to redress the French system of biologically defined filiation by withholding shared parental status from a person acting as a step-parent to his or her civil partner's child. Blanc thus calls for the legal endorsement of the care-based family forms represented in these texts.

The texts can therefore be said to foreshadow the recent politicization of same-sex parenting during the 2012 same-sex marriage campaign. Blanc exemplifies her interest in and commitment to engineering legal and political change by citing an extract from the 1994 bioethics legislation:

> *'L'homme et la femme formant le couple doivent être vivants, en âge de procréer, mariés ou en mesure d'apporter la preuve d'une vie commune d'au moins deux ans et consentants préalablement au transfert des embryons ou à l'insémination.'*

> […] Le législateur n'a même pas cru nécessaire de préciser que le couple doit être formé d'un homme et d'une femme, à ses yeux il l'est, par définition. (HFH 88)

> ['The man and woman who make up the couple must be living, of procreative age, married or able to provide evidence of a relationship of at least two years and consenting to the transfer of embryos or to the insemination.'

> […] The law did not even think it necessary to specify that the couple must be composed of a man and a woman. In its eyes, by definition, this is the case.]

The extract from the bioethics laws reveals the heteronormative discourses that define Western kinship. As we saw in Chapter 4, the heterosexual union is the gold standard against which all affective relationships are compared, and the mother–father–child triangulation the dominant mode of kinship.

The texts further expose ideas about which groups have the 'right' to have children. The fact that the bioethics laws prevented single women, as well as lesbian couples, from accessing fertility treatment reflects and reinforces the view that the heterosexual couple is the ideal parenting framework. *Mais qui va garder le chat?* goes some way towards questioning this view when Cécile's friend, a heterosexual, single woman, decides to create a child with the sperm donor used by Cécile and Fanny. For Célier, disabled and same-sex couples are less likely to receive sympathy for infertility than able-bodied, heterosexual couples:

> Devant le risque de transmettre une maladie héréditaire, beaucoup pensent qu'une stérilité naturelle serait très opportune. Les gens que l'on appelle communément normaux ont des difficultés à imaginer que des handicapés mentaux, sensoriels ou physiques souhaitent eux aussi donner la vie s'ils ont un risque réel de transmettre leur handicap. (MM 26)

> [When faced with the risk of passing on a hereditary condition, many think that being naturally infertile is highly convenient. People who are commonly referred to as normal struggle to imagine that people with mental, sensory or physical disabilities also want give life if there is a real risk of them passing on their disability.]

Similarly, '[s]'il s'agit [...] de l'infertilité due à l'impossibilité de faire un enfant au sein d'un couple homosexuel, la réflexion s'oriente différemment. La morale prend le relais des préoccupations affectives, économiques ou matérielles' [if the infertility is caused by the impossibility of creating a child within a homosexual couple, people think differently. Morality takes precedence over emotional, financial or material concerns] (MM 26–7). Célier suggests that society imposes on disabled and same-sex couples a moral duty to act in children's interests by remaining childless and, in this way, exposes how these attitudes towards infertility intersect with those towards disability and sexuality. Infertility is regarded as an obstacle to the fulfilment of able-bodied, heterosexual couples but as desirable, even necessary, for those who fall outside this group.

Gross argues that France's bioethics laws intended to preserve the normative appearance of parenting as a biogenetic process by erasing the couple's need to procreate artificially, which rendered infertility a source of shame by implying that recourse to methods of artificial conception needs to be covered up.[12] Bénard's *Prince Charmante* mocks the attempt to maintain the appearance of parenting as a biological process when Zélie and Alice travel to Barcelona to receive fertility treatment. Although Alice will have no biological connection to the child, she must go through the motions of becoming a biological parent. For instance, she must undergo the same health check undertaken by men providing sperm to a heterosexual couple, and she and Zélie must list their physical characteristics so that their baby might look like them:

> Deux colonnes. Mère. Père. Sourire. Dans chaque colonne, déclinaison d'identité, puis une trentaine de critères physiques: couleur de peau, teint, type, couleur des cheveux, des yeux, morphologie ...
>
> Il est précisé que si on nous demande tout ça, c'est pour faire en sorte que notre môme nous ressemble.
>
> 'Aaaaahhhhh?' s'amuse Alice, 'parce qu'on peut choisir la couleur de ses yeux?'
>
> 'C'est pas l'but, non. C'est pour éviter que des couples caucasiens se retrouvent avec un p'tit black. De toute façon, il faut joindre une photo de chacune.' (PC 409)

---

12   Gross, *Parent ou homo*, 80.

[Two columns. Mother. Father. Smile. In each column, self-declaration of identity, followed by thirty or so physical criteria: skin colour, complexion, look, hair and eye colour, body type …

It is stated that they are asking us all this to make sure that our kid looks like us.

'Aaaaahhhhh?' Alice joked. 'Because we can choose what colour eyes it'll have?'

'No, it's not for that. It's so that Caucasian couples don't end up with a black child. We both need to attach a photo anyway.']

Although lesbian couples have the right to access reproductive technologies in Spain, the documentation that the couple must complete reinforces heteronormative assumptions: firstly, the form presumes that the patients are male and female; and secondly, the doctor instructs Zélie to fill out the mother's form and Alice to fill out the father's. While it is perhaps reasonable, in a medical context, to see Zélie as the mother, the documentation reveals the heteronormative view of the couple and family and recalls Blanc's observation – discussed in Chapter 4 – that during her partner's pregnancy she was perceived as the 'man' in her relationship. Furthermore, the couple mock the protocol that aims to make the conception of their child appear natural when Alice ironically suggests that they can choose the baby's eye colour. In this respect, the text questions the desirability of parent–child resemblance and, therefore, the biologistic definition of kinship. On the other hand, Alice's indifference to the child's eye colour conflicts with the importance that Zélie unquestioningly attaches to its skin colour. By reiterating the norm of racial resemblance within the family, the text declines to radically deconstruct the biologistic definition of kinship. Finally, this quotation touches on deep, polemical questions about the role that technology should have in the creation and manipulation of life. If, as Alice remarks, attempting to decide the baby's eye colour is superficial, the use of fertility treatment to prevent the transmission of severe chronic illnesses, for example, is arguably in the best interests of the child and family. Bénard's text thus raises the question of what limitations, if any, should be imposed on the relationship between life and science.

Overall, the texts emphasize the common ground between heterosexual and same-sex parents. While they concede the obvious point that the

make-up of same-sex families differs from the heterosexual model, and that
this is a relatively new phenomenon, they ultimately contend that family
structure matters less than the desire to have children and the quality of
the parent–child relationship. This claim to sameness has a clear political
function: to acquire marriage and adoption rights, as well as access to fertility treatment, for same-sex couples. Interestingly, while some of the texts
recognize that same-sex families provide an opportunity to redefine gender
roles within the family, they stop short of explicitly advocating anti-sexist
or feminist parenting, to which, according to some scholars, families that
challenge the male-dominated, heterosexual family are particularly suited.[13]
Given the requirement of the French legal system to apply rights univer-
sally, the claim to sameness for the purpose of acquiring legal rights seems
effective and exposes the continued othering of same-sex families within
the French Republic at the time of the texts' publication. Perhaps this explains why the texts suggest a degree of value in identity politics.

Identity Politics

Although the texts largely refrain from subscribing to an ideological defence of difference, they suggest the need for certain identity-based rights
for same-sex families. Identity politics refers to the promotion of the interests of social groups on the grounds that these groups are, by virtue of their
identity, victims of discrimination and oppression. Central to this cause
is the groups' cultural, political and social visibility. The modern LGBT+
movement has its roots in identity politics. Early gay liberationist tracts
such as Denis Altman's *Homosexual: Oppression and Liberation* (1971)
and Jeffrey Weeks's *Coming Out* (1977), as well as modern concepts such
as gay pride, called on gays and lesbians to publicly declare their sexuality

---

13   See, for example, Colleen Mack-Canty and Sue Marie Wright, 'Feminist Family
      Values: Parenting in Third Wave Feminism and Empowering All Family Members',
      in Andrea O'Reilly, ed., *Feminist Mothering* (Albany, NY: SUNY Press, 2008),
      143–59.

in order to expose and challenge their oppression.[14] The development of queer theory since the 1990s has given rise to doubts about the effectiveness of identity politics as a force of ideological change. In *Gender Trouble*, Butler warns that identity politics is limited by its reliance on categories that serve to support normative regimes: 'The mobilization of identity categories for the purposes of politicization always remain[s] threatened by the prospect of identity becoming an instrument of the power one opposes'.[15] By taking as its starting point social groups with which people identify, identity politics presupposes the stability and universality of identity categories. Against this, Butler advocates a permanently unstable notion of identity. For Butler, identity is performatively constituted: it is the always-incomplete product, rather than a fixed prerequisite, of constantly reproducing behaviour. In Butler's view, then, political change lies not in fighting for social groups with a supposedly shared identity but in the radical critique of identity itself: if identity is performative, the norms to which we are expected to conform have no fundamental legitimacy. In *Beyond Identity Politics: Feminism, Power & Politics* (2005), Moya Lloyd rejects the assumption made by identity politics that a stable subject precedes and is independent of politics; rather, the subject 'is itself a political effect'.[16] While she acknowledges that the 'idea of "woman" and her pain has mobilized many feminist campaigns', Lloyd suggests that these campaigns do not 'act on behalf of a pre-existing subject' but, rather, 'produce a subject through their activity'.[17] For Lloyd, destabilizing the subject does not foreclose politics but, on the contrary, makes it possible. She therefore argues that feminism, instead of clinging to the belief that it requires a stable subject for the purpose of political action, must adopt a conception of the subject as permanently in-process.[18] Identity politics has also

14   Dennis Altman, *Homosexual: Oppression and Liberation* (New York: New York University Press, 1993 [1971]); Jeffrey Weeks, *Coming Out: Homosexual Politics in Britain from the Nineteenth Century to the Present*, 2nd edn (London: Quartet Books, 1990 [1977]).

15   Butler, *Gender Trouble*, xxvii–xxviii.

16   Moya Lloyd, *Beyond Identity Politics: Feminism, Power & Politics* (London: SAGE, 2005), 30.

17   Lloyd, *Beyond Identity Politics*, 5.

18   Lloyd, *Beyond Identity Politics*, 27.

been criticized for reifying differences. Even Altman and Weeks oppose the separatism of gay liberationists and concede that the movement's insistence on coming out risks ghettoizing homosexuals.[19] Yet not to come out is to remain invisible. Gross makes a similar point about the term 'homoparentalité' [same-sex parenting]: while the term's emphasis on homosexuality implicitly marks the same-sex family as different from the 'ordinary', heterosexual norm, without denomination same-sex families would struggle for visibility.[20] The desire for visibility versus the danger of self-othering is, then, the dilemma of identity politics.

A way around this paradox is Gayatri Spivak's notion of strategic essentialism or, in her words, 'a *strategic* use of positivist essentialism in a scrupulously visible political interest'.[21] Strategic essentialism, then, operates on a false notion of identity as fixed and universal in order to engineer political change. This does not preclude the nuanced vision of identity just outlined. As Lloyd argues in her study of feminism and identity politics, '[r]ecognizing that the subject is permanently in-process does not mean that politically feminists cannot act, at times, *as if* women share features in common, even an essential, unchanging womanliness'.[22]

In the present context, strategic essentialism entails falsely presenting same-sex parents as a unified category in order to secure their legal and social parity. One way to do this is through same-sex parenting associations. The formation of same-sex parenting associations, such as the *Association des Parents et Futurs Parents Gays et Lesbiens* [Association of Gay and Lesbian Parents and Future Parents], the *Association des Familles Homoparentales* [Association of Same-Sex Families], and the *Enfants d'Arc en Ciel* [Rainbow Children], testifies to the impact that same-sex couples' desire to become parents is having on French society. The APGL, the country's leading same-sex parenting association, was founded in 1986. Until the end of the 1990s, it had just seventy members. In tandem with the increasing visibility of gay and lesbian parenting at the time of the PACS debate, membership rose

19   Altman, *Homosexual*, 238; Weeks, *Coming Out*, 7.
20   Gross, *Qu'est-ce que l'homoparentalité?*, 7–8.
21   Gayatri Chakravorty Spivak, *In Other Worlds: Essays in Cultural Politics*, Routledge Classics (London: Routledge, 2006 [1987]), 281.
22   Lloyd, *Beyond Identity Politics*, 27–8.

sharply to 600 between 1996 and 1999 and to 1,500 by 2002. In 2016, the association had 2,000 fully paid-up members. The APGL aims to offer information to gay and lesbian parents and future parents and to provide a forum for the sharing of their experiences. In addition, it fights for the legal recognition of gay and lesbian families, irrespective of their mode of conception, and to end the discrimination against gay and lesbian parents and their children. Thanks to the APGL, the neologism 'homoparentalité' entered the *Petit Robert* in 2001. As a result of its political and social activism, the APGL is, with growing frequency, being consulted by politicians and the media on matters of the family, both in France and in Europe, and has, since 2015, held a position in the *Union Nationale des Associations Familiales* [National Union of Family Associations].[23]

The portrayal of same-sex parenting associations in Girard's *Mais qui va garder le chat?* and Cinq-Fraix's *Family Pride* suggests that there is still a need for strategic forms of identity politics. *Family Pride* makes explicit reference to the APGL, thus blurring the divide between fiction and reality. These associations are important because they show same-sex parents that they are not alone in their situation. Indeed, Anna takes heart from finding accounts of other same-sex parents, as she tells Cécile: ' "Nous ne sommes pas seules au monde, comme tu vas pouvoir le constater" ' ['We are not alone in the world, as you will see'] (FP 108). The information that these associations offer provides the couple with a sense that their desire to have children is both feasible and legitimate:

> Coparentalité, homoparentalité, parent biologique, parent social, parent légal …, un Nouveau Monde familial s'ouvrit alors sous mes yeux. Oui, c'était intéressant et surtout nouveau. Des études, des témoignages, une réalité, une réflexion, des actions. Tout un vocabulaire inédit que je découvrais avec curiosité. (FP 109)
>
> [Co-parenting, same-sex parenting, biological parent, social parent, legal parent … A New World of the family appeared before my eyes. Yes, it was interesting and

---

23   For details of the association's aims and membership figures, see 'L'APGL a 30 ans! 30 ans de combats et d'avancées', APGL (6 March 2016), <https://www.apgl.fr/article/item/503-30-ans-apgl-dates>, accessed 21 April 2016. The most recent membership figure was obtained through direct correspondence with the APGL.

above all new. Studies, accounts, a reality, a reflection, actions. A whole body of new
vocabulary that I was discovering curiously.]

It is significant, given that Anna discovers her pregnancy in 2000 – that
is, before the term 'homoparentalité' entered the dictionary – that the
text engages with the 'language' of same-sex parenting and that it refers to
the APGL at a time when the association had fewer than 1,000 members.
In this respect, Cécile and Anna are represented as frontrunners in becoming lesbian mothers and making same-sex families visible. Cécile and
Anna's unsuccessful internet search for same-sex parenting – amusingly,
the search engine yields no results and suggests that 'homoparentalité' is
a spelling error – is a reminder of the invisibility of this phenomenon at
the time when the novel is set. The novel goes on to cite definitions of
'homoparentalité' and 'co-parentalité':

> Homoparentalité: terme englobant plusieurs situations différentes de parentalité dans
> lesquelles au moins un parent est homosexuel: enfants nés d'une union hétérosexuelle
> antérieure, enfants adoptés, enfants nés grâce à la procréation médicalement assistée,
> insémination artificielle avec donneur ou participation d'une mère pour autrui, en-
> fants nés dans le cadre d'une coparentalité.
>
> Coparentalité: projet de parentalité impliquant un homme et une femme dont l'un
> au moins est homosexuel, et leurs partenaires éventuels. (FP 109)
>
> [Same-sex parenting: a term referring to several different parenting situations in
> which at least one parent is homosexual: children born from a previous hetero-
> sexual relationship, adopted children, children born via fertility treatment, artificial
> insemination with a donor or involvement of a surrogate mother, children born in
> a co-parenting arrangement.
>
> Co-parenting: a parenting arrangement involving a man and women, at least one of
> whom is homosexual, and their possible partners.]

In this passage, the novel develops its engagement with the jargon of
same-sex parenting. By deploying and explaining these terms, the novel
works to legitimize the social phenomenon that they represent – that is
to say, the fact that homosexuals are and aspire to be parents.

Mais qui va garder le chat?, although it too alludes to the language
of gay and lesbian parenting, also points to the limitations of this lexicon.
As we saw in Chapter 4, Fanny dismisses the term 'co-mère' [co-mother]

as ugly and mockingly compares the term 'co-parent' to the words 'co-équipier' [teammate] and 'co-propriétaire' [co-owner]. While these terms meet the needs of the social scientific literature on same-sex parenting, they are too scientific to be used as names for parents. The texts thus expose the inevitability of difference and the limitations of the language that is used to talk about same-sex parenting. Nonetheless, the incorporation of a neatly and newly coined language of same-sex parenting into the French lexicon reflects the repercussions of homosexuals' desire to become parents on wider society. The words 'homoparentalité' and its adjectival cognate 'homoparental' have no direct equivalent in English. Indeed, their possible direct translations – 'homoparentality', 'homoparenting', 'homoparenthood' and 'homoparental' – are rarely used, even in academic and activist circles. Instead, English speakers prefer to modify the root term, 'parenting', using adjectives, thereby creating terms such as 'same-sex parenting', 'LGBT+ parenting' and 'gay and lesbian parenting'. The opposing linguistic strategies for inscribing a shared phenomenon are a mark of the culturally constructed nature of kinship and of how different cultures are, on a linguistic level, dealing with, and having to deal with, the demands of gay and lesbian couples to become parents. While this might in part be attributed to the differing linguistic norms of English and French, it is interesting that the term 'same-sex parenting' – perhaps the most common translation of 'homoparentalité' – explicitly foregrounds the same-sex couple, whereas the word 'homoparentalité' underscores the homosexuality of the parent(s). On the one hand, the meaning of 'homoparentalité', which refers to any family configuration in which at least one parent is homosexual, is thus broader than that of 'same-sex parenting'. On the other hand, the French emphasis on the *homo*sexuality of the parents seems to preserve the heterosexual–homosexual binary.

Whereas *Family Pride* refers explicitly to the APGL, *Mais qui va garder le chat?* fictionalizes a same-sex parenting association, which Cécile joins. As in *Family Pride*, same-sex parenting associations give the lesbian couple a sense that their desire to become parents is legitimate. This legitimacy is vital in the context of the novels, which were published before same-sex families obtained legal recognition, and remains important even after the adoption of the marriage law, given the ongoing attempts of anti-same-sex marriage groups, most notably the Manif pour Tous, to spread negative discourses of same-sex parenting. Through the fictional association in *Mais qui va garder le chat?*, Cécile and Fanny go to a picnic organized by and for gay and lesbian parents and their families. Similarly, in *Family Pride* Anna, Cécile, Éric and Benoît receive an invitation to a gathering of would-be gay and lesbian parents. In both texts, the couples benefit from being able to meet other gay and lesbian couples with children. From the start, Cécile and Fanny have gay and lesbian friends who have children. Indeed, the novel's opening scene depicts Cécile and Fanny attending a gathering organized by their friends, Anne, Laetitia and Serge, to mark their daughter's seventh birthday. By beginning the novel in this way, Girard immediately positions her protagonists alongside another gay and lesbian family and gives the reader a sense of what will come to pass. The presence of other gay and lesbian families in the novel works also to normalize them and to create, as Cécile puts it, ' "[u]ne vraie pub" ' ['a real ad'] for same-sex families (MQV 72). Moreover, Anne participates in a documentary about same-sex parents; thus, the novel fictionalizes the increasing interest in and wider social and cultural impact of same-sex parenting, as Cécile reflects at the end of the novel: 'La cause des parents homos commençait à devenir intéressante pour les politiques' [The cause of same-sex parents was beginning to interest politicians] (MQV 211).

Although *Mais qui va garder le chat?* fictionalizes same-sex parenting networks and recognizes the entry of same-sex parenting into the political sphere at the time of publication, the narrator, Cécile, is relatively resistant to lesbian identity politics. Her and Magali's decision to be discreet about their relationship to all but their closest friends and the fact that Cécile remains closeted at work challenge gay liberationists' insistence that coming out is integral to homosexuals' emancipation. Unlike gay liberationists, Cécile sees little need to claim and proclaim a lesbian identity. Moreover, she is reluctant to join and attend the events organized by the same-sex parenting network discussed above. Most strikingly, Cécile is annoyed by her friend Claire's commitment to lesbian activism and dismisses her critique of the heterosexist and patriarchal norms that curtail expressions of lesbian sexuality. Claire laments that women, unlike men, are stigmatized if they 'pull' overtly or change sexual partners frequently; and that butch lesbians are degraded as failed men if they do not conform to norms of femininity, whereas camp gay men are branded as effeminate but not as women. Although the novel thus acknowledges the lesbian activist perspective, the narrator's immediate disavowal of this perspective suggests the novel's overall scepticism of identity politics: 'Ce discours m'agaçait. Je n'avais jamais été attirée par un militantisme quelconque et la cause lesbienne était pour moi une nébuleuse à laquelle je n'avais pas l'impression d'appartenir' [This argument annoyed me. I had never been drawn to any form of activism, and the lesbian cause was for me a bubble to which I did not feel that I belonged] (MQV 102). For some lesbian readers, it is perhaps frustrating that the novel's narrator rejects the radical stance of the character in the minor role and that Cécile's view reads more like a backlash against lesbian freedom than a queer-inspired critique of the limits of identity. Her position is, however, representative of those LGBT+ people who feel excluded by the LGBT+ scene or for whom sexuality is but one aspect of their identity and not something that they wish to politicize.

Other characters in the novel are less resistant to forms of identity politics seeking to normalize lesbianism. Anne's perspective on the talk-show in which she participates defends the merits of seeking visibility for oppressed groups: 'Elle pensait que plus on parlerait de ce genre de sujet, plus ils entreraient dans les mœurs' [She thought that the more people talked about subjects such as this, the more widely accepted they would become] (MQV 86–7). Furthermore, Fanny is willing to participate in the same-sex parenting association that Cécile resists. She is also undecided on the matter of gay and lesbian separatism. Following a scene in which Cécile's former partner and her new girlfriend are harassed, Fanny writes in her diary:

> Je n'ai jamais été confrontée à ce genre de situation. Cécile dit que c'est parce que je me protège en restant le plus possible dans un milieu homo. Si c'est vrai je m'en félicite. Je m'en veux aussi, ça me coupe des réalités. Celles de la société. Sont-elles vraiment nécessaires à affronter? Ne vaut-il pas mieux se créer sa propre réalité, un monde à soi? (MQV 64)

> [I have never been faced with this kind of situation. Cécile says that that is because I protect myself by remaining in gay circles as much as possible. If this is the case, I congratulate myself for it. I also feel bad about it; it cuts me off from the realities

of society. Is it really necessary to confront them? Is it not better to create one's own
reality, a world of one's own?]

For Fanny, gay and lesbian spaces afford her a degree of protection from
the harassment of heterosexist society. Fanny suggests the need for a specifically homosexual space where homosexuality can be practised freely.

Unlike *Mais qui va garder le chat?*, *Elles eurent beaucoup d'enfants* explicitly supports lesbian identity politics. Indeed, the very fact that Blanc
updated and republished the 2005 edition of the text testifies to her commitment to increasing the visibility of same-sex parenting. Furthermore,
Blanc explains that she briefly worked for the APGL, which suggests her
belief that same-sex parents need to be politically represented. Strikingly,
Elles eurent beaucoup d'enfants functions as a call to same-sex parents to
come out: 'Montrons-nous, et montrons-nous heureux, montrons nos
enfants épanouis, nous le leur devons bien!' [Let us show ourselves, let us
show ourselves as happy, let us show our happy children, we owe it to them!]
(HFH 52). Here, in what would be the introduction to the first edition,
Blanc insists on the need for same-sex parents to claim their identity; the
use of the first-person imperative functions almost as a call to arms and is
a mark of the collectiveness integral to identity politics. Blanc reinforces
her claim to a lesbian identity when she explains, perhaps ironically, that
she wanted to give her text the provocative title *Comment l'enfant vient
aux goudoues* [*How Lesbians*[24] *Have Children*]. Forced to renounce this
title due to its potential offensiveness, Blanc settles for writing: 'Goudoue
je suis, donc. J'ai cédé pour le titre, mais ne vous croyez pas quittes pour le
reste du livre!' [A lesbian I am, then. I gave in for the title, but do not think
that you have been let off for the rest of the book!] (HFH 53). Sarcastic
intent or not, the text's alternative title illustrates a defiance that resonates
with Blanc's defence of gay pride. Although she questions the notion of
being proud to be gay, she recognizes the need for an event that lifts the
traditional shame surrounding homosexuality. Unlike Cécile in *Mais qui*

---

24   'Goudoue' is a colloquial term for a lesbian. Blanc uses it ironically and states that it
      is preferable to 'gouine' – the French word for 'dyke'. To avoid this derogatory term
      that the author herself dislikes, I have chosen to translate 'goudoue' as 'lesbian'. As a
      result, Blanc's ironic intent is somewhat lost in translation.

va garder le chat?, Blanc opposes the need felt by some same-sex couples to hide. While she and her partner avoid public displays of affection – or 'exhibitionnisme' [exhibitionism], as Blanc puts it (HFH 60) – for fear of harassment, the specificity of their family is known to their immediate community. For Blanc:

> Si nous voulons que nos princesses soient bien dans leurs godasses d'enfants de goudoues, le moins que nous puissions faire pour elles, c'est de montrer que nous n'avons pas honte de ce que nous sommes, ni de notre famille. D'être visibles enfin. (HFH 60)

> [If we want our princesses to be happy in their boots as children of lesbians, the least we can do for them is to show that we are not ashamed of who we are or of our family. To be visible basically.]

Blanc argues that it is in her children's interests that she and her partner publicly identify with their lesbianism and that visibility is essential to establishing the legitimacy of same-sex families: 'Si nous homoparents restons des fantasmes, nous suscitons peur ou dégoût. C'est en nous montrant que nous désamorçons la bombe' [If we same-sex parents remain fantasies, we provoke fear or aversion. It is by showing ourselves that we defuse the bomb] (HFH 60).

Blanc's subscription to identity politics recalls Spivak's notion of strategic essentialism. Like Spivak, Blanc uses identity as a means through which to push for legal rights for same-sex parents. For example, Blanc insists on the need to legalize same-sex marriage and adoption in order to protect same-sex parents and their children: 'Ils ont un besoin urgent de ces droits' [They urgently need these rights] (HFH 47); 'Oui, la loi sur le mariage et l'adoption est urgente!' [Yes, the marriage and adoption law is urgent] (HFH 48). Blanc's recourse to identity aims not to group all same-sex families into an essentialist, homogeneous category – indeed, Blanc does not claim to speak for all same-sex parents or deny the specificities of all families – but to secure legal recognition for them. In her study of coming out narratives, Judith Roof criticizes the logic of strategic essentialism, arguing that it fails to account for the constructed nature of identity categories: 'Even imagining visibility as a politically effective ploy for the establishment of gay male and lesbian rights and recognition

means understanding visibility as bound up with a knowledge of identity'.[25] This view is undoubtedly inspired by queer theory's emphasis on
the performativity of identity. Roof's argument is pertinent, but Blanc's
approach also has merit in that it puts practical concerns ahead of somewhat abstract theoretical drawbacks.

The above readings are supported by the fact that, beyond the narratives, some of the authors are working hard to engrain gay and lesbian
couples' desire to become parents into the French collective imaginary.
Blanc's commitment to increasing the visibility of same-sex families is further underlined by the appearance of her story in mainstream newspapers,
magazines and on the radio, and the text has been the object of several
book signings. In an interview with Michel Duponcelle for TQ Magazine,
Blanc says that her family is, on a small scale, 'contributing to more open-
mindedness and understanding towards gays in general and same-sex families in particular'.[26] This is a statement not just about the importance of
visibility for same-sex parents but is Blanc's claim to be making an impact.
Indeed, Blanc refers at another point in the interview to her contribution to
same-sex parents' activism. The appearance of Blanc's story in mainstream
media testifies not only to the need for visibility but also to a public interest
in same-sex parents, since it is reasonable to assume that media production
is in part dictated by the interests of readers. Articles about Blanc's text
have appeared in well-reputed broadsheet newspapers, such as *France Soir*,
and the regional newspaper *Le Dauphiné Libéré*, as well as in the Belgian
newspaper *Le Soir*. The journalists' overwhelmingly positive reception of
the author and her text – the article published in *Le Soir* refers to it as 'a
delightful and powerful little book' – is evidence of changing attitudes towards homosexuality and same-sex parenting.[27] Like Blanc, Célier seems
committed to promoting the visibility of same-sex families. In 2009, she,
her partner and her daughter featured in a one-hour documentary that,

25   Judith Roof, *Come As You Are: Sexuality and Narrative* (New York: Columbia
      University Press, 1996), 146.
26   Michel Duponcelle and Myriam Blanc, 'Myriam Blanc: "et elles eurent beaucoup
      d'enfants ..."', *TQ Magazine* 237 (2005), 30–1 (31).
27   Hugues Dorzée and Jean-Pierre Borloo, 'Deux "goudoues" et un couffin', *Le Soir*
      (30 May 2005).

like Célier's text, seeks to undermine stereotypes about the negative effects of same-sex parenting on children. A story about Célier and her partner's marriage in 2013 featured in the regional newspaper *La Montagne*, and an interview with Célier was published in the gay and lesbian magazine *Têtu*.[28] Blanc's and Célier's participation in the public sphere, both as writers and in the media, reinforces the claims made in their texts about the need to make same-sex parenting visible.

Regardless of the authors' opinions on identity politics, their decision to publish their work and appearances in interviews and newspapers are ultimately ways of demanding visibility. By virtue of their very presence in the public sphere, the texts contribute to the visibility of same-sex parents. The texts have yet to receive attention from renowned literary critics, suggesting that the texts have largely appealed only to a niche market. However, on the websites of Amazon and Fnac, a leading French high-street store, a small number of readers have commented, mostly positively, on the texts and rated them four or five stars. Of course, only a fraction of readers take the time to review a text; only readers with strong feelings, positive or negative, are likely to comment, and those vehemently opposed to gay and lesbian parenting are perhaps less likely to purchase these texts. This partly explains why the reception of these texts seems positive.

The readers' reviews of these texts exhibit three principal trends that shed light on how readers are dealing with the alternative family forms presented in the texts. Firstly, and most significantly, a number of readers relate the texts' representation of lesbian mothering to the wider social and political debates on same-sex parents. For example, one reviewer of *Maman, Mamour* writes:

> The story of *Maman* and *Mamour* is highly topical. Faced with the words of protestors, this is a story full of love and tenderness. Questions are asked and tackled without taboo, and there is an attempt to offer answers.

28 Véronique Lacoste-Mettey, 'Une très longue manche de fiançailles', *La Montagne* (7 July 2013); Taina Tervonen and Brigitte Célier, '*Maman, Mamour, ses deux mamans*: Interview de Brigitte Célier', Univers-L.com (30 June 2008), <http://www.univers-l.com/maman_mamour_ses_deux_mamans_interview_brigitte_celier.html>, accessed 31 March 2017.

A lovely account that may raise the debate![29]

Similarly, a reviewer of *Family Pride* writes: 'A story describing the fight to feel like a parent, the loneliness of the characters when society abandons or rejects them'.[30] Finally, a reviewer of *Mais qui va garder le chat?* refers to it as 'a novel that is useful for the public' and that 'raises and answers many questions that the public might ask about lesbian couples and same-sex parenting'.[31] The readers' references to same-sex parenting testifies to the social and political visibility of this phenomenon in contemporary France. The review of *Mais qui va garder le chat?* is particularly significant in that it alludes to the power of literature to engineer ideological and political change. One reader of *Elles eurent beaucoup d'enfants* evokes the text's questioning of negative stereotypes about the effects of same-sex parenting on children: 'Their daughters have grown up, they are as crazy and stable as mine. They want to get married; I am getting divorced! And people say that it's gay couples who don't work properly …'.[32] Blanc's text has seemingly compelled this reader to publicly challenge the view that same-sex parenting is bad for children and that a same-sex couple cannot provide the stable environment required to raise a child. Another review echoes Blanc's own view that lesbian families are, at least in terms of the emotional attachment between parents and children, no different from other families: 'This is their story […], that of same-sex families,

29   <https://www.amazon.fr/Maman-Mamour-deux-mamans-homoparentale/dp/284337488X/ref=sr_1_1?__mk_fr_FR=ÅMÅŽÕÑ&dchild=1&keywords=maman+mamour&qid=1596558376&sr=8-1>, accessed 4 August 2020.

30   <https://www.amazon.fr/Family-Pride-Laurence-Cinq-fraix/dp/2848760567/ref=sr_1_1?__mk_fr_FR=ÅMÅŽÕÑ&dchild=1&keywords=family+pride+cinq-fraix&qid=1596558500&quartzVehicle=184-694&replacementKeywords=family+cinq-fraix&sr=8-1>, accessed 4 August 2020.

31   <https://livre.fnac.com/a16649139/Eliane-Girard-Mais-qui-va-garder-le-chat#omnsearchpos=1>, accessed 4 August 2020.

32   <https://www.amazon.fr/Elles-eurent-beaucoup-denfants-marièrent-ebook/dp/B00B2NAWKC/ref=sr_1_3?__mk_fr_FR=ÅMÅŽÕÑ&dchild=1&keywords=myriam+blac&qid=1596558931&sr=8-3-spell>, accessed 4 August 2020.

that of a family pretty much like any other.'[33] Studying readers' responses
to the texts reveals that they are keen to use their reviews as a chance to
make their own largely progressive ideological and political statements
about gay and lesbian parenting. This points to the gradual erosion of
norms of the family in contemporary France and is suggestive of the potentially positive impact of texts such as these on wider society. That said,
one particularly long review of Blanc's text illustrates the continued entrenchment of these norms. The text, this reader argues, is sexist in that
it reduces men to 'jets of sperm' and disturbs children's filiation.[34] This
reviewer justifies their conservatism by painting their argument as a defence of the rights of fathers and children and by supporting it with references to associations and texts opposed to same-sex parenting, which
they describe as a slight variation on political correctness. The reviewer
misguidedly equates Blanc's defence of lesbian mothering with an attack
on fatherhood – an interpretation that recycles patriarchal images of lesbians as women who hate men. Defending the rights of lesbian mothers
does not amount to taking away rights from fathers.

Secondly, it is notable that a handful of reviews interpreted the texts
as 'truth claims' about same-sex parenting. Although undeniably problematic – indeed, Blanc and Célier resist the interpretation of their experiences
as truth claims, instead presenting them merely as contributions to the
debate on same-sex parenting – readers' references to the 'authenticity',
'realism' and 'truth' of the works grant same-sex parents a legitimacy that
they have traditionally been denied. Moreover, they presuppose the existence of negative stereotypes that, according to readers, are rightly being
challenged. This attitude underscores the increasing acceptance of same-sex
families in contemporary France.

Finally, what becomes most evident in reading the reviews is the
pleasure that reviewers obtained simply from reading the texts. Indeed,

---

33   <https://www.amazon.fr/Elles-eurent-beaucoup-denfants-marièrent-ebook/dp/
     B00B2NAWKC/ref=sr_1_3?__mk_fr_FR=ÅMÅŽÕÑ&dchild=1&keywords=
     myriam+blac&qid=1596558931&sr=8-3-spell>, accessed 4 August 2020.

34   <https://www.amazon.fr/Elles-eurent-beaucoup-denfants-marièrent-ebook/dp/
     B00B2NAWKC/ref=sr_1_3?__mk_fr_FR=ÅMÅŽÕÑ&dchild=1&keywords=
     myriam+blac&qid=1596558931&sr=8-3-spell>, accessed 4 August 2020.

most reviewers refer to the authors' agreeable style, charm, light touch and good sense of humour. The enjoyment derived from reading these texts demonstrates that, for readers, representations of lesbian mothering serve not only to inform political and social debate but to entertain. It would be cynical to interpret this as a transformation of lesbian mothering into an object of consumption. Rather, it is surely a sign of the gradual integration of lesbian mothering into the definition of the accepted family and of the sense of legitimacy that lesbian-parent readers acquire through reading the text. Since to publish a text is, by definition, to make it public, to demand visibility, it also demonstrates the effectiveness of visibility as a force of ideological change.

Broadly, the texts suggest that identity politics is useful in the pursuit of greater visibility and specific legal rights. The same-sex parenting associations in the novels by Girard and Cinq-Fraix are portrayed as means of legitimizing the desire to become a lesbian parent. Despite its largely positive portrayal of these associations, Girard's novel is, in keeping with French universalism and its corresponding problematization of group identity, sceptical of identity politics in general. In contrast, Célier and Blanc are committed to the cause of coming out as a lesbian parent, both in the texts and in their activities beyond them.

Concluding Thoughts

Although the texts necessarily challenge the traditional notion of the family as a heterosexual unit, the lesbian mothers that they represent largely lay claim to ordinariness, specifically in relation to their desire to start a family and their relationship to their children. In this respect, the texts do not seek to radically reimagine the family but to create a space for same-sex parenting within it. This meant altering the legal framework regulating the family at the time of the texts' publication. The texts therefore call for legal change, particularly by legalizing same-sex marriage, making fertility treatment available to lesbian couples and giving a legal status to the co-mother.

To some extent, it is a pity that none of the texts offers a more radical, separatist stance on same-sex families or that they do not suggest the potentially transgressive ways in which same-sex couples might raise their children (though the absence of the latter may well be due to the texts' focus on the characters' journeys to motherhood, rather than their experience of it). However, it is worth recalling Virginie Descoutures's observation, cited in Chapter 1, that lesbian mothers generally aspire to ordinariness. In this light, the normalization of lesbian mothers in these texts probably reflects how most lesbian mothers see themselves: not as radically different but as mothers who just happen to be lesbian. It is also worth remembering Stephen Hicks's point, again noted in Chapter 1, that any sense of difference is only ever a product of dominant discourses. Assertions that same-sex families are a radical family form thus only work to prop up the dominant discourse of the family and, by extension, the othering of the same-sex family. This is not to say that all families are the same; but it is to say that differences between families are likely due to a range of factors of which sexuality is but one example.

Conclusion

The ten texts studied in this book are marked by two commonalities. Firstly, they all present families that divert from the traditional, heteronormative model. In doing so, they not only reflect recent changes in family life; they also intervene in the political debates on same-sex families that have been happening in France since the late 1990s. Secondly, they all give a voice to lesbian mothers and thus offer some insight into what it means to be a lesbian mother in twenty-first-century France. By exposing the challenges of being a lesbian mother, as in the texts examined in earlier chapters, or demanding equal rights and treatment more explicitly, as in those analysed in later chapters, this is literature that strives to make a difference.

How, then, do these texts reimagine the family? Clearly, they challenge the heteronormative assumption that the family is an inherently heterosexual unit. On a deeper level, though, the range of family forms represented even in this relatively small corpus shows that same-sex families are not reducible to a singular, unitary category. The texts by François, Monferrand, Mallet and Dumont portray women who are or will become lesbian but who have children in a heterosexual relationship. These narratives primarily centre on the difficulty of being an openly lesbian mother in a homophobic and patriarchal context. Importantly, though, in all these texts the mother is ultimately able to assume her sexuality, and her lesbian lover is positioned as, or at least imagined to be, a step-parent to her children. This is an important step towards the planned lesbian families portrayed by Girard, Cinq-Fraix, Célier, Blanc and Bénard. By representing families headed by a lesbian couple, these authors challenge not only the equation of the family with heterosexuality but also the longstanding image of the father as head of the family and the traditional understanding of the family as a biological unit, which is particularly significant given the emphasis placed on the supposed biological basis of the family by opponents of same-sex marriage and families in France. In contrast, these authors portray the family as a social unit founded on care-giving as well as biology. This reflects, and perhaps builds on, the turn in much feminist and queer theory towards the idea of gender and sexuality as social constructs rather than biological givens. Despite these shared features, the texts by Girard, Cinq-Fraix, Célier, Blanc and Bénard are different in several ways, the most significant of which is the presence or absence of father figures. Whereas the couples in Girard's, Blanc's and Bénard's texts choose to become parents without a present father, Cinq-Fraix's and Célier's couples decide that the father needs to be involved in their child's life. For Cinq-Fraix's couple, this means becoming parents with a gay couple. Taken together, the texts studied in this book demonstrate the multiple ways of forming and living in a homosexual family, and this suggests the limitations of thinking about the same-sex family as a singular, essentializing entity, especially if done so in opposition to an equally reductive notion of *the* heterosexual family. Collectively, the texts emphasize the plurality of the family in France today.

The fact that the texts present families that differ significantly from the heterosexual, biology-based, nuclear family does not, however, translate into the use of difference as a political position. They reimagine the family but tend to underline the common ground between all families, particularly in terms of the desire to have and love a child. Célier and Blanc frequently lay claim to ordinariness, trivializing their wish to start a family and emphasizing that their children are happy, healthy and loved. On this basis, they also call for the equal rights that were lacking at the time of the texts' publication. Blanc is particularly insistent on this point, arguing that same-sex marriage is in the best interests of children in same-sex families, while Girard explores the negative impact of unequal rights on the non-biological mother. Another way in which the texts emphasize the common ground between all families is their treatment of themes that potentially affect all mothers, regardless of their sexuality. From Mallet's exploration of the relationships between mothers and daughters and between children and step-parents, to Monferrand's representation of maternal ambivalence, to Bénard's references to the gendered division of unpaid labour, these texts show that while a mother's sexuality is important and interesting, it is but one factor that shapes the experience of mothering. This strongly indicates a broad resistance to those who would argue that same-sex families provide a radical alternative to the heterosexual norm. Rather, the attempts by the authors to normalize lesbian mothers and same-sex families suggest their belief that there is more to be gained from focusing on similarities rather than differences and a strong scepticism of the existence of, and need for, a same-sex specificity.

On a less positive note, the difficulties faced by the lesbian mothers in these texts speak volumes about the challenges of lesbian mothers living in contemporary France. In addition to the lack of legal recognition for same-sex families, the characters must confront the arguments used to oppose same-sex families at the time of the same-sex marriage debate. The claim that children need a mother and a father and references to 'real', defined as biological, mothers resurface in these texts, and the fact that the lesbian mothers themselves initially struggle with these ideas indicates how powerful and widespread they are.

Given that opposition to same-sex families is usually just homophobia disguised as concern for the welfare of children, it is perhaps unsurprising that some of the challenges facing the lesbian mothers in these texts extend to lesbians without children. The pressure felt by the characters in the texts by François, Mallet and Dumont to end their lesbian relationships testifies to the obstacles preventing love between women. Even in Monferrand's novels, in which the lesbian characters are readily accepted by those within their social circle, lesbianism is not affirmed publicly. Bénard reveals the aversion to lesbianism in society, while Dumont explores the invisibility of lesbianism and lack of lesbian social spaces. Girard and Cinq-Fraix present a range of coming out experiences, testifying to the varying degrees to which homosexuality is accepted by members of the family. The challenges facing the lesbian characters in these texts are a reminder that, despite the extension of rights and recognition to LGBT+ people in recent years, being LGBT+ remains far from straightforward. The representation of homophobia is, perhaps, a call not to forget or overlook the struggles of LGBT+ people.

In addition to representing a range of family forms, the texts cover an impressive variety of literary genres, from autobiography to popular fiction. Interestingly, the texts by Célier and Blanc suggest that autobiography has a potentially significant role in the literary representation of lesbian families and other non-normative experiences of parenting.[1] This points to a desire among mothers who mother outside the norm to voice their experiences and, perhaps, a need to raise awareness among readers. Turning to the popular fiction novels, the broadly conventional form adopted by Girard, Cinq-Fraix and Mallet might be read as a further attempt to normalize same-sex parenting. The autobiographical and popular fiction texts share a somewhat didactic function. In Célier's and Blanc's cases, this is self-declared; in the novels by Girard and Cinq-Fraix, this occurs through conversations in which the characters act as mouthpieces for positions, conservative and progressive, in the debates on same-sex families.

It is hoped that this book will act as a springboard for further research on non-normative family forms in French literature. However, the exact focus of this research is to a large extent dependent on how the French literary landscape evolves. For instance, an obvious starting point would be to examine narratives of gay fathering, but these are currently few and far between. This may be because, on a demographic level, there are fewer gay fathers than lesbian mothers, and this in turn may be due to the more considerable legal and social obstacles facing gay couples who want children relative to those facing lesbian couples. Surrogacy is currently illegal in France, meaning that would-be gay fathers have to travel abroad. Added to this is the fact that, for some, gay fathering is less acceptable than lesbian mothering due to the traditional idealization of the maternal role.[2] Gay men and lesbians therefore face slightly different challenges when becoming parents, so research on literary portrayals of gay fathering is likely to expose different norms of the family and how literature is challenging

---

1   See, for example, Karine Degunst, *Félicitations, c'est une FIV! Le parcours drôle et vrai d'une PMA heureuse* (Paris: Pixl, 2015); Sandrine Derohr, *PMA pour mon ange* (Nantes: Amalthée, 2015); Amandine Forgali, *Un GPS pour la cigogne*, 2 vols (Paris: Terriciae/Forgali, 2011–13); Mireille Margarito, *Une vie à t'espérer: Mon combat pour être mère* (Paris: Michalon, 2014); Martine Silberstein, *Ma princesse est atteinte de leucodystrophie: Témoignage d'une mère à sa fille* (Paris: L'Harmattan, 2010).

2   Martine Gross, Danielle Boyer and Sandrine Dauphin, 'Penser la paternité en dehors du lien à la maternité: Un questionnement à partir de la paternité gay', *Informations sociales* 176 (2013), 76–85 (83–4).

them. Work on bisexual and transgender parents would be equally valuable and welcome, if the literary landscape permitted it. Another potentially fruitful avenue for future research is to take the argument made in this book that the family is a social, as well as biological, unit as a starting point for looking at other forms of non-biological parenting, such as adoptive and step-parent families, as well as the extended family. A crucial point made by the texts in this study is that the family is not reducible to the biology-based mother–father–child triangulation. The novels by Girard, Cinq-Fraix and Mallet show the role of grandparents in the family, while the many texts that envisage the lesbian mother's lover as a potential step-parent highlight how common this parental role is today. By examining literary portrayals of other family forms, future studies can shed greater light on how litera-ture is reimagining the family on levels other than gender and sexuality.

This book has also highlighted the ongoing need to engage with LGBT+ literature more generally. Recent legal changes, notably same-sex marriage, have created a new context for LGBT+ literary expression – a context not just of tolerance but of recognition. On the other hand, the difficulties of being openly lesbian and the range of coming out experiences represented in the texts in this study should remind us not to take accept-ance of LGBT+ people for granted. With this in mind, it is worth asking how far twenty-first-century literary representations of LGBT+ identities are evolving in tandem with these legal changes. Do authors represent LGBT+ characters who lay claim to these rights, or are they seen as un-necessary? Do they create characters who deliberately position themselves outside the mainstream? Given the recent visibility of queer sexualities in the mainstream, studies aiming to explore literary depictions of sexual identities and practices that transcend the heterosexual–homosexual di-chotomy would also be most interesting.

Finally, it is probable that this book will need to be extended in the future. Although still relatively rare, texts focusing on lesbian mothering are likely to become more numerous. This is a theme still in its infancy and will therefore need to be revisited as the corpus expands and diversifies. A possible evolution is the emergence of lesbian-parented children as au-thors of or characters in the texts. Of the texts studied in this book, only the novels by Monferrand and Mallet feature children with a significant role. As real-life lesbian-parented children grow up, they are likely to claim a literary voice of their own. Moreover, despite this book's focus on contemporary literature, it is clear that the social, legal and political landscape has changed dramatically since the texts studied in this book were published. With the legalization of same-sex marriage and adoption in 2013 and the right to access fertility treatment granted in 2019, many of the obstacles facing the lesbian mothers in these texts were removed. Writing about lesbian mothering in the 2020s is thus markedly different from writing about lesbian mothering just a decade ago. This fast-changing backdrop makes for an exciting context for literary creation and criticism.

Bibliography

Altman, Claire, *Deux femmes et un couffin* (Paris: Ramsay, 2005).

Altman, Dennis, *Homosexual: Oppression and Liberation* (New York: New York University Press, 1993 [1971]).

Angot, Christine, *Interview* (Paris: Fayard, 1995).

'L'APGL a 30 ans! 30 ans de combats et d'avancées', APGL (6 March 2016), <https://www.apgl.fr/article/item/503-30-ans-apgl-dates>, accessed 21 April 2016.

Badinter, Élisabeth, *L'Amour en plus: Histoire de l'amour maternel, XVIIᵉ–XXᵉ siècle* (Paris: Flammarion, 1980).

——, *Le Conflit: La femme et la mère* (Paris: Flammarion, 2010).

Barthes, Roland, 'La Mort de l'Auteur' (1968), in Éric Marty, ed., *Œuvres complètes*, 5 vols (Paris: Seuil, 1993–2002), II (1994), 491–5.

——, *The Pleasure of the Text*, trans. Richard Miller (New York: Hill and Wang, 1975 [1973]).

Beauvoir, Simone de, *Le Deuxième Sexe: L'Expérience vécue*, Folio Essais, 38 (Paris: Gaillmard, 1976 [1949]).

Bénard, Claire, *Prince Charmante: Que fait-on quand on tombe amoureuse d'une femme?* (Paris: La Boîte à Pandore, 2013).

Béraud, Céline, 'Un front commun des religions contre le mariage pour tous?', *Contemporary French Civilization* 39/3 (2014), 335–49.

Blanc, Myriam, *Elles eurent beaucoup d'enfants … et se marièrent: Histoire d'une famille homoparentale*, new edn (Marseille: Le bec en l'air, 2012 [2005]).

——, '*Et elles eurent beaucoup d'enfants … Histoire d'une famille homoparentale*: témoignage ou "roman vrai"?', unpublished paper given at 'LGBT and Parenting: An Emerging Theme?', Institute of Modern Languages Research, University of London, 19 October 2018.

Borrillo, Daniel, 'Biologie et filiation: les habits neufs de l'ordre naturel', *Contemporary French Civilization* 39/3 (2014), 303–19.

——, 'La vérité biologique contre l'homoparentalité: le statut du beau-parent ou le "PaCS de la filiation"', *Droit et société* 72 (2009), 361–71.

Bos, Henny M. W., *Parenting in Planned Lesbian Families* (Amsterdam: Amsterdam University Press, 2004).

——, and Frank van Balen, 'Children in Planned Lesbian Families: Stigmatisation, Psychological Adjustment and Protective Factors', *Culture, Health & Sexuality: An International Journal for Research, Invention and Care* 10/3 (2008), 221–36.

Boutignon, Béatrice, *Tango a deux papas, et pourquoi pas?* (Issy-les-Moulineaux: Le Baron Perché, 2010).

Breton, Claire, *J'ai 2 mamans, c'est un secret* (Paris: Leduc.s, 2005).

Brisac, Geneviève, *Week-end de chasse à la mère* (Paris: Éditions de l'Olivier, 1996).

Butler, Judith, *Gender Trouble: Feminism and the Subversion of Identity*, Routledge Classics, 2nd edn (London: Routledge, 2007 [1990]).

——, 'Is Kinship Always Already Heterosexual?', *differences: A Journal of Feminist Cultural Studies* 13/1 (2002), 14–44.

Cadoret, Anne, *Des parents comme les autres: Homosexualité et parenté* (Paris: Odile Jacob, 2002).

Cairns, Lucille, *Lesbian Desire in Post-1968 French Literature* (Lewiston, NY: Edwin Mellen, 2002).

——, *Marie Cardinal: Motherhood and Creativity* (Glasgow: University of Glasgow Press, 1992).

Cameron, Paul, 'Children of Homosexuals and Transsexuals More Apt to Be Homosexual', *Journal of Biosocial Science* 38/3 (2006), 413–18.

Campbell, Elizabeth, 'Re-visions, Re-flections, Re-creations: Epistolarity in Novels by Contemporary Women', *Twentieth Century Literature* 41/3 (1995), 332–48.

Célier, Brigitte, *Maman, Mamour, ses deux mamans: Grandir dans une famille homoparentale* (Paris: Anne Carrière, 2008).

Cervulle, Maxime, 'Les Controverses autour du "mariage pour tous" dans la presse nationale quotidienne: du différentialisme ethno-sexuel comme registre d'opposition', *L'Homme & la Société* 189–90 (2013), 207–22.

Chodorow, Nancy, *The Reproduction of Mothering: Psychoanalysis and the Sociology of Gender* (Berkeley: University of California Press, 1978).

Cinq-Fraix, Laurence, *Family Pride* (Paris: Philippe Rey, 2006).

Cixous, Hélène, 'The Laugh of the Medusa', trans. Keith Cohen and Paula Cohen, *Signs: Journal of Women in Culture and Society* 1/4 (1976 [1975]), 875–93.

——, 'Le Rire de la Méduse', *L'Arc* 61 (1975), 39–54.

Dally, Ann, *Inventing Motherhood: The Consequences of an Ideal* (London: Burnett, 1982).

Davis, James D., Jr, *Beautiful War: Uncommon Violence, Praxis, and Aesthetics in the Novels of Monique Wittig* (New York: Peter Lang, 2010).

Degunst, Karine, *Félicitations, c'est une FIV! Le parcours drôle et vrai d'une PMA heureuse* (Paris: Pixl, 2015).

Delphy, Christine, 'Proto-féminisme et anti-féminisme', *Les Temps modernes* 346 (1975), 1469–1500.

Derohr, Sandrine, *PMA pour mon ange* (Nantes: Amalthée, 2015).

Descoutures, Virginie, *Les Mères lesbiennes* (Paris: PUF, 2010).

Despentes, Virginie, 'A terme' (1995), in *Mordre au travers* (Paris: Librio, 1999), 61–3.

Dorzée, Hugues, and Jean-Pierre Borloo, 'Deux "goudoues" et un couffin', *Le Soir* (30 May 2005).

Douru, Muriel, *Deux mamans et un bébé* (Paris: KTM, 2011 [2008]).

——, *Dis … mamanS* (Paris: Éditions Gaies et Lesbiennes, 2003).

Downing, Jordan B., and Abbie E. Goldberg, 'Lesbian Mothers' Constructions of the Division of Paid and Unpaid Labor', *Feminism and Psychology* 21/1 (2011), 100–20.

Dumont, Paula, *La Vie dure: Éducation sentimentale d'une lesbienne* (Paris: L'Harmattan, 2010).

Duponcelle, Michel, and Myriam Blanc, 'Myriam Blanc: "et elles eurent beaucoup d'enfants …"', *TQ Magazine* 237 (2005), 30–1.

Duthel, Yean-Yves, *Deux hommes et trois couffins: Une tranche de vie réelle* (Saint-Zénon, Québec: Louise Courteau, 2013).

Edwards, Natalie, 'Babykillers: Véronique Olmi and Laurence Tardieu on Motherhood', in Amaleena Damlé and Gill Rye, eds, *Women's Writing in Twenty-First-Century France: Life as Literature* (Cardiff: University of Wales Press, 2013), 98–110.

——, *Shifting Subjects: Plural Subjectivity in Contemporary Francophone Women's Autobiography* (Newark: University of Delaware Press, 2011).

——, *Voicing Voluntary Childlessness: Narratives of Non-Mothering in French* (Oxford: Peter Lang, 2016).

'Emma', 'Fallait demander', (9 May 2017), <https://emmaclit.com/2017/05/09/repartition-des-taches-hommes-femmes/>, accessed 20 June 2017.

Engelking, Tama Lea, 'Renée Vivien and The Ladies of the Lake', *Nineteenth-Century French Studies* 30/3–4 (2002), 362–79.

Fassin, Éric, 'Same-Sex Marriage, Nation, and Race: French Political Logics and Rhetorics', *Contemporary French Civilization* 39/3 (2014), 281–301.

Fell, Alison S., *Liberty, Equality, Maternity in Beauvoir, Leduc and Ernaux* (Oxford: Legenda, 2003).

Fillod, Odile, 'L'invention de la "théorie du genre": Le mariage blanc du Vatican et de la science', *Contemporary French Civilization* 39/3 (2014), 321–33.

Firestone, Shulamith, *The Dialectic of Sex* (London: Cape, 1971 [1970]).

Fisher, Dominique D., 'A propos du "Rachildisme" ou Rachilde et les lesbiennes', *Nineteenth-Century French Studies* 31/3–4 (2003), 297–310.

Follet, Fanny, and Hélène de Monferrand, 'La Trilogie d'Hélène vingt ans après', *Lesbia* (2010), <https://fr.calameo.com/read/0030409913326df5f2847>, accessed 26 January 2019.

Forgali, Amandine, *Un GPS pour la cigogne*, 2 vols (Paris: Terriciae/Forgali, 2011–13).

Fraisse, Geneviève, and Michelle Perrot, eds, *Histoire des femmes en Occident: Le XIXᵉ siècle* (Paris: Perrin, 2002 [1991]).

François, Jocelyne, *Les Bonheurs* ([n.p.]: Lacombe, 1982 [1970]).

——, *Joue-nous 'España'* (Paris: Mercure de France, 1980).

Freud, Sigmund, 'Three Essays on the Theory of Sexuality' (1905), in Elisabeth Young-Bruehl, ed., *Freud on Women: A Reader* (London: Hogarth, 1990), 89–145.

Friedan, Betty, *The Feminine Mystique* (London: Norton, 2001 [1963]).

Frosh, Stephen, *The Politics of Psychoanalysis: An Introduction to Freudian and Post-Freudian Theory*, 2nd edn (Basingstoke: Macmillan, 1999 [1987]).

Fulcher, Megan, Raymond W. Chan, Barbara Raboy, and Charlotte J. Patterson, 'Contact with Grandparents among Children Conceived via Donor Insemination by Lesbian and Heterosexual Mothers', *Parenting: Science and Practice* 2/1 (2002), 61–76.

——, Erin L. Sutfin, and Charlotte J. Patterson, 'Individual Differences in Gender Development: Associations with Parental Sexual Orientation, Attitudes, and Division of Labor', *Sex Roles* 58/5 (2008), 330–41.

Garnier, Éric, *L'Homoparentalité en France: La Bataille des nouvelles familles* (Vincennes: Thierry Marchaisse, 2012).

Gasparini, Philippe, *Est-il je? Roman autobiographique et autofiction* (Paris: Seuil, 2004).

Gibson, Margaret F., ed., *Queering Motherhood: Narrative and Theoretical Perspectives* (Bradford, ON: Demeter, 2014).

Giorgio, Adalgisa, ed., *Writing Mothers and Daughters: Renegotiating the Mother in Western European Narratives by Women* (New York: Berghahn, 2002).

Girard, Éliane, *Mais qui va garder le chat?* (Paris: JC Lattès, 2005).

Goldsmith, Elizabeth C., ed., *Writing the Female Voice: Essays on Epistolary Literature* (London: Pinter, 1989).

Gross, Martine, 'Être grand-parent dans un contexte homoparental en France: Chassez le biologique par la porte, il revient par la fenêtre', *Recherches féministes* 22/2 (2009), 69–76.

——, *Parent ou homo, faut-il choisir? Idées reçues sur l'homoparentalité* (Paris: Le Cavalier Bleu, 2013).

——, *Qu'est-ce que l'homoparentalité?* (Paris: Payot & Rivages, 2012).

——, Danielle Boyer, and Sandrine Dauphin, 'Penser la paternité en dehors du lien à la maternité: Un questionnement à partir de la paternité gay', *Informations sociales* 176 (2013), 76–85.

Gunther, Scott, *The Elastic Closet: A History of Homosexuality in France, 1942–Present* (Basingstoke: Palgrave Macmillan, 2009).

——, 'Making Sense of the Anti-Same-Sex-Marriage Movement in France', *French Politics, Culture & Society* 37/2 (2019), 131–58.

Hall, Stuart, ed., *Representation: Cultural Representations and Signifying Practices* (London: SAGE, 1997).

Hanscombe, Gillian, and Jackie Forster, *Rocking the Cradle: Lesbian Mothers: A Challenge in Family Living* (London: Owen, 1981).

Herbrand, Cathy, 'Les rendre grands-parents: l'enjeu des relations intergénération-nelles au sein de coparentalités gaies et lesbiennes en Belgique', in Jérôme Courduriès and Agnès Fine, eds, *Homosexualité et parenté* (Paris: Armand Colin, 2014), 175–88.

Herrera, Cristina, '"The Girls Our Mothers Warned Us About": Rejection, Redemption, and the Lesbian Daughter in Carla Trujillo's *What Night Brings*', *Women's Studies: An Interdisciplinary Journal* 39/1 (2009), 18–36.

Hicks, Stephen, *Lesbian, Gay, and Queer Parenting: Families, Intimacies, Genealogies* (Basingstoke: Palgrave Macmillan, 2011).

Hirsch, Marianne, *The Mother/Daughter Plot: Narrative, Psychoanalysis, Feminism* (Bloomington: Indiana University Press, 1989).

Holmes, Diana, 'The Comfortable Reader: Romantic Bestsellers and Critical Disdain', *French Cultural Studies* 21/4 (2010), 287–96.

——, *French Women's Writing, 1848–1994* (London: Athlone, 1996).

——, *Romance and Readership in Twentieth-Century France: Love Stories* (Oxford: Oxford University Press, 2006).

Honoré, Christophe, *Ton père* (Paris: Mercure de France, 2017).

Hughes, Alex, *Violette Leduc: Mothers, Lovers, and Language* (London: W.S. Maney/MHRA, 1994).

Irigaray, Luce, 'And the One Doesn't Stir without the Other', trans. Hélène Vivienne Wenzel, *Signs: Journal of Women in Culture and Society* 7/1 (1981), 60–7.

——, 'The Bodily Encounter with the Mother', trans. David Macey, in Margaret Whitford, ed., *The Irigaray Reader* (Oxford: Blackwell, 1991), 34–46.

——, *Ce sexe qui n'en est pas un* (Paris: Minuit, 1977).

——, *Le Corps-à-corps avec la mère* (Montreal: La Pleine Lune, 1981).

——, *Et l'une ne bouge pas sans l'autre* (Paris: Minuit, 1979).

——, 'Petite annonce: Égales ou différentes?' (1990), in *Je, tu, nous: Pour une culture de la différence* (Paris: Grasset, 1990), 9–15.

——, 'Pourquoi définir des droits sexués?' (1988), in *Je, tu, nous: Pour une culture de la différence* (Paris: Grasset, 1990), 101–15.

Jensen, Katherine A., 'Male Models of Feminine Epistolarity; or, How to Write Like a Woman in Seventeenth-Century France', in Elizabeth C. Goldsmith, ed., *Writing the Female Voice: Essays on Epistolary Literature* (London: Pinter, 1989), 25–45.

Jones, Ann Rosalind, 'Writing the Body: Toward an Understanding of "L'Ecriture Feminine"', *Feminist Studies* 7/2 (1981), 247–63.

Jones, Elizabeth H., *Spaces of Belonging: Home, Culture and Identity in 20th-Century French Autobiography* (Amsterdam: Rodopi, 2007).

Jordan, Shirley-Ann, 'Figuring Out the Family: Family as Everyday Practice in Contemporary French Women's Writing', in Marie-Claire Barnet and Edward Welch, eds, *Affaires de familles: The Family in Contemporary French Culture and Theory* (Amsterdam: Rodopi, 2007), 39–58.

Juhasz, Suzanne, 'Lesbian Romance Fiction and the Plotting of Desire: Narrative Theory, Lesbian Identity, and Reading Practice', *Tulsa Studies in Women's Literature* 17/1 (1998), 65–82.

Julien, Danielle, Marie-France Bureau, and Annie Leblond de Brumath, 'Grand-parentalité et homoparentalité au Québec: Nouvelles dispositions législatives et proximité des liens en fonction de la composition familiale', in Benoît Schneider, Marie-Claude Mietkiewicz, and Sylvain Bouyer, eds, *Grands-parents et grands-parentalités* (Ramonville Sainte-Agne: Érès, 2005), 199–217.

Klein, Melanie, 'Early Stages of the Oedipus Conflict' (1928), in *'Love, Guilt and Reparation' and Other Works, 1921–1945* (London: Vintage, 1998 [1975]), 186–98.

Knibiehler, Yvonne, and Catherine Fouquet, *L'Histoire des mères du Moyen Âge à nos jours* (Paris: Montalba, 1980).

Kristeva, Julia, 'Stabat Mater' (1977), in *Histoires d'amour* (Paris: Denoël, 1983), 225–47.

Kurdek, Lawrence A., 'The Allocation of Household Labor by Partners in Gay and Lesbian Couples', *Journal of Family Issues* 28/1 (2007), 132–48.

Laclos, Choderlos de, *Les Liaisons dangereuses*, Le Livre de Poche (Paris: Librairie Générale Française, 2002 [1782]).

Lacoste-Mettey, Véronique, 'Une très longue manche de fiançailles', *La Montagne* (7 July 2013).

Lacroix, Xavier, '"Une mesure discriminatoire pour l'enfant"', (7 January 2013) <http://www.eglise.catholique.fr/actualites/dossiers/dossiers-2013/le-mariage-pour-tous/359669-une-mesure-discriminatoire-pour-lenfant/>, accessed 2 February 2017.

Laurens, Camille, *Philippe* (Paris: P.O.L., 1995).

Lawler, Steph, 'Stories and the Social World', in Michael Pickering, ed., *Research Methods for Cultural Studies* (Edinburgh: Edinburgh University Press, 2008), 32–49.

Leclerc, Annie, *Parole de femme* (Paris: Grasset, 1974).

Lejeune, Philippe, *Le Pacte autobiographique*, new edn (Paris: Seuil, 1995 [1975]).

Lerner, Sasha, and Ada L. Sinacore, 'Lesbian Mother–Heterosexual Daughter Relationships: Toward a Postmodern Feminist Analysis', *Journal of GLBT Family Studies* 8/5 (2012), 446–64.

Lloyd, Moya, *Beyond Identity Politics: Feminism, Power & Politics* (London: SAGE, 2005).

Lyonette, Clare, and Rosemary Crompton, 'Sharing the Load? Partners' Relative Earnings and the Division of Domestic Labour', *Work, Employment and Society* 29/1 (2015), 23–40.

MacArthur, Elizabeth J., *Extravagant Narratives: Closure and Dynamics in the Epistolary Form* (Princeton, NJ: Princeton University Press, 1990).

Mack-Canty, Colleen, and Sue Marie Wright, 'Feminist Family Values: Parenting in Third Wave Feminism and Empowering All Family Members', in Andrea O'Reilly, ed., *Feminist Mothering* (Albany, NY: SUNY Press, 2008), 143–59.

Mallaval, Catherine, 'Adoption pour tous: les juges récalcitrants prennent une claque', *Libération* (16 April 2015), <http://next.liberation.fr/vous/2015/04/16/adoption-pour-tous-les-juges-recalcitrants-prennent-une-claque_1243918>, accessed 15 February 2019.

Mallet, Axelle, *Le Choix de la reine* (Paris: KTM, 2009).

Margarito, Mireille, *Une vie à t'espérer: Mon combat pour être mère* (Paris: Michalon, 2014).

Moi, Toril, *Sexual/Textual Politics: Feminist Literary Theory*, 2nd edn (London: Routledge, 2002 [1985]).

Monferrand, Hélène de, *Les Amies d'Héloïse*, Le Livre de Poche (Paris: Fallois, 1990).

——, *Les Enfants d'Héloïse* (Paris: La Cerisaie, 2002 [1997]).

——, *Journal de Suzanne* (Paris: Fallois, 1991).

Nordqvist, Petra, ' "I've Redeemed Myself by Being a 1950s 'Housewife' ": Parent–Grandparent Relationships in the Context of Lesbian Childbirth', *Journal of Family Issues* 36/4 (2015), 480–500.

Oakley, Ann, *From Here to Maternity: Becoming a Mother* (Harmondsworth: Penguin, 1986 [1979]).

——, *Housewife* (Harmondsworth: Penguin, 1976 [1974]).

——, *The Sociology of Housework* (London: Martin Robertson, 1974).

Olmi, Véronique, *Bord de mer* (Paris: Actes Sud, 2001).

O'Reilly, Andrea, ed., *Feminist Mothering* (Albany, NY: SUNY Press, 2008).

——, ed., *From Motherhood to Mothering: The Legacy of Adrienne Rich's 'Of Woman Born'* (Ithaca, NY: SUNY Press, 2004).

——, ed., *Mother Outlaws: Theories and Practices of Empowered Mothering* (Toronto: Women's Press, 2004).

——, 'Mothering against Motherhood and the Possibility of Empowered Mothering for Mothers and Their Children', in Andrea O'Reilly, ed., *From Motherhood to Mothering: The Legacy of Adrienne Rich's 'Of Woman Born'* (Ithaca, NY: SUNY Press, 2004), 159–74.

——, ed., *Twenty-First-Century Motherhood: Experience, Identity, Policy, Agency* (New York: Columbia University Press, 2010).

Parachini-Deny, Juliette, and Marjorie Béal, *Mes deux papas* (Nice: Tom'poche, 2015 [2013]).

Park, Shelley M., *Mothering Queerly, Queering Motherhood: Resisting Monomaternalism in Adoptive, Lesbian, Blended, and Polygamous Families* (Albany, NY: SUNY Press, 2013).

Parker, Rozsika, *Torn in Two: The Experience of Maternal Ambivalence* (London: Virago, 1995).

Patterson, Charlotte J., 'Children of Lesbian and Gay Parents', *Child Development* 63/5 (1992), 1025–42.

——, Erin L. Sutfin, and Megan Fulcher, 'Division of Labor among Lesbian and Heterosexual Parenting Couples: Correlates of Specialized versus Shared Patterns', *Journal of Adult Development* 11/3 (2004), 179–89.

Patterson, Yolanda Astarita, *Simone de Beauvoir and the Demystification of Motherhood* (Ann Arbor, MI: UMI Research, 1989).

Payne, Robert, 'Lesbianism and Maternal Ambivalence in Hélène de Monferrand's *Les Amies d'Héloïse* (1990) and *Les Enfants d'Héloïse* (1997)', *Revue critique de fixxion française contemporaine* 12 (2016), 120–9.

Pellegrino, Pascal, *Papa gay: Lettre à mon enfant interdit* (Lausanne: Favre, 2009).

Perreau, Bruno, *Queer Theory: The French Response* (Stanford, CA: Stanford University Press, 2016).

Rich, Adrienne, 'Compulsory Heterosexuality and Lesbian Existence', *Signs: Journal of Women in Culture and Society* 5/4 (1980), 631–60.

——, *Of Woman Born: Motherhood as Experience and Institution*, 2nd edn (London: Norton, 1986 [1976]).

Robcis, Camille, 'How the Symbolic Became French: Kinship and Republicanism in the PACS Debates', *Discourse* 26/3 (2004), 110–35.

——, *The Law of Kinship: Anthropology, Psychoanalysis, and the Family in France* (Ithaca, NY: Cornell University Press, 2013).

——, 'Liberté, Égalité, Hétérosexualité: Race and Reproduction in the French Gay Marriage Debates', *Constellations: An International Journal of Critical and Democratic Theory* 22/3 (2015), 447–61.

Roof, Judith, *Come As You Are: Sexuality and Narrative* (New York: Columbia University Press, 1996).

Roudinesco, Élisabeth, *La Famille en désordre* (Paris: Fayard, 2002).

Rousseau, Jean-Jacques, *Julie, ou la Nouvelle Héloïse*, Le Livre de Poche (Paris: Librairie Générale Française, 2002 [1761]).

Ryan-Flood, Róisín, *Lesbian Motherhood: Gender, Families and Sexual Citizenship* (Basingstoke: Palgrave Macmillan, 2009).

Rye, Gill, 'Lost and Found: Mother–Daughter Relations in Paule Constant's Fiction', in Gill Rye and Michael Worton, eds, *Women's Writing in Contemporary France: New Writers, New Literatures in the 1990s* (Manchester: Manchester University Press, 2002), 65–76.

——, 'Marginal Identities and New Kinship Paradigms: Surrogate Motherhood in Contemporary Women's Writing in France', in Gill Rye and Amaleena Damlé, eds, *Experiment and Experience: Women's Writing in France, 2000–2010* (Oxford: Peter Lang, 2013), 109–24.

——, 'Mums or Dads? Lesbian Mothers in France', in Gill Rye, Victoria Browne, Adalgisa Giorgio, Emily Jeremiah, and Abigail Lee Six, eds, *Motherhood in Literature and Culture: Interdisciplinary Perspectives from Europe* (Abingdon: Routledge, 2017), 98–110.

——, *Narratives of Mothering: Women's Writing in Contemporary France* (Newark: University of Delaware Press, 2009).

——, 'New Representations and Politics of Procreation: Surrogate Motherhood, Artificial Insemination and Human Cloning in Contemporary Women's Writing in France', in Margaret Atack, Diana Holmes, Diana Knight, and Judith Still, eds, *Women, Genre and Circumstance: Essays in Memory of Elizabeth Fallaize* (Oxford: Legenda, 2012), 109–21.

——, 'Registering Trauma: The Body in Childbirth in Contemporary French Women's Writing', *Nottingham French Studies* 45/3 (2006), 92–104.

——, and Michael Worton, eds, *Women's Writing in Contemporary France: New Writers, New Literatures in the 1990s* (Manchester: Manchester University Press, 2002).

Saigal, Monique, *L'Écriture: Lien de fille à mère chez Jeanne Hyvrard, Chantal Chawaf, et Annie Ernaux* (Amsterdam: Rodopi, 2000).

Saussure, Ferdinand de, *Cours de linguistique générale*, 3rd edn (Paris: Payot, 1949 [1916]).

Schumm, Walter R., 'Children of Homosexuals More Apt to Be Homosexuals? A Reply to Morrison and to Cameron Based on an Examination of Multiple Sources of Data', *Journal of Biosocial Science* 42/6 (2010), 721–42.

Schwarz, Jennifer, *Une histoire de famille* (Paris: Robert Laffont, 2014).

Schwarzer, Alice, and Simone de Beauvoir, '*Le Deuxième Sexe*: Trente ans après' (1976), in *Simone de Beauvoir aujourd'hui: Six entretiens* (Paris: Mercure de France, 1984), 71–85.

Séguin, Nathalie, *Une maman, une papa: récit d'une homoparentalité* (Paris: Société des Écrivains, 2013).

Shaktini, Namascar, 'Displacing the Phallic Subject: Wittig's Lesbian Writing', *Signs: Journal of Women in Culture and Society* 8/1 (1982), 29–44.

——, 'Monique Wittig's New Language', *Pacific Coast Philology* 24/1–2 (1989), 83–93.

Sheringham, Michael, *French Autobiography: Devices and Desires: Rousseau to Perec* (Oxford: Oxford University Press, 1993).

Silberstein, Martine, *Ma princesse est atteinte de leucodystrophie: Témoignage d'une mère à sa fille* (Paris: L'Harmattan, 2010).

Spivak, Gayatri Chakravorty, *In Other Worlds: Essays in Cultural Politics*, Routledge Classics (London: Routledge, 2006 [1987]).

Stacey, Judith, and Timothy J. Biblarz, '(How) Does the Sexual Orientation of Parents Matter?', *American Sociological Review* 66/2 (2001), 159–83.

Stambolian, George, and Elaine Marks, eds, *Homosexualities and French Literature: Cultural Contexts/Critical Texts* (Ithaca, NY: Cornell University Press, 1979).

Stambolis-Ruhstorfer, Michael, and Josselin Tricou, 'Resisting "Gender Theory" in France: A Fulcrum for Religious Action in a Secular Society', in Roman Kuhar and David Paternotte, eds, *Anti-Gender Campaigns in Europe: Mobilizing against Equality* (London: Rowman and Littlefield, 2017), 79–98.

Stanton, Domna C., 'Contesting the Exclusive Nation and the Republican Subject: For a New Universalism and Cosmopolitanism', *Contemporary French and Francophone Studies* 17/2 (2013), 123–40.

Sullivan, Maureen, *The Family of Woman: Lesbian Mothers, Their Children, and the Undoing of Gender* (Berkeley: University of California Press, 2004).

Sutfin, Erin L., Megan Fulcher, Ryan P. Bowles, and Charlotte J. Patterson, 'How Lesbian and Heterosexual Parents Convey Attitudes about Gender to Their Children: The Role of Gendered Environments', *Sex Roles* 58/7 (2008), 501–13.

Tardieu, Laurence, *Le Jugement de Léa* (Paris: Arléa, 2004).

Tervonen, Taina, and Brigitte Célier, '*Maman, Mamour, ses deux mamans*: Interview de Brigitte Célier', Univers-L.com (30 June 2008), <http://www.univers-l.com/maman_mamour_ses_deux_mamans_interview_brigitte_celier.html>, accessed 31 March 2017.

Texier, Ophélie, *Jean a deux mamans* (Paris: L'École des Loisirs, 2004).

Tôn, Émilie, 'La "charge mentale", le syndrome des femmes épuisées "d'avoir à penser à tout"', *L'Express* (10 May 2017), <http://www.lexpress.fr/actualite/societe/la-charge-mentale-le-syndrome-des-femmes-epuisees-d-avoir-a-penser-a-tout_1906874.html>, accessed 20 June 2017.

Toonder, Jeanette M. L. den, *"Qui est-je?" L'écriture autobiographique des nouveaux romanciers* (Bern: Peter Lang, 1999).

Vincent-Gérard, Armelle, and Julie Poncet, 'Les Français et la lecture en 2019', an Ipsos study for the Centre National du Livre (2019), <https://www.centrenationaldulivre.fr/fichier/p_ressource/17602/ressource_fichier_fr_les.frana.ais.et.la.lecture.2019.03.11.ok.pdf>, accessed 3 January 2020.

Waelti-Walters, Jennifer, *Damned Women: Lesbians in French Novels, 1796–1996* (Montreal: McGill-Queen's University Press, 2000).

Wainright, Jennifer L., and Charlotte J. Patterson, 'Peer Relations among Adolescents with Female Same-Sex Parents', *Developmental Psychology* 44/1 (2008), 117–26.

Walkowitz, Judith, 'Sexualités dangereuses', trans. Geneviève Faure, in Geneviève Fraisse and Michelle Perrot, eds, *Histoire des femmes en Occident: le XIXᵉ siècle* (Paris: Perrin, 2002 [1991]), 439–78.

Webster, Roger, *Studying Literary Theory: An Introduction* (London: Arnold, 1990).

Weeks, Jeffrey, *Coming Out: Homosexual Politics in Britain from the Nineteenth Century to the Present*, 2nd edn (London: Quartet Books, 1990 [1977]).

Winnicott, D. W., 'Transitional Objects and Transitional Phenomena' (1951), in *Collected Papers: Through Paediatrics to Psycho-Analysis* (London: Tavistock, 1958), 229–42.

Wittig, Monique, *Le Corps lesbien* (Paris: Minuit, 1973).

——, *Les Guérillères* (Paris: Minuit, 1969).

——, 'The Point of View: Universal or Particular?' (1980), in *'The Straight Mind' and Other Essays* (London: Harvester Wheatsheaf, 1992), 59–67.

——, 'The Straight Mind' (1980), in *'The Straight Mind' and Other Essays* (London: Harvester Wheatsheaf, 1992), 21–32.

<https://livre.fnac.com/a1649139/Eliane-Girard-Mais-qui-va-garder-le-chat#omnsearchpos=1>, accessed 4 August 2020.

<https://www.amazon.fr/Elles-eurent-beaucoup-denfants-marièrent-ebook/dp/B00B2NAWKC/ref=sr_1_3?__mk_fr_FR=ÅMÅŽÕÑ&dchild=1&keywords=myriam+blac&qid=1596558931&sr=8-3-spell>, accessed 4 August 2020.

<https://www.amazon.fr/Family-Pride-Laurence-Cinq-fraix/dp/2848760567/ref=sr_1_1?__mk_fr_FR=ÅMÅŽÕÑ&dchild=1&keywords=family+pride+cinq-fraix&qid=1596558500&quartzVehicle=184-694&replacementKeywords=family+cinq-fraix&sr=8-1>, accessed 4 August 2020.

<https://www.amazon.fr/Maman-Mamour-deux-mamans-homoparentale/dp/284337488X/ref=sr_1_1?__mk_fr_FR=ÅMÅŽÕÑ&dchild=1&keywords=maman+mamour&qid=1596558376&sr=8-1>, accessed 4 August 2020.

Index

Studies in Contemporary Women's Writing

Series Editor

GILL RYE
Emerita Professor,
Centre for the Study of Contemporary Women's Writing,
Institute of Modern Languages Research, University of London

Editorial Board

ADALGISA GIORGIO
University of Bath

EMILY JEREMIAH
Royal Holloway, University of London

CLAIRE WILLIAMS
St Peter's College, University of Oxford

CARAGH WELLS
University of Bristol

This book series supports the work of the Centre for the Study of Contemporary Women's Writing at the Institute of Modern Languages Research, University of London, by publishing high-quality critical studies of contemporary literature by women. The main focus of the series is literatures written in the languages covered by the Centre – French, German, Italian, Portuguese and the Hispanic languages – but studies of women's writing in English and other languages are also welcome. 'Contemporary' includes literature published after 1968, with a preference for studies of post-1990 texts in any literary genre.

Studies in Contemporary Women's Writing provides a forum for innovative research that explores new trends and issues, showcasing work that makes a stimulating case for studies of new or hitherto neglected authors and texts as well as established authors. Connections are encouraged between literature and the social and political contexts in which it is created and those which have an impact on women's lives and experiences. The goal of the series is to facilitate stimulating comparisons across authors and texts, theories and aesthetics, and cultural and geographical contexts, in this rich field of study.

Proposals are invited for either monographs or edited volumes. The series welcomes single-author studies, thematic analyses and cross-cultural discussions as well as a variety of approaches and theoretical frameworks. Manuscripts should be written in English.

Printed in Great Britain
by Amazon

43846809R00126